Brothers & Sisters—
A Special Part
of Exceptional Families

Second Edition

by

Thomas H. Powell, Ed.D.

Dean
School of Education and Human Services
Eastern Montana College
Billings, Montana

and

Peggy Ahrenhold Gallagher, Ph.D.

Department of Special Education
Georgia State University
Private Consultant
Atlanta, Georgia

·P·A·U·L·H·
BROOKES
PUBLISHING C°

Baltimore · London · Toronto · Sydney

Paul H. Brookes Publishing Co.
P.O. Box 10624
Baltimore, Maryland 21285-0624

Typeset by The Composing Room of Michigan, Inc., Grand Rapids, Michigan.
Manufactured in the United States of America by
The Maple Press Company, York, Pennsylvania.

First printing, October 1992.
Second printing, January 1996.

Library of Congress Cataloging-in-Publication Data

Powell, Thomas H.
    Brothers & sisters—a special part of exceptional families /
by Thomas H. Powell and Peggy Ahrenhold Gallagher. —
2nd ed.
        p.   cm.
    Includes bibliographical references (p.   ) and index.
    ISBN 1-55766-110-3
    1. Handicapped children—Family relationships.   2.
Brothers and sisters.   I. Gallagher, Peggy Ahrenhold,
1952–   . II. Title.   III. Title: Brothers and sisters—a special
part of exceptional families.
HV903.P69   1993
362.82—dc20   92-14205
                                               CIP

British Library Cataloguing-in-Publication data are available
from the British Library.

Contents

Foreword

I was a little brother, so it is only fair to remind you that big sisters and brothers have strong needs to prove that little ones are noxious little asses who should be done in. Somehow I got the feeling that their first experiences of evil in the world focused on little ones like me. At least that is what I gathered from my big sister's statements: "Why do we have to have him in our family?" and "I love everybody in the whole world except for the devil and my little brother." (All that because it was fun to do things like putting grasshoppers down her back?) On the other hand, we little ones often saw big brothers and sisters as overwhelming powers of darkness who would get us if we did not move fast enough. We learned the true meaning of "the *quick* and the dead." (Perske, 1981, p. 74)

In later life, my sister and I laughed about these earlier situations when our own families got together.

Then came this book from Tom Powell and Peggy Gallagher, casting an array of clarifying lights on brother–sister relationships. Even though it was written about "exceptional" families, it heightened my longing to thank my sister for the good things I always took for granted—for sticking up for me during an embarrassing situation so shameful it won't be described here, for helping me with my studies, for being extremely tender when I was sick, for taking some of my turns at wiping dishes so I could have extra playtime with my friends, and for protecting me from two bullies who *really* wanted to do me in. And that only scratches the surface of the good fighting, teaching, caring, sharing, shaming, supporting, and surviving we did together. This book also reinforced my belief that my sister nurtured me in ways my mother and father never could.

I see this book as one of the first "rocks thrown into a pond"—a pond that has always been there, but for the most part has only been taken for granted and has received little professional scrutiny until the last decade or so.

Now, Powell and Gallagher come along, educators with a keen sense for how people really learn, an ability to do applied research on what they're teaching, and a commitment to gather principles, skills, and data on relationships between persons with disabilities and their siblings from wherever they can find them. I predict that the material between these covers will serve as a base from which will come an ever-increasing fountain of information on siblings.

The fact that Powell and Gallagher are the founders of the Sibling Information Network (I joined it to get their splendid newsletter) has had a profound positive influence on this book. They have a great wealth of information about what happens in exceptional families, and they share this wealth in a number of important ways:

- *Siblings speak out.* Candid quotes from brothers and sisters who have "been there" and have reflected on their own family relationships—(people like Robert Meyers, a former *Washington Post* correspondent who has written so vividly about his experiences in news articles, a book, and a two-hour television drama)—enhance the book's interest and keep it relevant to real family situations.
- *Professionals help siblings speak out clearly.* An amazing number of strategies are described, like Shapiro's 13 crucial questions that need to be posed in a skillful manner, enabling siblings to ponder and answer as honestly as they can.
- *Siblings get recognition as powerful components in family systems.* Now that Ann Turnbull has quietly revolutionized this field's view of exceptional families by carefully searching for every component in these systems, Powell and Gallagher—in harmony with Turnbull—have focused on siblings alone and have expanded the field in the same fashion.
- *The effect of a sibling with disabilities on brothers and sisters is scrutinized.* This begins with the earlier studies in this decade, like the one conducted by Frances Grossman prior to 1972 in which she found that half of the "normal" siblings felt they were better off for having a brother or sister with a disability and half felt they weren't.
- *Information from literature on typical sibling relationships is described and applied.* A wise move: it will help parents and professionals recognize that relationships between "normal" siblings can harbor seeds for nurturing and destructive interactions as well.
- *Special concerns and unique needs are addressed.* This comes after discussions on typical situations, and helps the reader to see clearer differences between the two situations.
- *Thought-provoking, critical human situations appear throughout the book* (e.g., the story about Kathy, a college student studying special education who suddenly discovered she had a sister with mental retardation). Stories like that haunted me and made me wonder if the day is near when all mothers and fathers will feel free enough and strong enough to share with their children, as early as possible, information about the one with the disability.
- *Strategies for assisting sibling relationships fill much of the book.* Although one section is devoted to this issue and describes no less than 14 systematic professional approaches, others emerged elsewhere in the

book. And although readers may never create a perfect copy of a single strategy for their own area, they may be inspired to consider all components in these strategies and come up with their own unique and much improved programs.

- *The fact that siblings can be excellent teachers is explored.* Today, "regular" students in many public schools across the country are taking special training as one-to-one tutors of persons in special education classes. Sometimes they get better results than the teachers. The authors apply this new strategy to sibling interactions.

By now, you may be wanting to move into this book and ponder the wide array of illuminating components on your own. Good. But as you do, think again about Grossman's report as stated earlier in which she found that half of the siblings in her survey felt they were harmed because a brother or sister with a disability was present in the family, and half felt they were better for it. If a researcher did a similar survey, say, 5 years from now, one wonders if *more* than half of these siblings might feel they were better off for the experience . . . because of fresh breakthroughs in assisting brother and sister interactions . . . because of organizations like the Sibling Information Network . . . and because of this book.

Robert Perske
author of *Hope for the Families,*
New Life in the Neighborhood,
Show Me No Mercy,
Circle of Friends,
and *Unequal Justice*

Preface

Siblings play a critical role in our lives. Brothers and sisters know us like no one else. They have been with us during the good times and the bad. Siblings constitute our first social network, and their early influence affects us throughout our lives. Our sibling relationships are typically the longest relationships we will have in life. With all its importance, seldom do we take time to consider this relationship; seldom do we take time to recognize it; seldom do we take time to celebrate it.

This book is devoted to special sibling relationships, that is, relationships between brothers and sisters in which one sibling has a disability. We believe that in such family situations, sibling relationships take on new meaning and significance. Just like parents who have children with disabilities, brothers and sisters are also in need of special attention, understanding, and support. Most of all, these siblings need to be recognized for their unique contribution to the family system.

We have spent the last 15 years actively engaged in work with brothers and sisters. Our work has involved both research and the provision of direct service to siblings and their families. During that time, we learned to listen to siblings, to identify some of their needs, and to understand their unique role within exceptional families. Throughout this book, we have included a number of stories that have been shared with us, as well as a number of our own observations of siblings and their families.

It is important to recognize two fundamental principles that have guided our work with brothers and sisters. First, siblings, whether they have brothers or sisters with mental retardation, cerebral palsy, epilepsy, autism, learning disabilities, cancer, hearing/speech/vision loss, arthritis, Down syndrome, or other disabilities, have similar experiences and needs. Siblings typically discuss the same feelings and emotions, often sharing their joys, fears, and problems. As we put this book together, it made little sense to discuss siblings in terms of specific disabilities. The special concerns and unique needs of siblings are universal. Second, we have learned to respect that each sibling is unique. At first glance, this may seem to be in conflict with the previous statement; however, although siblings have similar concerns, needs, and experiences, the intensity and chronicity will vary from sibling to sibling. Since each sibling is a member of a unique family system, every sibling experiences life differently and so must be respected as an individual. The immediate and future influence that a sibling with a disability will have on his or her brother or sister will differ depending on a number of the family system's individual characteristics. A number of these characteristics are reviewed in Chapters 3 and 4.

We wrote this book for both professionals and parents who wish to learn about special siblings and to help family members. The second edition provides an update of the latest research and service programs, which have focused on the needs of brothers and sisters. The model of *theory to research to practice*, which must guide the development of human services, has also provided a format for the revisions. We believe our book will be helpful to researchers, practitioners, and families.

The book is divided into two sections. Section I, "Families & Siblings," provides a brief overview of the importance of siblings in the family system and the special aspects of having a brother or sister with a disability. Section II details a number of "Strategies To Help Siblings." Appendices then follow with resource listings for professionals and parents that should be helpful in working with siblings.

Fortunately, we live in a society where the power of words and labels are recognized. We have listened to many individuals who reminded us that people must be recognized, first and foremost, for their human characteristics. In keeping with this reminder, we have attempted to follow the example of Bob Perske in his many sensitive books. Therefore, we have written the second edition so that the important and ennobling descriptors (e.g., brother, sister, sibling, son, daughter, friend, person) appear before the word disability. Words that describe disabilities have been used sparingly and only when necessary.

It is our hope that this book will provide greater recognition of the needs and experiences of children and adults who have brothers and sisters with disabilities. We hope this book will help to stimulate the continued development of research and services to meet their special needs.

Acknowledgments

Throughout the production of the first edition of this book and during work on the second edition, we relied on the assistance of many people. We would like to thank Sally Burton, Judy Itzkowitz, Susan McHale, Donald Meyer, Milton Seligman, Zo Stoneman, and Ann Turnbull, who graciously shared materials with us; Eva Holbrook for her flexible childcare arrangements; Wes Townsend, Aloma Jess, Gloria Brown, Denise Clayton, Kathy Kelker, Heather Bush, and Pat O'Shaughnessy-Clark, who diligently assisted with the preparation of the second edition; the many families who provided lovely photographs of their children; and Susan Gregory, Dan Steere, Lucia Bohorquez, and Bev Rainforth, who reviewed the manuscript and provided feedback that substantially improved the final copy; and Irene and Kevin who provided us with love, time, encouragement, and support.

Finally, we would like to thank all the brothers, sisters, and parents who have shared their experiences with us during the past few years. The book contains many of your stories. We have changed your names to protect the trust that you placed in us; however, we hope you recognize your story so you will know how you influenced us.

To
Stedman, Nick, Tom Henry, and Cate
and
James and Mary Grace

Recognition has been slow in coming that the sisters and brothers of children with mental retardation and/or other handicaps are important people in the total picture of human exceptionality. They have their own special needs, which must be recognized and met. Their ability to contribute to the growth and happiness of their handicapped sibling is substantial. Their investment is large, and they have the right to assistance and support (p. 147).
Allen C. Crocker, 1983

Brothers & Sisters—
A Special Part
of
Exceptional Families

I

Families & Siblings

Listening
to Siblings

*From the time Roger began going to physicians and consultants,
it seemed to me that I carried a five-hundred-pound lead weight
around in front of my brain. Never out of my mind was the idea
that my brother was retarded, needed special attention, needed
special care and that I had to provide some of it (p. 36).*
Robert Myers, 1978

There is something unique, something special, about growing up in a family in which a brother or sister has a disability. Sibling relationships, normally critical to a child's overall development, take on special significance when one of the siblings has a disability. Unfortunately, a thorough understanding of just why the sibling relationship is altered when a child has a disability is not easily discerned. Perhaps it is because of stress experienced by the siblings; perhaps it is because the siblings spend more, or less, time together; or maybe it is because they rely on each other so much. Considering the multitude of factors involved and the individual nature of each family situation, it may, in fact, be impossible to clarify the uniqueness, the specialness, of such distinct sibling relationships.

For many years, professionals have maintained a fragmented view of families who have children with disabilities. They have looked mostly at mothers' views, while scant attention was being given to siblings (Seligman, 1983; Trevino, 1979). More recently, however, there has been a growing interest in the experiences of persons who have brothers or sisters with disabilities (Lobato, 1983; Schreiber, 1984; Skrtic, Summers, Brotherson, & Turnbull, 1984; Zeitlin, 1986). This interest is clearly evidenced by the increase in research efforts

3

directed toward brothers and sisters and inservice programs aimed at providing siblings with support services. In addition, parents and professionals are beginning to take the time to listen to siblings. Siblings are being brought together, interviewed, and encouraged to discuss their experiences. Parents and professionals are learning from siblings.

Living closely and intensely with a sibling who has a disability can be both rewarding and stressful. Reports from many siblings indicate a full range of strong feelings, from burden to joy. All reports from siblings clearly demonstrate that deep emotions surround the experience of growing up with a brother or sister who has special needs.

Professionals have begun asking siblings questions in an effort to learn how they can help them deal effectively with their special situations. As Sullivan (1979) observes:

> What must it be like when you first realize that other families you know don't have bloodstains or feces on the living room curtains or smeared on the front wallpaper (put there by an autistic sibling who likes that medium to fingerpaint)? . . . What must it tell you about how your community views your family when you see your sibling denied a chance to go to school where all children go? . . . How does it affect the view of your own eligibility for parenthood? Does it leave a lifetime mark? (p. 287)

Shapiro (1983) has suggested that professionals need to ask siblings a number of questions in order to learn more about their differing experiences. The siblings' answers to such probing questions will help professionals develop meaningful services to help families. It is Shapiro's hope that further information about siblings can be gathered by asking questions such as the following:

> How did you become aware of your sibling's disability?
> Have you had any special responsibilities assigned to you as a direct result of your sibling's condition?
> Do you volunteer to help your sibling or are you required to help?
> As you perceive your family's relationships, do you think that they have been affected by your sibling's condition?
> Is there a difference when the sibling is older than you? Younger?
> Has the family become more united? Less?
> What have been the financial effects on you, your education, your activities?
> Have you been included in plans made for your sibling (e.g., parents' will, guardianship, respite care, transportation, vacations)?

Are you anxious or fearful about a time when you may need to assume significant responsibility for him or her?

Has having a sibling with a disability affected your social life, relationships, dating?

Do you perceive changes in the behavior of others toward you when they learn that you have a sibling who has a disability?

Has the presence of this sibling affected goals and plans you have for your future?

Has his or her presence played a role in your choice of vocations?

As we talk with siblings we must offer them a safe haven to discuss their issues and feelings without reprise. Such interaction, of course, may be difficult for many parents and professionals, as the information shared may cause feelings of pain or guilt. Miller (1985), a sister of a woman with mental retardation, describes a sibling group she formed in order to encourage open discussion in an accepting environment. In the following, she recounts some of the critical conditions:

> There were many times that parents and professionals that heard about our Sunday meetings felt excluded. We heard questions like, "Why are siblings so unwilling to include us?", "What makes them so angry and resentful?", "Why don't they talk to us?" The answer is we could not. We needed to face ourselves and to get in touch with what was happening. This could only be done if we could be sure that we would:
>
> 1. Not inflict pain on those that we loved
> 2. Not be judged and found selfish, unkind, maybe even cruel
> 3. Not have someone who would try to make us see the other side (All the positives and the advantages of having a sibling with a handicap—we know them. Those are easy to acknowledge and talk about.)
> 4. Be able to talk and to connect to someone who could truly understand. (p. 4)

Ellifritt (1984), whose sister has Down syndrome, notes her feelings when this safe haven was not provided:

> I remember several times trying to tell my Mom how I felt and she would say, "Your feelings are wrong and you'd better change them." . . . It was devastating to be told that my feelings were wrong, and yet still not be able to get rid of them. Besides feeling guilty about having angry feelings, I began to think that there was something definitely wrong with me. (p. 19)

Siblings have much to share. They can teach those who are willing to listen to their message, and they can guide the actions of parents and professionals who want to help them. By listening carefully, we can learn how siblings' needs can best be met. First, however, we must learn to listen. By closely listening to their stories and

probing their experiences, we can learn to minimize problem situations and maximize opportunities for growth. Learning from their collective experiences, we can begin to help other brothers and sisters turn a potentially painful, burdensome experience into a rewarding one.

Fortunately, a few siblings have shared some of their experiences with others. This sharing has provided parents and professionals with opportunities to begin to understand their feelings and needs. In an effort to set the stage for the subsequent chapters of this book, excerpts from several siblings' candid descriptions of their feelings and experiences appear on the following pages. Their insights and comments provide opportunities to learn about the special nature of growing up with a brother or sister who has a disability.

Conway (1986) has a brother with prolonged mental illness. She opens her account of her relationship with a set of mixed feelings that expresses the emotions experienced by many siblings:

> Being the sibling of a person with a disability is a paradoxical experience. It can be stressful and difficult, but it can also impart a deep sense of meaning to life. It can provoke concern and compassion, which these days seems increasingly rare. It can also elicit feelings which are powerful and contradictory. (p. 4)

Bodenheimer (1979) offers a brief description of several of her experiences with her brother, Chris, who has autism. She tells of her concern over his diagnosis and the etiology of his disability:

And I remember the turmoil surrounding the pursuit of his elusive diagnosis. The whole family shared in the knowledge that "something" was wrong—he doesn't talk, he doesn't seem to hear, yet he loves music and keeps rhythm, he will only eat bananas, he's fascinated with water, never wants to cuddle, won't sleep through the night. . . . Knowing all these things made it even more difficult when those professionals sought out gave confusing and conflicting reports. . . . An especially difficult part of living with an autistic sibling is the ever-present question of etiology. Why??? As a child, it's hard to live with someone who has difficulty learning, gets upset, and acts strangely when no one seems to know why. Children expect adults to have the answers, but so often in the case of the autistic child, the siblings are left on their own to grapple with this question. (pp. 291–292)

Consider what McCallum (1981) felt when he learned that his younger brother was both deaf and blind: "It seemed terrifically unfair to me. I was perplexed and very confused by it" (p. 2). His statement, displaying emotions that are not unlike parental feelings, seems typical of those made by other siblings, and provides a clue to the needs that siblings have when children are diagnosed.

All too often it seems that siblings are excluded from information and from the search for answers concerning the disability. Ellifritt (1984), whose sister has Down syndrome, describes the situation she faced:

My parents never sat me down and said, "This is the problem, this is what's wrong with her. Do you understand? Do you have any questions?" My attempts to communicate were all in vain. (p. 19)

Fortunately, some brothers and sisters have different experiences when learning about the disability. Itzkowitz (1989) interviewed a sibling who reported:

When I found out that John was handicapped, I had plenty of questions. I'm lucky my parents were there to help me understand more about the handicap of my brother and handicaps of other people similar to John. (p. 182)

Some siblings tell us of the extra responsibilities and burdens they experienced as a result of their sister or brother. Hayden (1974), a sister of a child who was deaf, notes some of the tremendous responsibilities placed on her shoulders at an early age and some of her parents' unrealistic expectations:

When Daddy spent a year in Korea, I became Mother's sole helper. My role as second mother to Mindy held some prestige and much responsibility. It took away from play time with children my own age. And, just as a mother serves as an example for her children, I was expected to be an exceptionally "good" little girl. The high standards my mother set for my behavior, though, had not only to do with my setting an example; her reasons were also practical. Mindy's impetuous behavior left her with little patience, energy, or time to put up with shenanigans from me. . . . The responsibility I felt for Mindy was tremendous. One year, when my "babysitting" duties involved periodic checking on my sister, Mindy wandered away between checks. After a thorough but fruitless search of the neighborhood, my mother hysterically told me that if anything happened to Mindy, I would be to blame. I felt terrified and guilty. I was seven. (p. 27)

Myers (1978) also reminds us of the additional responsibility siblings are often given and of the pressure applied to mature quickly:

My role in those days was someone who was always around to help care for Roger. That was my mother's phrase. My father called me his "good right arm." Roger himself called me "Dad" before he corrected himself and called me "Bobby". . . . I never felt I dressed like a kid, never felt comfortable with the clothes I wore, never felt I knew how to act as a boy or a teenager. I was a little man. (p. 36)

Zatlow's (1982) strong emotional feelings about her brother, Douglas, who has autism, are evident in her writing. She shares a loving relationship with him, yet reminds us of his tremendous needs and her subsequent responsibilities:

There was no relief from Doug. Day in and day out, his needs had to be tended to regardless of our wants and desires. He always came first. . . . Because Douglas's presence dominated everything, there was not real time for myself. Under these conditions, childhood takes on an uneasy dimension. A sibling denied the fundamental right of being a child. An opportunity to have friends over does not often materialize because visits were dependent on my brother's moods and behavior. Going out was governed by my mother's need for my assistance in any way. My mother nicknamed me "the other mother" as I took my responsibility with seriousness and maturity in excess of my young years. Unfortunately, the pattern became a way of life. (p. 2)

Helsels (1985) is a sister of a sibling with mental retardation, epilepsy, and cerebral palsy. She tells of some of her feelings of embarrassment: "I was certain that everyone was looking at my brother with his obvious handicap and then wondering what was wrong with the rest of us" (p. 110).

Klein (1972) talked with Diane, a young college student, who recalled a particularly memorable experience:

I can remember being embarrassed about Cathy because she is really, I guess, quite upsetting to see for the first time. . . . I can remember in a bus terminal we had to spread a blanket on the floor so Cathy could crawl around and get a bit of exercise. A crowd gathered and I hated the people so much. I was just terribly embarrassed and I wanted to hide Cathy and I wanted to protect her from these people who were glaring. . . . (p. 25)

Hayden (1974) lets us have a glimpse of some of her feelings about the unequal attention her sister received:

Mindy's achievements always met with animated enthusiasm from our parents. In contrast, it seemed Mother and Daddy's response to my accomplishments was on the pat-on-the-back level. I was expected to perform well in every circumstance. I wanted my parents to be enthusiastic about my accomplishments too. . . . I wanted to be noticed. (p. 27)

Laureys (1982), whose brother Brian has autism, suggests that the experience of having a sibling with a disability varies among families:

Another aspect of Brian's life in our family is the rather distinct difference between the way the older and younger siblings reacted to him. I really can't recall being embarrassed that much of Brian in public or with friends. Since he was younger and pretty passive, we older brothers could just explain that this was our cute retarded little brother who just acted kind of "odd." Later, our friends thought he was real COOL because he dug rock and roll music so much. Also, there was security in numbers . . . with all those brothers around, not many ignorant kids would dare make fun of him. But for the younger half of the family, it was a bit different. Just how do you explain to your friends that this big (5 ft., 10 in., 175 lbs.) and strong, and normal-looking guy running around the house, braying incomprehensive sounds and flicking little lint balls, is really OK? Some of their friends (especially girls—high school age) would be terrified! Most understood when Brian was explained to them. . . . Some did not. (p. 5)

Klein (1972) talked with a group of siblings and reported the content of their simple, but powerful messages. One of these siblings, Richard, whose brother suffered from a hearing loss and severe physical disabilities, experienced the pain of watching his brother being teased on the playground:

They made a circle around my brother and started looking at him and I just didn't know what to do. On the one hand I felt like saying, and it upsets me now to think that I would say what I wanted to say, "Jim, hurry up and get out of here." Even now that I say it, it is totally disgusting and at the same time I wanted to say to all those little kids, "If you don't move now, I am going to throw you all over the fence." Even now I have not resolved it—more than anything else, it shows me that I have not really come to terms with the whole thing. Furthermore, it gives me some appreciation for what my brother has to go through. (p. 13)

Other siblings have also reported problems they have had with children teasing and poking fun at their brothers and sisters with disabilities. Seligman (1983) notes that this teasing puts many siblings in a double bind. Parents may demand the sibling protect the child with a disability, while playmates encourage shunning the child; consequently, the sibling has confused feelings (both anger and love) toward the child with a disability. Consider Hayden's (1974) story about her playmates and her sister Mindy:

They often did mock her, of course, and we would leave—except one time which, to this day, gives my conscience no rest; when I joined in. I lost many playmates by having to side with Mindy. I felt neglected by my family and shunned by my peers. I was a very lonely little girl. (p. 27)

Bodenheimer (1979) shares the important role her parents played in her acceptance of her brother, Chris:

> But in time I was helped to understand that the best we could do was to meet his needs as we saw them, enjoy his engaging personality, and accept what seemed impossible to change. The model of caring consistently displayed by our parents made it easier for my brother and me to assume this kind of acceptance. (p. 292)

Some siblings tell of their initial jealousy and subsequent realization of their brother's or sister's needs. Mark's brother, Chad, had Down syndrome and died at the age of six of congestive heart complications. Mark notes:

> One thing I couldn't understand was why Chad got what he wanted more than I did. He got to eat ice cream every morning for breakfast and he got first choice of things that Daddy brought home. When we both wanted the same coloring book, or candy, Chad always got it and it didn't always seem fair back then, but now that I am older I realize why he got them. All this happened years ago and I can remember some things like they were yesterday, while some things I can just barely remember, but now I realize, more than I did years ago, how much Chad meant to me. All of this may have happened long ago but the memories of Chad will always be stored in the very front of my brain and I will never forget him. (M. Langston, personal communication, April 24, 1984)

Siblings often talk about the future and the chance that they may someday be responsible for their brother or sister. As McCallum (1981) notes, because of his brother, he experienced a number of fears, hopes, and expectations regarding his future spouse:

> I needed a girl who was willing to look at a kid that sat in the living room, wiggling his wrist at the light and squawking . . . a kid who scooted from room to room on his butt. I needed someone who was willing to see all that and still accept him as a human being. I also needed someone who would be willing to bear the burden of taking care of my brother if we had to assume that responsibility. (p. 2)

Similarly, Itzkowitz (1989) interviewed another sibling who told her:

> The most frightening feeling growing up was . . . what will I do if something happens to my parents? For years I have asked God to take my sister before my parents. (p. 183)

While many brothers and sisters have shared some of their pain, fears, and frustrations with us, these stories present only one side of the picture. The sibling experience can also be quite rewarding and have a profound, positive influence on the individual brothers and sisters. Konig (1986) shares a bit of what he has received from his brother who is deaf:

Frank has taught me a great deal. But most of all he has helped me understand the difficult but certainly manageable situation all people with handicaps face. There may be things Frank can't do or can't do as well as hearing people, but there are a lot of things he does much better. I'm happy and privileged to have a brother like Frank. (p. 4)

Westra (1986), in her letter to the Sibling Information Network, gets directly to the point:

I never felt my sister was a burden or a shame. I was proud of the way she responded to me. She influenced my life, education and career immeasurably. She taught me about unconditional love. She was and still is a joy to me. (M. Westra, personal communication, June 10, 1986)

And consider these statements of other siblings:

Being in a family with someone "special" to take care of not only makes you mature faster but gives you more experience and a better understanding of how to handle people as well. (Torisky, 1979, p. 290)

I consider myself to have had a very special upbringing. I learned so much from my brother, indirectly. I enjoy being around people like him, although, of course, there is no one as special as my brother Ben. (Lettick, 1979, p. 294)

I always felt there was something very different about our family. Of course, you know, Cathy being that difference. Because of her difference there was a degree of specialness or closeness about us that, I do not know, it was sort of a bond that made us all very, very close. (Klein, 1972, p. 25)

I have learned to look for a deeper meaning in life; I have learned to question "normalcy." Finally, I have learned hope. (Conway, 1986, p. 4)

In her interview of siblings across the United States, Itzkowitz (1989) reported numerous positive statements from brothers and sisters. For example, a sibling of a sister with mental retardation wrote:

My experience with my retarded sister has been one of the most important in my life. It has at times been stressful and emotional, but ultimately a very positive influence. It has definitely shaped my life and channeled my interests in ways I would otherwise have not pursued. (p. 23)

Helsels (1985), although reporting a full range of feelings and emotions, summarized her experience in the most positive way:

All in all, though, I feel that Robin has brought much good into the lives of my family. He has taught us a great deal about acceptance, patience, individual worth, but most of all about love. (p. 96)

SOME FINAL THOUGHTS ON LISTENING

Siblings have much to teach us. We can only learn if we are willing to take the time to listen and to better understand their powerful messages. It seems clear that it is difficult, at best, to make generalizations about the experiences of siblings. Upcoming chapters show that research and clinical practice have proven that although siblings share a number of similar characteristics and feelings, each brother and sister is affected differently by a sibling with a disability. It is important that neither parents nor professionals make any assumptions without first listening and offering support.

By listening to siblings, we know that the experience of growing up with a brother or sister who has a disability is not easily defined. It is certainly not unidimensional. The experience is complex. Like all sisters and brothers, siblings report that they have powerful feelings about their siblings. Whether positive or negative, we have yet to meet a sibling who reported that the experience did not in some way influence his or her life.

Attending to their messages, we can begin learning how to help enhance their experience so that more siblings will benefit from it, and so that families will also be strengthened. It all starts by listening.

2

Siblings—A Special Relationship

*Still—whether one celebrates or denies the sibling bond—
as long as one has a brother or sister alive, there is always
another human being who has known one as a child, who has
experienced one in a unique and intimate way over which one has
had little control, who has been a mirror, however distorted,
of one's childhood and youth—someone, in short, who has been
a child of, and has shared the same parents (p. 336).*
Stephen P. Bank and Michael D. Kahn, 1982a

Sitting around the kitchen table in Janet's house seemed so comfortable and familiar to her siblings. Her home was much like the home they had grown up in as siblings; in fact, many of their parents' possessions could be found throughout the house. These four siblings had decided to keep their sibling relationship vibrant when their parents died, and gathered together often on Saturday nights. At these gatherings, they shared news, compared notes, reminisced about the past and, most importantly, celebrated their sibling relationship. Bob and David talked about going fishing together and their previous hikes to the lake. Joan and Janet talked about family vacations and shared experiences at school. All four openly talked about their parents, remembering their strong points as well as their weak ones. Each had a slightly novel perspective on their parents, which made the other siblings think, laugh, and sometimes cry. Each sibling had a different relationship with the other. Although they shared many experiences as a group, they also shared uniquely personal experiences with each other. As adults, with growing children of their own, their sibling relationships have taken on a new significance. Each one contributes in different ways to helping the others. David helped Joan and her husband with a down payment on their new house. Janet helped Bob secure his new job. Joan watches Janet's

13

children when she travels for business. Bob always has time to help the others with household projects and chores. Their present and past relationships have helped them to find meaning in their current lives. These siblings continue to rely on each other, which emphasizes the value of their unique family relationship. The bond between these siblings ties them together for a lifetime and grows stronger every day. They have shared a special time together—their childhood. They have shared the same parents, and as adults, they continue to share their lives with each other.

Although it is unclear what unique social characteristics only children possess (Falbo, 1982), it is clear that siblings have a powerful influence on the lives of their brothers and sisters. For instance, Jiao, Ji, and Jing (1986) found that children with siblings are rated more persistent and cooperative and have greater peer prestige than the more "egocentric" only children. What *is* so critical about siblings? Throughout this chapter, a number of aspects of the sibling relationship are reviewed. The forthcoming pages focus on relationships between siblings in general. The special relationship between siblings and their brothers and sisters with disabilities is considered in detail in Chapter 3.

THE IMPORTANCE OF SIBLINGS

A Special Relationship

Unlike any other relationship, the sibling relationship provides two people with physical and emotional contact at critical stages throughout their lives. Siblings provide a continuing relationship from which there is no annulment. This permanent relationship allows individuals to exert considerable influence over each other through longitudinal interactions.

Simply put, siblings are socialization agents. Siblings often provide the first and probably the most intense peer relationship for a child. This special relationship provides a context for social development. Through ongoing, long-term interactions, siblings teach social skills to one another. From these social interactions, the child develops a foundation for later learning and personality development. Experiences in the areas of sex-role, moral, motor, and language development are all found in the context of social interactions.

Social interaction with siblings plays a critical role in overall development. As Bossard and Boll (1960) note, the relationship between siblings is one of "mutual interdependency." Siblings, for instance, are available as long-term playmates and companions. As such, they help each other and teach each other, either directly or incidentally. The relationship also provides opportunities for sharing and the open and direct expression of their feelings.

Through their social interactions, siblings also learn a "give-and-take" process. They learn to share. Siblings help each other learn to compromise. They teach each other the benefits of mutual collaboration and learn about resolving differences. This socialization process has a profound influence on the life of the sibling.

Siblings also serve as a unique support system for one another. Besides being a playmate, the sibling may be a confidant and a counselor. Siblings typically provide advice to each other. This support system, important throughout the sibling relationship, takes on additional significance as the siblings mature and leave home. The sibling support network can continue throughout adulthood.

An Increasing Significance in Today's Society

Bank and Kahn (1982a) propose that current social changes in American society may result in greater levels of sibling contact and emotional interdependence. These changes, summarized below, may ultimately increase the importance of brothers and sisters:

1. Family size is decreasing. Couples are having fewer children and these children tend to be closer in age, fostering more intense contact with each other.
2. Individuals are living longer, and siblings provide a longitudinal source of support to each other—especially in their later years.
3. Families tend to move often, and the difficulties in establishing friends inherent in such moves may force siblings to rely on each other more intensely.

4. As more mothers seek employment outside of the home, young siblings will spend greater amounts of time in environments supervised by individuals other than parents. As siblings grow older, they may spend even greater amounts of time in unsupervised situations.
5. As our technological society advances, there is greater pressure on young people to compete. As society becomes more exacting and competitive, siblings will increasingly compare each other's progress.
6. Parents are experiencing more stress and, as a result, are becoming "unavailable" to children for longer periods of time. These periods of parental emotional absence influence sibling relationships.

A Lifelong Relationship

The sibling relationship is perhaps the most long-lasting and most influential relationship of a person's life. The sibling relationship begins with the birth of a brother or sister and continues throughout a person's lifetime. The duration of that relationship is certainly substantial. Unlike parental relationships, which may last 40–60 years, the sibling relationship may last 60–80 years.

The sibling relationship, like any meaningful relationship, changes and develops as do the siblings. As Bank and Kahn (1982a) note, the sibling relationship has periods of intense activity as well as periods of inactivity. Sibling relationships follow a life cycle of their own. In early childhood, siblings provide a constant source of companionship for one another. As young children, they interact with each other frequently and share not only toys, clothes, rooms, and parents, but also important family experiences. During the school years, siblings begin to reach out to nonfamily members. Siblings use the social skills they have learned from each other to establish relationships with others outside the family constellation. Throughout adolescence, many siblings seem ambivalent about their relationships with brothers and sisters; however, they rely on siblings as confidants and advisors, especially regarding relationships with friends, use of drugs, sexuality, and other concerns (Lamb, 1982). In adulthood, the sibling relationship takes on new characteristics. The sibling leaves home and establishes an independent life. Young adult siblings may provide critical support or encouragement. These instances, however, are usually infrequent. As siblings have their own children, their brothers and sisters, as aunts and uncles, provide unique experiences to each other's children. They provide an additional network of love and support to their siblings' children. In old age, when children move away and spouses die, siblings provide a support network to each other (Cicirelli, 1982; Seltzer, 1991). They may again re-establish frequent contact and, in some cases, move in together to provide companionship and share the final experiences of life as they shared the first stages of their lives together.

SIBLINGS WITHIN THE FAMILY SYSTEM

Families have always been a very meaningful and substantial part of life. It is from the support of the family that a child develops the strength and spirit to meet the challenge of the future. We first learn of the outside world and ourselves as part of that world from the family. Families provide children with their first opportunities to explore, to communicate, and to interact with other human beings.

Families change as children grow older, as parents change, and as the community changes. Family members' relationships are adjusted and social contacts outside the family expand and mature. However the family changes, it still remains the social point of departure. Children leave the family and go to school, to church, to recreational activities, and on to their adult lives—frequently to marriage and their own families. The family is a stepping stone to the future.

Interactional Dynamics

Families can be viewed as an interrelated system that supports the interdependence of the individual family members. Each member of the family is a critical element whose personality and interactions affect those of other family members. As one member of the family changes, so, too, will the other members. As Beckman and Bristol (1991) point out, the fundamental concept of a family systems focus is that the family consists of a number of interdependent subsystems. Events or circumstances that affect one part of the system likewise influence the other parts (Fewell, 1986; Minuchin, 1974; Stoneman & Brody, 1984; Turnbull & Turnbull, 1990). The extended family, the community, and any policies that regulate resources are all outside influences that affect the nuclear family (Bronfenbrenner, 1977).

Family interactions are never as simple as they may first seem. An interaction between parents often influences future interactions between the parents and children or one parent and child. As a toddler learns to use language, for instance, the child influences the way parents and even siblings relate to him or her. Likewise, the relationship between a father and his second daughter influences the interaction between his two daughters. Any one family member exerts influence on his or her individual relationship with every other family member. This influence, in turn, affects the relationships *between other* family members.

Schvaneveldt and Ihinger (1979), in their analysis of sibling interactions and interdependence, assert the importance of considering families as systems. They have outlined five basic assumptions in regard to sibling relationships:

1. Within most families, there exist three subsystems of interaction. Each of these subsystems (spouse–spouse, parent–child, and sibling–sibling) operates semi-independently within the family structure.
2. Family members both initiate and receive social interactions. Family interaction is dynamic—with husbands and wives affecting each other, parents and children affecting each other, and siblings affecting each other.
3. Sibling interaction is a continuous process of development that occurs throughout the life span.
4. The personality development and social behaviors of family members are partially determined by family composition and interaction.
5. Sibling groups have properties similar in characteristics to other small groups.

Thus, in conceptualizing sibling relationships, the group or dyad of siblings must be first thought of in the context of the larger family system. These patterns of influence are transactional in nature; that is, one sibling affects the other sibling and vice versa, and this interaction changes across time (Bell, 1968; Sameroff & Chandler, 1975).

RESEARCH ON SIBLING RELATIONSHIPS

Exactly what influence do brothers and sisters have on each other? Do birth order and age-spacing really affect a child's personality? Research on siblings and their unique relationships with each other is beginning to help separate the facts from countless tales about siblings.

As Teti and Ablard (1989) note, Levy, in 1934, was one of the first authors to address the role of family context in shaping sibling relationships. A shift away from the family systems focus then occurred. Sibling status (constellation) variables such as age, sex, or birth order became the focal point. This change was probably precipitated by the historical interest in these variables as predictors of intelligence and personality factors (Sutton-Smith & Rosenberg, 1970). These studies on the effects of sibling status variables as predictors of sibling relationships have been inconclusive (Abramovitch, Corter, & Lando, 1979; Dunn & Kendrick, 1982), and more recently, the trend in studying sibling relationships has again shifted back to a family systems interactional focus. Both of these research trends are discussed in this chapter. Such research findings have led to the development of pragmatic techniques to enhance or alter the effects siblings can have on one another. Later in this book, in Chapters 5–11, many techniques useful for children who have a brother or sister with a disability are thoroughly discussed.

Constellation Variables

Much of the earlier research on sibling relationships involving children without disabilities has concentrated on linking certain factors about the individual siblings, such as age-spacing, gender, or ordinal position, to differences in such variables as achievement, conformity, dependency, intelligence, or personality (Jacobs & Moss, 1976).

Age-Spacing   Koch (1955) concluded that age-spacing was an important consideration in explaining sibling relationships. He found that children closest in age (less than 4–6 years apart) played both with each other and with each other's friends more, and had more common interests than did children further apart in age.

Gender   On the assumption that siblings do, in fact, influence the behavior of each other, several authors conducted studies on sibling gender related to learning tasks. Cicirelli (1972) found female siblings more effective than male siblings or female nonsiblings in teaching a simple conceptual task to younger brothers and sisters. In contrast, he also indicated that boys tend to be more effective in teaching younger, unrelated children than in teaching their own brothers and sisters.

A similar study to determine the differences in mother–child versus sibling–sibling interactions on a problem-solving task was also conducted by Cicirelli (1976a). He discovered that the older sibling's behaviors and the younger child's responses depended on the sex of the older sibling. Cicirelli found that mothers tended to help younger children more when the older child in the family was a male, suggesting that when a child has an older sister, mothers relinquish portions of their helping roles to the older sister.

Cicirelli (1976a) uncovered another pattern revealing that, with siblings of the opposite sex, younger children were more independent and received more feedback on tasks from the mother or older sibling than did children with the same-sex siblings. However, a 1980 study by Dunn and Kendrick offered different findings. In a study of social behaviors of infants, Dunn and Kendrick found marked differences between same- and mixed-sex sibling pairs at 14 months of age. The authors observed 40 pairs of siblings at various times in their homes. They noted that by the time the younger child was 14 months of age, more frequent positive social behaviors were shown by both siblings in same-sex pairs. In contrast, more negative behaviors were displayed by the first child in different sex pairs. Two laboratory studies (Lamb, 1978a, 1978b), however, seem to dispute the Cicirelli and the Dunn and Kendrick conclusions. Lamb found that the sex composition of sibling pairs had no influence on the interactions of the children.

Such diverse findings highlight the difficulties faced by researchers; the issues are complex and hard to distill to single variables. Stoneman, Brody, and MacKinnon (1986) discuss two broad theoretical perspectives of research studies on sibling status in sex-role development. The first (Brim, 1958) has focused on sibling modeling of stereotypical sex-role behavior in which researchers predict that children in same-sex pairs should be the most stereotypically sex typed while children from cross-sex pairs should be more androgynous. Another perspective (Schachter, 1982) proposes a rivalry-defense hypothesis which predicts that same-sex pairs become more different than opposite-sex siblings in order to avoid comparison and competition.

Birth Order   Unruh, Grosse, and Zigler (1971), focusing on birth order and number of siblings in a family, compared groups of firstborn, later-born, and only-born children on a task used to assess the effectiveness of social reinforcement. Firstborn children played significantly longer without social reinforcement than did later-borns; however, "the number of siblings was not found to be related to

playing time" (p. 1154). In their discussion, the authors pointed out that using "number of siblings" or birth order as a variable has not yielded consistent results, and they suggested that "age gap between siblings" might be an important variable for consideration.

Others (Belmont & Marolla, 1973; Bossard & Boll, 1960; Harris, 1964; Weiss, 1970), too, have tried to establish a pattern of personality characteristics for the "first child" or for the "baby" of the family. Some children seem to fit easily into these typical stereotypes. Studies (Belmont, Stein, & Zybert, 1978; Davis, Cahan & Bashi, 1977; Sutton-Smith & Rosenburg, 1970; Zajonc & Bargh, 1980) suggest that sibling birth order variables do influence individual styles, preferences, and adult self-esteem, but the importance of such patterns may have been overestimated. The constructs are inadequate in explaining the complexity of sibling relationships.

Transition from Constellation Variables

Despite the complexity, researchers of varying backgrounds, from sociology to medicine, have stressed the importance of the sibling relationship. The key word here may be *relationship*. Factors beyond sibling age-spacing or ordinal position are now believed to be important in describing and explaining the nature of sibling relationships. There has been a recent shift in the literature from the study of sibling-status constellation variables (birth order, age-spacing, etc.) to a study of the formative process of developing sibling relationships and the complexity of those relationships within a systems framework.

Furman and Buhrmester (1985) have begun developing a systematic framework for describing and assessing the quality of sibling relationships. The authors argue for the importance of studying relationship qualities directly in conjunction with family constellation variables such as ordinal position, gender of sibling, or age-spacing. Such a framework should also capture the parent–child relationship as it relates to the quality and management of sibling relationships as well as characteristics of individual children including temperament and cognitive factors.

Relationship Patterns

Recent sibling research shows an increased appreciation both of variability in cultural styles and of the development of sibling relationships across the life span rather than just in the early childhood years. Researchers are beginning to examine the effects of how parents treat and respond to children in their family in different ways (parental differential treatment), and how such patterns, or the perception of such treatment, affect sibling relationships. At the same time, researchers are beginning to search for developmental interaction patterns in sibling relationships. Both of these areas of research—differential experiences and developmental-age patterns—are outlined below.

Differential Experiences   Daniels and Plomin (1985), Plomin and Daniels (1987), and Rowe and Plomin (1981) have argued that events within a family are often experienced in very different ways by individual children, creating what they call nonshared environmental influences. As Schachter and Stone (1985) note, the *nonshared within family environment* is the environment that children in the same family do *not* share in common. Previous studies of environmental influences that have focused on variables such as social class, maternal employment, or father absence are generally shared by all siblings in the family, and therefore, can account for similarities but not differences.

Parental differential treatment is viewed as one component of the nonshared environment (Daniels & Plomin, 1985; Plomin & Daniels, 1987). Researchers have begun establishing links between such differential treatment and differences in siblings' adjustment (Dunn & Plomin, 1990; McHale & Pawletko, 1992). Dunn and Plomin (1990) recently completed a series of research studies and concluded that siblings, even though they may grow up in the same family with the same parents, experience their environments quite differently.

Dunn and Plomin (1990) believe that any resemblance among siblings is due to hereditary similarity and not to the experience of growing up in the same family. Their premise is that siblings are remarkably different from each other, that they are treated differently by parents and siblings, and that they experience this treatment differently. Whether it is actually being treated differently by parents or the *perception* that they are being treated differently that affects siblings is still unknown. Daniels, Dunn, Furstenberg, and Plomin (1985) found that differences in siblings' perceptions of maternal closeness, influence in family decision-making, and chore expectations accounted for significant portions of the variance in their adjustment.

Children as young as 14 months of age appear to be vigilant monitors of their mothers' interactions with older siblings. Even though a mother may treat her children similarly at a particular age/stage, the siblings (unless they are twins) are not at that age/stage at the same time, and thus, focus on the differential parental behavior (Dunn & Plomin, 1990).

A further question, of course, is how much the differences in parental behavior are responses to differences in the child's behavior or personality (Dunn & Plomin, 1990). Developmental changes in children may elicit differences in maternal behavior (Dunn, Plomin, & Daniels, 1986). Varying experiences within the sibling relationship may also contribute to individual outcomes.

Maternal Behavior   Dunn et al. (1986) have looked at maternal behavior toward siblings over time. They examined tapes of each sibling at 24 months in the home and found that while mothers were consistent in affection and verbal responsiveness, they differed in their controlling behavior toward the two siblings. The authors compared the same mother's behavior toward the siblings at 12 and 24 months. They found little stability in maternal behavior toward the same child during the course of a year. While consistent in their responses to advances in their children at the same age, mothers differ in their responses to the same child over time.

Stocker, Dunn, and Plomin (1989) examined the links with child temperament, maternal behavior, and family structure in sibling relationships. Home visits included interviews and observations of 96 families with siblings grouped by ages 3–6 and 5–10 years. They found that differences in sibling relationships are, to a significant extent, related to maternal behavior, temperamental characteristics of the children, their age, and family structure variables. The child's temperamental characteristics accounted for a significant amount of the unique variance in sibling relationships. Groups in which the second-born siblings were older had more cooperative and less conflictual relationships than those groups in which siblings were younger.

Stewart, Mobley, VanTuyl, and Salvador (1987) conducted a longitudinal assessment of firstborn children's adjustment to the birth of a sibling. At the birth, the older children were from 2 to 4 years of age. Observations at 1, 4, 8, and 12 months after the birth showed the sibling responding by imitating the infant or by confronting the mother or infant. Over time, interactions were primarily confrontations with the increasingly "intrusive" infant. Observational data supported earlier results found by Dunn and Kendrick (1982). The data indicated that mothers had dramatically decreased their interactions with the firstborn over time, while fathers' relative frequency of interaction with the older child had remained stable (Stewart et al., 1987).

These results confirm those of previous studies showing connections between differential parental behavior and conflictual sibling relationships. They found that, as in the previous studies by Bryant and Crockenberg (1980) and Brody, Stoneman, and Burke (1987), most mothers directed more affection, attention, control, and responsiveness to the younger sibling. This powerful predictor, maternal differential behavior, provides support for the significance of non-shared environmental factors. The causal direction, of course, is still unclear since maternal behavior may be a consequence of the negative relationship between siblings rather than its cause.

Developmental/Age Patterns Vandell and Wilson (1987) note that studies on early relationships involving siblings have focused on the content and affective quality of sibling interactions. Young siblings are naturally influenced by the presence of a brother or sister, and the actions of one child influence the actions and reactions of others. Some of the effects of these sibling–sibling interactions have been documented. Researchers are also documenting the patterns of sibling relationships at various ages throughout the life cycle. While many of the early studies have looked at the relationship during the infancy and preschool years, school-age and even adult sibling relationships are now being examined.

Studies in Infant and Preschool Years Studies in the early years of children's lives have looked specifically at language development and reciprocal and complimentary interactions, as well as the content and affective quality of the sibling interactions from a longitudinal perspective.

1. *Language:* Several recent studies (Barton & Tomasello, 1991; Mannle & Tomasello, 1987; Tomasello & Mannle, 1985) have investigated the effects of brothers and sisters on their younger siblings' (24 months and younger) language development. In looking at triads with a parent and two siblings present, it seems that compared to the mother–infant dyad, siblings are highly directive in their linguistic interactions with younger siblings and show little skill (or inclination) to provide nonverbal information to the infant. They neither adjust their sentence length and complexity nor add conversation-maintaining devices. At the same time, it seems that the younger siblings have a perfect opportunity to adapt their linguistic skills to meet the higher demands of this rich language environment. Although these younger siblings are capable of participating in triadic interactions, they are more likely to join into an ongoing topic than to initiate one.

Jones and Adamson (1987) also investigated language use in mother–child–sibling interactions. They found that, in their mother's presence, later-borns made significantly fewer utterances when siblings were present than when they played alone. While there were no qualitative differences in maternal speech during dyadic as compared to triadic situations, a striking quantitative difference was found. Mothers spoke much less to the younger sibling when the older sibling was present; however, the older sibling's language did not seem to compensate for the decrease. Woolett (1986) maintains that when an older sibling is present, while there may be a decrease in adult sensitivity to individual children and their needs, a more stimulating linguistic environment is also often found.

Dunn and Shatz (1989) stress the importance of language in a "multispeaker" world and see the sibling relationship as an important source of input and experience. Their observations indicate that second-born siblings intruded into others' conversations 22% of the time and, thus, were clearly involved in much of the talk between others present.

2. *Reciprocal and Complementary Interactions:* Dunn (1983), in a review of sibling relationships in early childhood, stresses the dual dimensions of such relationships—*reciprocal* and *complementary* interactions.

The reciprocal aspect of the sibling relationship can be assessed in terms of both the frequency and the quality of the interactions. Within each sibling dyad, both positive and negative interactions have been observed. Sibling reciprocity can be defined in terms of play and interaction with each other, familiarity and intimacy, and the emotional intensity of the relationship (Dunn, 1983).

Complementary features of sibling relationships include sibling caregiving, teaching, and the development of attachment. Dunn points out that most children are reported to be interested in a newborn sibling and concerned at any sign of distress from the infant. Although the development of attachment between siblings has not yet been well documented, the importance of teaching by the older sibling seems to contribute to both children's intellectual development. Cicirelli (1972, 1976b), for instance, has documented that older siblings of 6 and 7 years can effectively teach their younger siblings in structured situations. These types of actions contribute to strengthening the sibling bond.

For instance, Samuels (1980) assessed the effect of an older sibling's presence upon numerous 23-month-old infants while they were exploring a new environment. Samuels found that, when older siblings were present, the infants tended to leave their mothers more quickly, stay away longer, and move farther away from their mothers than they did when no older siblings were present. Infants also inspected and manipulated objects more in the presence of their older siblings.

Dunn (1983) concludes that sibling relationships provide a context for social learning and understanding. She notes that sibling influence can be seen in the imitative behaviors of younger siblings, as well as in the development of social and intellectual skills. Dunn suggests that the complementary features of sibling interactions are areas of importance in the developmental patterns of sibling relationships. She stresses the importance of individual differences in siblings' characteristics, such as temperament, to the development of the relationship, rather than the previously studied sibling-status variables.

3. *Longitudinal Studies:* Vandell and Wilson (1987) contrasted observations of mother–infant turn-taking exchanges with sibling–infant and peer–infant exchanges at 6 and 9 months. While infants spent more time in turn-taking exchanges with their mothers, their experiences with older siblings were related to subsequent peer interaction. The infants who had more extensive turn-taking experiences with skilled social partners engaged in more extensive turn-taking with a peer. They confirmed studies by Abramovitch and her colleagues that show that the older child is more likely to initiate behavior while the younger infant is more likely to respond.

Abramovitch and her colleagues (Abramovitch et al., 1979; Abramovitch, Corter, & Pepler, 1980; Abramovitch, Corter, Pepler, & Stanhope, 1986; Corter, Abramovitch, & Pepler, 1983; and Pepler, Abramovitch, & Corter, 1981) have conducted a notable series of research projects documenting the relationships of siblings longitudinally. Their basic goal has been to provide information on the content and affective quality of sibling interactions in the preschool years. They have looked at how variables such as gender or age affected these patterns.

In the beginning study, the younger siblings averaged 20 months of age and age intervals between the siblings were either extensive (2½–4 years) or minimal (1–2 years). Using observational ratings, the authors found that the oldest child in the sibling dyad initiated prosocial acts more often than did the younger siblings, while younger siblings imitated more often. These effects were found regardless of age-spacing between siblings.

These researchers also looked at interactional patterns in both same-sex and mixed-sex sibling pairs and found girls to be more prosocial than boys in both the 1979 and 1980 studies. In the same-sex (1979) study, pairs of sisters responded more positively, overall, in prosocial behavior than did brothers. In the mixed-sex (1980) study, younger siblings responded more positively to social initiations than did their older siblings. Also, in the same-sex pairs, older boys were more physically aggressive than older girls, while no differences emerged on any measures of aggression in mixed-sex pairs.

Corter et al. (1983) found that mothers are less consistent in their treatment of children in mixed-sex sibling dyads, and propose increasingly sex-typed interests and activities as factors in less positive interactions between mixed-sex dyads. Overall, though, they documented reciprocity in the sibling relationship from an early age with prosocial and play-oriented behaviors constituting a majority of sibling interactions in the preschool years.

In a first longitudinal follow-up study by Pepler et al. (1981) of 28 pairs of mixed-sex and 28 pairs of same-sex siblings, it was found that the above-documented pattern of interaction remained quite stable during the 18 months following the initial observations. Older children still initiated more prosocial behaviors while younger siblings imitated more often. However, a marked increase in prosocial behavior by both the older and younger siblings was noted over the 18-month time period. Interestingly, gender differences found in the earlier study, in which girls initiated more prosocial behaviors, were not found in the follow-up observations.

Abramovitch et al. (1986), in a second follow-up study of sibling interaction, observed 24 pairs of same-sex and 24 pairs of mixed-sex sibling dyads in their homes. This study, conducted 18 months after a first follow-up study and 3 years after their initial observations, found patterns of interaction similar to those observed earlier. In their ongoing longitudinal observations in naturalistic and laboratory settings, Abramovitch et al. have observed the older sibling consistently initiating more aggressive and prosocial behaviors, while the younger sibling displayed more imitative behaviors. The older sibling thus dominated the relationship even as both siblings grew older. They suggest that birth order is a critical component of sibling interaction. Neither of the variables, age-spacing nor gender composition, showed consistent effects.

Dunn and Kendrick (1979), Lamb (1978a), Samuels (1980), and Wishart (1986) also point out that older children serve as models initiating actions while the younger siblings pay attention to and tend to imitate their older brothers and sisters. Wishart found that sibling modeling could possibly be an effective method of facilitating cognitive development in infants.

School-Age Siblings Many studies of sibling interactions have looked at preschool-age children and their younger infant or toddler siblings. Older siblings offer toys to their siblings and attempt to engage in verbal exchanges (Abramovitch et al., 1979; Abramovitch et al., 1980; Lamb, 1978a, 1978b; Samuels, 1980) while the younger siblings model and monitor the behavior of their older brother or sister. Recently, several studies have investigated the interactions of school-age siblings. Sutton-Smith and Rosenberg (1968), for instance, found that on one hand, older preadolescent-age siblings (fifth- and sixth-graders) were perceived by themselves and their younger siblings as

being more "powerful" in social-structural terms. On the other hand, the younger siblings were perceived as showing more resentment and as having a tendency to turn more often to their parents for help.

Miller and Maruyama (1976), in an effort to explore whether the interaction of siblings in the home may require later-born children to develop more effective interpersonal skills (since they are viewed as having less "power"), argued that later-born children should be better liked in popularity measures. To test this hypothesis, the authors conducted a study of siblings in kindergarten through sixth grade in which they controlled for race, sex, and age variables. They found that, in school-setting measures of popularity in friendship, play, and school/work situations as well as in teacher ratings, later-born children did, in fact, rate as possessing greater social skills.

Stoneman et al. (1986) note that context, role relationships, and gender differences are three important factors in exploring sibling interactions for school-age children:

1. *Context* Brody and Stoneman (1986) note that in a contextual approach to sibling relationships, sibling interaction patterns cannot be understood apart from the contexts in which they occur. In

Stoneman et al.'s (1986) descriptive study of same-sex and cross-sex school-age sibling pairs, activities selected in the home by same-sex pairs were the most stereotypically sex-typed. Types of activities in cross-sex pairs tended to be influenced mostly by the gender of the older child.

2. *Role Relationships* A *role* is a patterned sequence of actions performed in an interactive or social context (Stoneman & Brody, 1982) that appears to have important developmental outcomes. The role relationships that occur during sibling interactions are important to explore. Studies of school-age siblings by Brody, Stoneman, and MacKinnon (1982); Brody, Stoneman, MacKinnon, and MacKinnon (1985); and Stoneman et al. (1984, 1986) looked at the roles of teacher, learner (or observer), manager, and managee in semistructured and naturalistic contexts. Consistent with earlier reported studies of preschool-age sibling dyads, older school-age siblings assumed teacher and manager roles more often while the younger siblings accepted the reciprocal roles of managee and learner. They also found greater role asymmetries in sibling interactions as contrasted with peer interactions, and in dyads having an older sister as contrasted with those containing an older brother.

Minnett, Vandell, and Santrock (1983) observed 73 pairs of siblings in the schools and focused on the 7- to 8-year-old firstborn siblings. The sibling pairs participated in unstructured, cooperative, and competitive contests. The authors found that firstborn siblings were significantly more likely than their younger siblings to praise, to teach, and to display dominant behaviors. The authors also noted that more positive behaviors were associated with siblings in pairs more widely spaced in age (3–4 years), while aggression was more common in pairs more closely spaced in age (1–2 years). This contrasts with a finding of Abramovitch, Pepler, and Corter (1982) who found that in preschool-age siblings, the age differences in dyads made little or no difference in their social interactions.

3. *Gender Differences* Stoneman et al. (1986) discussed gender differences in the role relationships of school-age children. Generally, female sibling pairs play together more than males (Brody et al., 1985; Stoneman et al., 1984) and among same-sex sibling pairs, older girls assume more of a teacher role than boys.

Adolescent and Adult Years Although information about adolescent sibling relationships is scarce (Bryant, 1982; Buhrmester & Furman, 1990), yielding discrepant findings in the areas of power (Bigner, 1974; Vandell, Minnett, & Santrock, 1987), warmth/closeness, and conflict (Vandell et al., 1987) as functions of age/development, some research has been completed. Bryant (1982) has written a chapter on sibling relationships in middle childhood. She suggests that "ambivalence," as well as rivalry and conflict, characterize the relationship of siblings during these years.

In a further attempt to clarify developmental trends, Buhrmester and Furman (1990) administered the Sibling Relationship Questionnaire to children in grades 3, 6, 9, and 12. They found that relationships were rated as progressively more egalitarian across the age groups. Adolescents reported reduced levels of dominance, nurturance, companionship, intimacy, and affection from their older siblings than did the younger participants. While levels of perceived conflict with younger siblings were moderately high across all four grades, ratings of conflict with older siblings were progressively lower. The authors suggest that sibling relationships become less asymmetrical and intense with age, and they point out the importance of a child's place in the family constellation when describing sibling relationships.

Daniels et al. (1985) also examined adolescent-age siblings when looking at within-family variance. Their research involving 348 families, each with two siblings from 11 to 17 years of age, confirmed that siblings in the same family experience different environments. These findings were reported by the parents, and to a great extent, the siblings themselves. It seems that environmental differences are related to dissimilarities in the development between siblings. The sibling who is reported by parents, teachers, and other brothers and sisters to be "psychologically better adjusted" also enjoys more maternal closeness, more sibling and peer friendliness, and more voice in family decision-making.

While there have been few studies of sibling relationships during the adult years, some researchers have begun to examine this important stage. For example, Aldous, Klaus, and Klein (1985) have looked at aging parents and their relationships with adult children. They found that although social prescriptions regulate a norm of equal attachment to each child in order to encourage family harmony and eliminate sibling rivalry, parents do, in fact, differentiate between children. In addition, the factors of proximity and gender were found to consistently promote close kinship ties.

Bank and Kahn (1982b) and Cicirelli (1982) have also begun to document sibling relationships throughout the life span into the adult years. Cicirelli has described the process of development for these ongoing relationships, suggesting that by the middle childhood years, sibling roles determined by the position in the family and various personality characteristics have been clearly established. He suggests that while siblings may be close throughout their adolescent years, supporting each other in new steps such as dating, there is often a period of separation in early adulthood, where contact is more dependent on external circumstances such as holidays. Later in their lives, siblings may share in the care for their elderly parents and the dismantling of the parents' home after their deaths (Cicirelli, 1982).

Relationship of Sibling Interactions to Family System

As noted by Brody, Stoneman, and MacKinnon (1986), only a few studies have directly focused on the relationship of siblings' interactions to other family subsystems. The findings suggest that such interaction *is* related to the quality of the sibling relationship. In their 1986 study, Brody and his colleagues observed 24 sibling pairs in their homes. Results revealed several associations between maternal child-rearing practices and the behavior of the older sibling toward the younger sibling. Managing and helping behaviors of the older sibling were positively related to maternal child-rearing practices that encouraged curiosity and openness. In contrast, these behaviors were negatively related to maternal inconsistency and anxiety induction. Maternal use of nonpunitive control techniques and her enjoyment of the maternal role were related to less agonistic behavior and more prosocial behavior, respectively. The authors also found that the particular play context influenced the types of behaviors observed and, thus, urge other researchers to focus on "context" as an important variable when looking at sibling interactions. Patterson (1976) found that coercive exchanges among siblings were predictable from similar interactions of parents and children.

Other studies (Brody & Stoneman, 1986; Brody et al., 1987; Bryant & Crockenberg, 1980; Teti & Ablard, 1989) have also suggested that sibling relationships are in large part a function of the parent–child relationship. Teti and Ablard found that dyads with a secure infant and a more secure older sibling appeared to be more likely to develop a nonagonistic relationship than those without such securely attached children; furthermore, the securely attached infants were less likely to protest and aggress against their mothers or older siblings when the mothers played only with the older sibling.

Corter et al. (1983) conducted naturalistic observations of mother–child and preschool-age sibling interactions. They found that when the mother was present, while the overall level of sibling interaction was reduced, it was also more agonistic than when the mother was not present. Brody et al. (1987) conducted research that suggests that younger siblings are less prosocial and more agonistic toward older siblings in times of family distress.

Wood, Vaughn, and Robb (1988) investigated concordance in the social-emotional and attachment behaviors of firstborn and second-born siblings in 65 families and found that the quality of infant–maternal attachment at 12 months showed significant concordance among siblings and was conditioned by the stability of maternal behavior. They suggest that caregiving experience is a fundamental influence on social-emotional development, and argue against the assumption that siblings in the same family necessarily show markedly different behaviors.

Beyond mother–child interactions, it seems that temperament of individual siblings also plays an important role in sibling relationships. Stocker et al. (1989) stress the importance of looking at temperamental and personality characteristics of each sibling as likely factors in the relationship that develops between them.

Temperament

Brody, Stoneman, and Burke (1988) conducted a study of child temperament and parents' perceptions of the child's adjustment. Seventy married couples with two children of the same gender were studied. They found that the perception of the child's adjustment was associated with the temperament of both siblings. Thus, for example, a child's absolute level of persistence or emotional intensity may be less important to parental perceptions than are the *differences* in absolute levels of temperament compared to the sibling. The authors urge researchers to continue focusing on the intrafamilial perspective and the family processes that create similar or dissimilar environments for children in the same family.

SUMMARY

It is clear that siblings play an important role in each other's development during their lifetime. Social interactions with siblings provide a context and foundation for the development of social and related skills such as language or motor skills. It is a foundation from which brothers and sisters are prepared for experiences with others outside of the family constellation.

Early research efforts focusing on the relationship between and among siblings were concerned primarily with the structure of the sibling relationship. Variables such as birth order and age-spacing were considered important in defining sibling relationships. More recent research has focused on the patterns of interaction within sibling and family relationships. Perceived or actual differential treatment of siblings by parents affects the quality of the sibling relationship, as well as the quality of mother–child interactions. Research in developmental patterns has focused on preschool and school-age children, and shows a role pattern of initiation on the part of the firstborn child and one of imitation for the second-born sibling.

Stocker et al. (1989) emphasize that longitudinal analyses of sibling relationships are needed to document the stability of patterns over time. They also suggest that in order to carefully understand the sibling relationship, characteristics of the children within the relationship (e.g., temperament), in addition to their relationships with other family members, must be examined. Brody and Stoneman (1986) and Stoneman et al. (1986) argue for the importance of context in describing sibling interactions.

Future research must contend with a myriad of issues. Research to date, for instance, has focused on only two siblings in any one family. In reality, of course, many families have more than two children and patterns of interaction between all siblings should be documented. Additional research must also continue to examine nonshared environmental factors and the influence of the father in sibling and mother–child relationships. The influence of divorce, separation, and remarriage on sibling relationships should also be addressed.

Special Brothers & Sisters in the Family System

To conclude, I want to relate that I, myself, and my other siblings all agree that despite the challenges and hassles of having a brother with autism, we feel we've benefited from the experience. We've learned to appreciate our blessings of health and to be compassionate toward others less fortunate. Certainly we've learned to not mind being different (p. 5).
Ken Laureys, 1982

Grace and Kevin wanted a large family. Gary, their third child, was born with Down syndrome. The doctors diagnosed Gary's condition at birth and were, for the most part, encouraging about his chances of attending school and of being accepted as part of their small rural community. The doctors had no idea of the effects, if any, Gary would have on the rest of the family, particularly Vivian and Linda, the oldest daughters, and any other children to come. Two years later, Gary was also diagnosed as being deaf, but the family had a relatively easy adjustment otherwise. Then Grace became pregnant again. Grace and Kevin decided it was time to find out what influence a child with a disability might have on brothers and sisters and vice versa.

The next few weeks were devoted to earnest research of information concerning what effects children with disabilities have on their siblings. Grace and Kevin read quite a few research reports. Some of the reports noted negative effects, others noted no significant effects, and still other reports claimed the effects were positive. They began to wonder about the value of such research if definitive answers were not to be found. So Grace decided to visit with other parents and inquire about sibling problems and the outcomes other families experienced. Again, no clear answers were evident. Finally, Grace and Kevin realized that they had to rely on their own feelings and judgment. They wanted a large family, and Gary was an integral part of that family already. His older sisters experienced difficulties with Gary, but also seemed to take great pride in his accomplishments. The couple resolved to try their best to create a loving family environment that fostered acceptance.

Like other parents in similar situations, Grace and Kevin came to realize that the time they spent reviewing some of the literature was worthwhile. They were convinced that if siblings' experiences could be both positive and negative, then they, as parents, could make the difference. Their readings and interviews gave them a new understanding of problems experienced by siblings and what parents could do to limit and/or minimize those problems.

Gary now attends a special education program in a public high school; the same high school attended by his two younger brothers. His two older sisters are attending a university. Grace and Kevin look back and know that they, indeed, made a difference. Gary is a most special part of their family.

THE FAMILY: A SOCIAL SYSTEM

It is helpful to take a broad perspective of the family when discussing a subset of that group such as siblings. Several authors have reviewed the general literature on families and adapted it to develop a framework for viewing families that include individuals with disabilities (Beckman & Bristol, 1991; Fewell, 1986; Mackeith, 1973; Minuchin, 1974; Stoneman & Brody, 1984; Turnbull & Turnbull, 1990). The fundamental concept of such a theory is that the family consists of a variety of subsystems each of which is interrelated. Of course, such a framework takes on an added dimension when one of the members in the system has a disability.

Turnbull and Turnbull (1990) have outlined a systems framework for the family of a person with a disability. This model includes four components as seen in Figure 3.1: 1) family characteristics, 2) family interaction, 3) family function, and 4) family life cycle. Each of these components is described briefly below.

Family characteristics are the descriptive factors, such as constellation variables (severity of disability or cultural background of the family), that describe a family and give input on family interaction. *Family interaction* is the ongoing process of family relationships that is responsive to individual and family needs; *family function* refers to the varying categories of needs that a family addresses such as economic or health needs. Finally, the *family life cycle* component represents the sequence of changes that affects families during the early childhood and school-age years as well as in adolescence and adulthood. Each of these components is important in considering the nature of sibling relationships. Elements of the family life cycle are addressed further below.

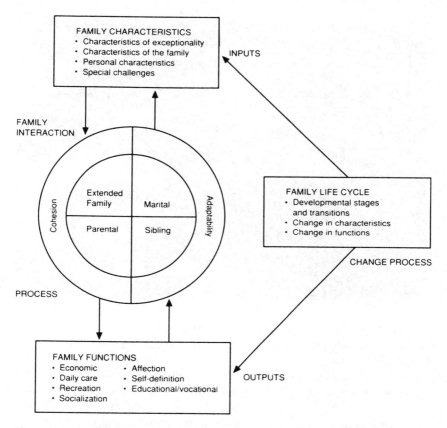

Figure 3.1. Family systems conceptual framework. (From Turnbull, A. P., & Turnbull, H. R., III. [1990]. *Families, professionals, and exceptionality: A special partnership* [2nd ed.] [p. 18]. New York: Merrill Publishing Company. As adapted by permission from A. P. Turnbull, J. A. Summers, & M. J. Brotherson [1984]. *Working with families with disabled members: A family systems approach* [p. 60]. Lawrence: The University of Kansas, University Affiliated Facility.)

For many families, the realization that a child has a disability is an unexpected shock. For example, no one imagined that Jonathan would be born with multiple disabilities; it was a surprise when Lisa was diagnosed as having a learning disability; Anthony's parents cried when they learned that he had mental retardation. However difficult, most families find ways to cope with new situations and new problems. The news of a disability forces families, particularly parents and siblings, to confront their dreams and expectations for the

child. Most likely, those dreams are altered by the reality of the disability. Learning about such a disability permanently changes the life of each family member.

The adjustment period in which family members learn to revise their dreams and accept the child with a disability into their framework differs from family to family. In some families, the process is long and difficult, for others, it seems to occur easily. Perske (1981) put it well:

> When a new youngster has a handicap, the family often expends energy beyond the ordinary. An increased sharpening of wits and widening of hearts become necessary so that the one with the handicap can be understood, loved, and accepted as a member of a close-knit family circle. On the other hand, some households become cold toward such a child, and more families change for the worse. (p. 14)

All families face a number of critical transitional periods in their lives that create stress. The birth of a new child, school entrance, a change in those living in the household—all are periods of stress. For the family with a child who has a disability, however, the stress of these times may be particularly acute. Mackeith (1973) has described four such periods:

1. When parents initially find out the child has a disability
2. When the child with a disability becomes eligible for educational services and, thus, faces academic expectations

3. When the family member with a disability leaves school and faces the personal confusion and frustration of all adults
4. When parents age and can no longer assume the responsibility and care for the person with a disability

These points in family life serve as a framework to help service providers identify potential periods in which family members, particularly parents and siblings, experience intense stress (Simeonsson & Simeonsson, 1981). Knowing when stress is likely to occur enables professionals to direct their services to alleviate or minimize the problems for family members during these critical times. Stress need not have completely negative effects, but can be turned into a positive force.

Turnbull and Turnbull (1990) have outlined a number of issues encountered by parents and siblings at life-cycle stages. These are included in Table 3.1. The authors note, for instance, that initially after the birth of a child who has disabilities, parents are concerned with "obtaining an accurate diagnosis," "informing siblings," and "establishing routines to carry out family functions" (Turnbull & Turnbull, 1990, p. 134). During a child's beginning school years, parents must decide the merits of mainstreamed versus specialized placement for their child. Perhaps arrangements for childcare and after-school activities need to be made as well. During the child's adolescent years, parents must make decisions surrounding important concerns, such as sexuality or vocational planning. After the school years, parents may be stressed with their continuing financial obligations toward the individual and with decisions on living arrangements. If the individual with a disability leaves home, the parents must adjust their relationship with each other and, perhaps, jointly face their daughter's or son's emerging interest in dating or marriage. During later years, parents worry about the placement and care of their child after their deaths.

All families must face times of decision, but transitions at these points may be more difficult for families with individuals who have a disability. Traditional symbols or rituals marking a transition may be delayed or nonexistent (e.g., no high school graduation ceremony). And, intensifying matters, critical periods for siblings without disabilities may occur simultaneously, forcing the family to deal with the differing needs of individual family members at the same time (Turnbull & Turnbull, 1990; Wikler, Wasow, & Hatfield, 1981).

Like all other families, families that have a member with a disability are facing the societal pressures and demands of today (Simeonsson & Simeonsson, 1981). Each family is unique and has varying needs. Families display both vulnerability and extreme strength, and when that family includes a child with a disability, the family may be

Table 3.1. Possible issues encountered at life-cycle stages

Life-cycle stage	Parents	Siblings
Early Childhood (ages 0–5)	• Obtaining an accurate diagnosis • Informing siblings and relatives • Locating services • Seeking to find meaning in the exceptionality • Clarifying a personal ideology to guide decisions • Addressing issues of stigma • Identifying positive contributions of exceptionality • Setting great expectations	• Less parental time and energy for sibling needs • Feelings of jealousy over less attention • Fears associated with misunderstandings of exceptionality
School Age (ages 6–12)	• Establishing routines to carry out family functions • Adjusting emotionally to educational implications • Clarifying issues of mainstreaming vs. special class placement • Participating in IEP conferences • Locating community resources • Arranging for extracurricular activities	• Division of responsibility for any physical care needs • Oldest female sibling may be at risk • Limited family resources for recreation and leisure • Informing friends and teachers • Possible concern over younger sibling surpassing older • Issues of "mainstreaming" into same school • Need for basic information on exceptionality
Adolescence (ages 12–21)	• Adjusting emotionally to possible chronicity of exceptionality • Identifying issues of emerging sexuality • Addressing possible peer isolation and rejection • Planning for career/vocational development • Arranging for leisure-time activities	• Overidentification with sibling • Greater understanding of differences in people • Influence of exceptionality on career choice • Dealing with possible stigma and embarrassment • Participation in sibling training programs

(continued)

Table 3.1. *(continued)*

Life-cycle stage	Parents	Siblings
	• Dealing with physical and emotional change of puberty • Planning for postsecondary education	• Opportunity for sibling support groups
Adulthood (ages 21–)	• Planning for possible need for guardianship • Addressing the need for appropriate adult residence • Adjusting emotionally to any adult implications of dependency • Addressing the need for socialization opportunities outside the family • Initiating career choice or vocational program	• Possible issues of responsibility for financial support • Addressing concerns regarding genetic implications • Introducing new in-laws to exceptionality • Need for information on career/living options • Clarify role of sibling advocacy • Possible issues of guardianship

Reprinted with permission of Merrill, an imprint of Macmillan Publishing Company from *Families, professionals, and exceptionality: A special partnership* (2nd ed.) by Ann P. Turnbull and H. Rutherford Turnbull, III. Copyright © 1990, 1986 by Merrill Publishing Company.

both stressed and strengthened by the experience. Featherstone (1980) speaks of the solitude, loneliness, and fear of being the parent of a child with a disability. She reminds us, however, that parents and families do endure and learn to live with difficult circumstances and, as Perske (1981) suggests, often turn a tough situation into a rich and rewarding experience.

SIBLINGS: EFFECTS OF A SPECIAL RELATIONSHIP

A special part of the family is, of course, siblings. The brothers and sisters of persons with disabilities are vital components in the family system. They influence the individual through their interactions and are, likewise, influenced by their brother or sister. This influence has preoccupied researchers, who have sought to describe the effects individuals with disabilities have on their siblings. The following pages review some of that research. Much of the early research efforts concentrated on the varying effects the child with a disability would have on brothers and sisters if the child lived at home or was institutionalized. Later research has been devoted to the process of the sibling relationship and the remediation of problems experienced by siblings.

This chapter reviews research that shows positive, negative, and mixed results regarding the effects a child with a disability has on his or her siblings, as well as factors that seem to contribute to the varied outcomes. Then more recent literature on actual interactional processes is discussed, and the research in context/role considerations, differential treatment, and stress/coping styles is reviewed.

Several authors (Cerreto & Miller, 1981; Lobato, 1990; McHale, Simeonsson, & Sloan, 1984; Seligman, 1983; Senapti & Hayes, 1988; Simeonsson & McHale, 1981) have recently reviewed research on the relationships between children with disabilities and their siblings. Basically, this research shows that there can be both positive and negative effects for the child without a disability.

On the positive side, some siblings report satisfaction in learning to live and cope with the demands of a child with a disability. They experience genuine joy and pleasure at the smallest accomplishments of the child, and feel a warmth and compassion for all people as individuals with unique needs and abilities.

It is a situation ripe for mixed emotions, however, and siblings also report negative effects. These negative effects include feelings of bitterness and resentment because of the extra attention given the child with the disability. Some siblings explain that they feel fearful and anxious about how to interact with the child, or even feel guilty because of their own good health.

Negative Effects

Farber (1959), one of the pioneers in exploring the psychosocial adjustment of siblings of a child with a disability, developed the Farber Role Tension Index. This index, which has been used extensively in studying family adjustment patterns, is a parental rating of the sibling without a disability based on 10 personality characteristics. In studies beginning more than three decades ago, Farber (1959, 1960, 1968) suggested that the more independent and higher functioning the child with the disability, the better adjusted the siblings tend to be. He also found that older sisters, who often had greater caregiving responsibilities for the child, scored higher in "role tension" when the child with a disability lived at home rather than in an institution. It is important to note that Farber's data came from parental assessments of their children, not from the siblings themselves. As Cerreto and Miller (1981) have pointed out, subsequent research has produced a set of complex observations that partly support and partly refute Farber's original contentions.

Fowle (1968), using Farber's Role Tension Index, concurred with Farber's finding that institutionalization of the child with a disability was especially beneficial to sisters. Again, since they were the ones who often assumed extra caregiving responsibilities associated with the child, sisters seemed to bear the brunt of tension. Lobato (1983, 1990) maintains, however, that extra caregiving responsibilities do not necessarily lead to negative adjustment. Such responsibilities may be balanced by an increase in the quantity or quality of attention given to the siblings by parents. According to Farber and Rychman (1965), "role tension" was also experienced by siblings of children with disabilities as the child became, in effect, the youngest child socially, regardless of chronological age.

Some corroboration of potential deleterious effects comes from an extensive study conducted by Grossman (1972). In her exploratory study, she interviewed college students, whose siblings had varying degrees of mental retardation. Her data revealed that about one-half of the group she interviewed had difficulties as the result of the child with a disability. These included ignorance concerning the feelings of the child with mental retardation and uneasiness about their own future children. Grossman also found that some siblings felt guilty for being in good health while, at the same time, they felt neglected because of their parents' preoccupation with the child who had a disability.

McHale and Gamble (1987) found that older sisters of children with mental retardation showed somewhat poorer adjustment in four measured areas than did siblings of children without disabilities. Older brothers were also more anxious and had lower levels of perceived competence in the areas of social acceptance and conduct when they had a sibling with a disability.

Positive Effects

Although Grossman (1972) found some negative effects on siblings, she also found a number of positive outcomes. She reported that about one-half of college students interviewed described the presence of a child with a disability as a positive, integrative experience in their family. These siblings showed increased tolerance for differences as well as higher levels of empathy and altruism. Grossman pointed out that the "humanness" of persons with mental retardation, as viewed by siblings, was influenced by the severity of the retardation, the extent to which the mother seemed to accept the child, and the amount of time the sibling played with the brother or sister with a disability. Grossman proposed that the manner in which a disability was interpreted and accepted delineated its impact on the siblings involved. Taylor (1974) agreed that a positive communication pattern between siblings without disabilities and mothers of children with mental retardation is instrumental in achieving optimal sibling adjustment.

Other authors have also concluded that there are positive aspects associated with the presence of a child with a disability in the family (Graliker, Fishler, & Koch, 1962). Schipper (1959), basing his results on parental histories and home observations, found that 75% of the siblings of children with Down syndrome in his study were happy and well adjusted. Schreiber and Feeley (1965) concluded that, for some siblings of children with disabilities, there is an increased sense of maturity and responsibility resulting from growing up with the child. Mates's (1982) study of 32 children with autism found that, as a group, their siblings displayed higher-than-average levels of self-concept. Additionally, Lloyd-Bostock (1976) found that parents reported that their child with a disability was generally loved and accepted by the other siblings in the family.

McHale, Sloan, and Simeonsson (1986) compared the sibling relationships of three groups of 6- to 15-year-old persons—those with siblings who: 1) had autism, 2) had mental retardation, or 3) had no known disabilities. All sibling relationships were rated by the siblings as generally positive with no significant differences found among groups. Mothers of children with a disability rated the sibling relationship more positively than did mothers of the comparison group. It is important to note that the data indicated that the experience of having a child with a disability in the family is highly variable, with a range of responses displayed. Children who have siblings without disabilities, however, tended to have responses that clustered around the mean.

Mixed Outcomes

Cleveland and Miller (1977) conducted a mail survey to obtain information on the long-range influences that a child with a disability would have on family members. The authors analyzed 90 surveys of adult siblings and focused particularly on their life commitments and career choices. Oldest female siblings reported having significantly more responsibility for the child with a disability. The older siblings also tended to enter the helping professions more often and sought professional counseling for personal problems. The authors found, too, that the adult siblings perceived the presence of the child with a disability as affecting their social relationships because in the course of almost daily contact with the child, they placed less emphasis on close friendships, marriage and family, and community membership. Female siblings reported having closer relationships with the child who has a disability than did their brothers. They also reported being more knowledgeable about mental retardation than their brothers. Self-reports from siblings in this study also suggested that siblings assumed responsibilities for inferred parental psychological needs, for example, and tended to overachieve and, thus, compensate for the limitations of the child with the disability.

As Cerreto and Miller (1981) emphasize, a major finding of the Cleveland and Miller study is that there may, in fact, be a positive outcome for the normal sibling who has a brother or sister with a disability. In general, adult siblings agreed that their families coped successfully, that they were adequately informed, and that both they and their parents had adapted successfully to the presence of the child with mental retardation. Other more recent studies have also found mixed outcomes in sibling relationships.

McHale and Gamble (1987) have supplemented behavior ratings with self-reports of sibling interactions and activities. Telephone interviews, conducted on a daily basis, found no differences between children who had a younger sibling with a disability and those without in terms of number of negative or positive behaviors directed at the siblings. Siblings having a brother or sister with a disability did

report greater intensity of any problems—that is, the events were seen as more troublesome. The authors point out that such intensity often leads to "internalized problems" involving worries and anxieties about the child's welfare. McHale and Gamble (1987) have found that such adjustment problems often become more negative with age.

Wilson, Blacher, and Baker (1989) found that, while siblings expressed a high degree of perceived responsibility for the child's welfare and a high proportion of siblings viewed their interactions as successful, the reports were not entirely positive. The siblings did acknowledge sadness, anxiety, and anger; for a minority, such negative feelings were the most evident.

Kirkman (1986), an Australian researcher, conducted a survey of adults who had a brother or sister with a disability and organized their responses around the following themes: family relationships; schooling, friendships, and social life; difficult and easy times; self-concept; and sibling relationships. She stressed that all siblings cause problems for their other siblings whether or not a child with a disability exists in the pair. She also found that while the problems or concerns may be more pronounced when there is a child with a disability, they are not necessarily of a different nature than those in other sibling relationships.

Lobato (1990) also agreed that, in general, siblings of children with disabilities do not have a higher instance of major personality or behavior disorders than their sibling peers. Granted, they are affected by the experience of living with a child who has a disability and may have special concerns and feelings; however, these do not often translate into measurable psychological adjustment problems.

Self-Concept/Behavior Ratings   When comparing children who have a sibling with a disability and children who have siblings with no known disability, a number of researchers have found mixed or no differences in self-concept or behavior problems. Gath and Gumley (1987) compared three groups of sibling pairs: the first had a child with Down syndrome; the second had a child with mild, non-specific mental retardation; and the third consisted of siblings with no known disability. Children related to a sibling with Down syndrome had fewer behavior problems and did better in school than those related to siblings with nonspecific mental retardation. Furthermore, the pairs with nonspecific mental retardation were also more likely to be associated with lower socioeconomic status (SES) groups. Sisters did not exhibit any more adjustment problems than brothers in this study.

Lobato, Barbour, Hall, and Miller (1987) found no differences in self-competence and acceptance, understanding of developmental disability, or childcare responsibility in preschool-age children, 24 of whom had a sibling with a disability and 22 of whom had a sibling without a disability. Interestingly enough, significant group differences were found in behavior ratings by mothers. Mothers rated their children, whether they were boys or girls, as more aggressive when they had a sibling with a disability.

Dyson, Edgar, and Crnic (1989) sent a questionnaire to 110 families, one-half of whom had a child with a disability and a control group of families with children having no disabilities. In the families having a child with a disability, they found that a combination of factors, such as parental attitude, social support, and family psychological environment, predicted the self-concept, presence or absence of behavior problems, and social competence of the older siblings. The same combination of factors was predictive only of social competence in the families where there were no children with disabilities. These siblings were also negatively affected (had lower self-concepts) by parental stress related to the condition of the sibling with the disability.

Dyson and Fewell (1989) compared the self-concept of 37 siblings who have brothers or sisters with a disability to a control group who had a sibling without a disability. These groups were matched by gender, geographical region, SES, and age. They found no differences in the levels of self-concept between the two groups and no significant effects for gender, birth order, SES, or type of disability. Dyson (1989) and Ferrari (1984) also found that siblings of children with a disability were comparable to children who had siblings with no disabilities in measures of self-concept, behavior problems, and social competencies. Dyson (1989) did find differences along psychological dimensions such as aggression and hyperactivity, and great variations within each group of siblings. Dyson and Fewell (1989) hypothesize that the actual effect of a sibling with a disability is slight because either the nature of self-concept is permanent or siblings have developed positive concepts through certain transactional processes. These processes include adaptive coping and additional responsibilities leading to increased competence. Dyson and Fewell conclude that the effect of a sibling with a disability on a person's self-worth is individualized and that further studies should investigate the importance of the type of disability, as well as expand on the instrumentation used.

FACTORS CONTRIBUTING TO THE SIBLINGS' ADJUSTMENT PATTERNS

It is evident that the impact a child with a disability has on siblings may vary a great deal. The relevance of research conducted 20–30 years ago is subject to question, especially given the increase in family support services (e.g., respite care and public school programs).

Wilson et al. (1989), for instance, stress the need to update sibling research since the Education for All Handicapped Children Act of 1975 was passed (since 1990 now known as the Individuals with Disabilities Education Act). They suggest that previously found negative effects on siblings may be moderated by the increased openness about, acceptance of, and services for those with disabilities. However, it is generally agreed that, even today, it can be stressful to have a brother or sister with a disability.

Cerreto and Miller (1981) and Trevino (1979) have noted that normal siblings of children with disabilities are potentially "at risk" for a wide variety of behavior or emotional problems, which may be long-lasting and may influence career choices and future family patterns. Past research has shown that a myriad of factors may contribute to the adjustment patterns of the child without a disability.

It is helpful to envision the effects of a child with a disability on the sibling in terms of a continuum, with very positive outcomes at one end and very negative outcomes (e.g., psychological disturbance) at the other. Many different factors seem to contribute to where the sibling without a disability functions on this continuum. Family characteristics, including size, SES, and religion, appear to be important factors contributing to sibling adjustment. Additionally, parental attitudes and expectations, as well as characteristics of both the siblings, such as age, gender, temperament, and the severity of the child's disability, also significantly influence the sibling relationship and affect sibling adjustment. A discussion of these four major contributing factors follows. Although all of these variables have not been studied extensively, it is thought that they often interact with each other to influence different feelings and relationships. It is important to remember that this continuum of outcomes for siblings is not static. Simply because a sibling seems to have a very healthy, positive relationship at one time does not mean that, at another time, the same sibling may not express some very negative behaviors and feelings.

Family Characteristics

Characteristics of the nuclear family appear to be important factors contributing to sibling adjustment. Family size, the socioeconomic status of the family, and religious involvement must also be considered as unique variables that influence the sibling relationship.

Family Size Taylor (1974) has suggested that siblings from larger families are generally better adjusted than those from smaller families. It seems natural that in two-child families where one child has a disability, parents are more likely to rest all their hopes and expectations on the other sibling. In larger families, however, these hopes and desires can be distributed to several children and, thus, prevent the pressure from resting on the one child. Dyson (1989) also found that the greater the number of children in the family, the better the psychological adjustment of the siblings. McHale et al. (1984) agreed that children from larger families are better adjusted, provided the families have adequate financial resources.

Socioeconomic Status Family SES can also affect sibling responses toward a child with a disability. Grossman (1972) found that siblings from middle-class families generally had a range of positive and negative feelings that were predictable from their parents' attitudes. Middle-class families often have problems lowering their high expectations for their child with a disability (McHale et al., 1984). At the same time, middle-class families tend to be more financially secure and better prepared to utilize outside resources, such as camps, respite care services, and a wide range of professionals, in securing help for any family needs. Conversely, families of lower SES typically have limited financial resources. Thus siblings, especially females, who are from poorer families may be overburdened with extra caregiving responsibilities that cannot be provided for through other channels.

Stoneman, Brody, Davis, and Crapps (1988) found that in families with greater income, siblings participated more in out-of-home activities as well as spent more time with friends. They also found that more educated parents placed fewer caregiving responsibilities on older siblings and facilitated more out-of-home activities.

Religion Stubblefield (1965), in review of the literature regarding the role of religion in parental acceptance of a child with a disability, noted that the birth of such a child often precipitates a theological crisis for many parents. Religious faith affects the parents' responses to the birth. Zuk, Miller, Bartram, and Kling (1961) established moderate but positive correlations between measures of religious background and maternal acceptance of a child with a disability. They found that Roman Catholic families tend to be more accepting of a child with mental retardation than are Jewish or Protestant families, and they explained such acceptance as deriving from the explicit definitions supporting the home and family life decreed by the Roman Catholic Church.

McHale and Gamble (1987) found that mothers who were more involved in religious activities used more coping strategies for dealing with the stress of having a child with a disability. The religious involvement of the mother was also related to higher self-esteem and fewer depression and anxiety symptoms in the siblings.

Parental Attitudes & Expectations

Siblings' perceptions of their parents' attitudes regarding the child with a disability can indeed be a powerful influence on their adjustment (Caldwell & Guze, 1960). In a study of the adjustment of parents and siblings, Caldwell and Guze (1960) looked at 32 families, one-half of which had a child with a disability living in the home and one-half of which had a child with a disability living in an institution; they found that, generally, the two groups were similar in adjustment. One area in which the two groups were clearly different was in the sibling's perception of the ideal living arrangement for the child with mental retardation. One group felt that the home was the appropriate place for the child; the other group felt that the institution was the best living situation. The siblings' responses were consistent with whether their brother or sister was at home or institutionalized. Holt (1958) also conducted personal interviews with parents in the homes of 201 families having children with mental retardation. Holt noted that 5% of the parents reported feelings of embarrassment and shame on the part of the children without a disability toward their sibling with mental retardation, and that such feelings were, to some extent, related to the parents' own adjustment.

Other researchers have stressed the importance of parental attitude in sibling adjustment. Grossman (1972) has suggested that one of the strongest factors affecting the sibling's acceptance of the child with a disability is the feelings of the parents, particularly the mother. After working with parents who were unable to participate in open discussions with their other children regarding the sibling who has a disability, she has proposed that the manner in which parents interpret and respond to a disability determines the impact on the siblings involved. Graliker et al. (1962), in their study a decade earlier, found that siblings without disabilities showed less disturbance in home, school, and social activities when both parents had the same positive attitude toward their child with mental retardation than did children of parents who did not share such a positive attitude. Clearly, parental attitudes exert a significant influence on a sibling's acceptance of a child with a disability. Siblings are better adjusted when their parents are more accepting of the condition of the child (McHale et al., 1984). As Lobato (1990) notes, a positive marriage with good communication predicts good psychological adjustment for the children. Lobato sees both good communication and closeness acting as critical buffers between the siblings and the stresses of having a brother or sister with a disability.

In McHale et al.'s 1986 study, status variables such as age, gender, and family size were not as highly correlated with the ratings of the quality of sibling relationships as were other factors such as perception of favoritism or coping ability (discussed later in this chapter). Specifically, children who have a sibling with a disability and their mothers rated the sibling relationship as being more positive when future concerns regarding the sibling, feelings of rejection, and pa-

rental favoritism are perceived as minimal by the children. The relationship is also improved when the child sees a positive response from parents and peers toward the sibling with a disability.

Characteristics of the Sibling without a Disability

It is difficult to separate demographic characteristics in families who have a child with a disability from those birth order characteristics found in all other families (Lobato, 1983). However, the gender and age of the sibling without a disability, in relation to the child with a disability, seem to be factors that contribute to the sibling's adjustment.

Gender—Caregiving As mentioned previously, several authors have found that older female siblings are most adversely affected by the presence of a child with a disability (Cleveland & Miller, 1977; Gath, 1974; Graliker et al., 1962; Grossman, 1972; McHale et al., 1984). Older siblings, particularly females, may experience this because they usually assume childcare responsibilities, and these responsibilities are often compounded when one of the children has a disability.

Wilson et al. (1989) suggest that, with the passage of PL 94-142 in 1975 and consequent greater availability of support services (including respite care), the task of caregiving for siblings has been reduced. Moreover, they suggest that recent shifts in the definitions of sex-roles may help to evenly distribute caregiving responsibilities among male and female siblings. Stoneman et al. (1988) did not find this to be true, however, and submit that the dramatic changes in the role of women in our society appear to have had minimal impact on the disproportionate role that older sisters of children with mental retardation still bear in childcare responsibilities. Their study found that the older sisters' responsibilities were associated with an increase in observed sibling conflict and a decrease in positive sibling interactions, as well as decreased opportunities for peer contacts and activities outside the home. As a group, though, the siblings of brothers and sisters with disabilities did not differ from comparison peers in the frequency of contact with friends or participation in activities outside the home.

In semi-structured home interviews with 24 siblings (ages 9–13), all of whom had a younger sibling with severe disabilities, Wilson et al. (1989) found that caregiving (teaching, dressing, feeding, babysitting, or disciplining) appears to be a regular and significant feature of the siblings' relationship. In this descriptive study, siblings reported that they interacted with the child on a daily basis and were "conversant" regarding the school activities of the child.

McHale and Gamble (1987) also found that children who had brothers or sisters with disabilities spent significantly more time taking care of their siblings, while those who had siblings without disabilities spent more time doing chores together. Thus, while the amount of time spent together was relatively the same, the tasks and activities were different.

Wilson et al. (1989) also found that age and sex (considered separately or in interaction) did not distinguish children who had generally positive interactions from others. Older children and those from lower SES families did report more caregiving, which suggests that services from PL 94-142 have not yet ameliorated differences in social class.

Gender—Age Some research shows that the psychological adjustment of siblings is more positive when the child with a disability is of the opposite gender from the sibling. Grossman (1972) found that siblings reported more embarrassment when the sibling with a disability was of the same gender and of close age to the child. Likewise, Schreiber and Feeley (1965) and Simeonsson and Bailey (1983) found that the greater the age difference between the child with a disability and the sibling, the more likely it is that the sibling will be well adjusted. Wider age-spacing of children is associated with less parental stress and reports of better marital relationships (Wagner, Schubert, & Schubert, 1985), which can lead to smoother sibling relationships.

Wilson et al. (1989), however, found that children who were of the same gender and relatively closer in age to the child with the disability described a more positive impact. The authors view the sense of "connectedness" reported between siblings as being a salient finding. While children of the same age and gender may enjoy the benefit of close companionship, such "togetherness" is also fertile ground for conflict (Lobato, 1990).

It also appears that when the sibling without a disability is older, particularly more than 10 years older, he or she will better adjusted (McHale et al., 1984; Simeonsson & Bailey, 1983). As Lobato notes, both Breslau (1982) and Dyson (1989) also found fewer indications of adjustment problems as differences in siblings' ages increased. Simeonsson and Bailey (1983) feel that the poorer adjustment found in siblings who are younger or closer in age may be attributable to identity problems. These siblings may have difficulty, for instance, adjusting expectations of what the "older brother" should do when he has a disability and may not even be able to feed himself. The sibling must learn to adjust his or her own identity in relation to a sibling who has a disability and, therefore, does not perform as a person that same age would typically perform. Simeonsson and Bailey (1983) have also proposed that the extent to which siblings perceive themselves as competent in relation to the child will help determine their adjustment. In effect, then, they suggest that older siblings, being innately more competent, or siblings who have been trained and who feel competent with the child with a disability, may be better adjusted than those who do not feel such confidence. They also feel that characteristics such as temperament may be of major importance when looking at the relationship between two siblings.

Characteristics of the Child with a Disability

The child with the disability, of course, also brings a unique personality and set of characteristics to the sibling relationship. Although the specific type of disability does not appear to be a major factor in sibling adjustment, the severity of the disability and concomitant caregiving requirements, as well as the ever-increasing age of the person with the disability, are influencing factors.

Type of Disability It seems that diagnosis of the particular type of disability involved is not a crucial factor in the adjustment of siblings with disabilities. One exception may be the diagnosis and subsequent residence, if the disability is one that requires any type of residential program, such as those offered in some states for persons with visual or hearing impairments. Correa, Silberman, and Trusty (1986) suggest that residence of the child with a disability is a factor in adjustment. Their review involves children who have a brother or sister with visual impairment who may be in a residential program for at least part of their life, reappearing in the family on weekends and holidays. Another exception seems to be in the case of families with higher incomes; siblings seem to be less well adjusted when their sibling's disability is ambiguous or undefined (McHale et al., 1984).

Lobato (1983) has detailed a series of studies on siblings of children with Down syndrome, cystic fibrosis, hearing impairments, autism, cerebral palsy, and childhood cancers, and notes that all the researchers describe similar results regarding the psychosocial adjustment of the siblings. Stressing that there must be factors other than the type of disability that determine adjustment for the siblings without disabilities, Lobato has suggested that these factors may include such characteristics as sex or age relative to the child with disabilities. It is also likely, she asserts, that parental attitudes toward the child with a disability, as discussed above, have a strong effect on the other children's sense of well-being. Simeonsson and Bailey (1983) have also suggested that other factors, such as individual traits, temperament, or functional behaviors of the child may transcend the influence of any particular disability.

Severity of Disability Farber (1959), Grossman (1972), and Kirk and Bateman (1964) found that siblings were more adversely affected when the child's disability was more severe and, thus, required more care. Again, the state of a family's financial resources interacts with the severity of the disability. In families of lower SES, where the financial resources for babysitters or tutors are unavailable, siblings typically have more caregiving responsibilities. Caregiving responsibilities, which include such tasks as feeding and bathing, have been discussed by several authors (Battle, 1974; Fotheringham & Creal, 1974; Korner, 1971; Robson & Moss, 1970; Schaffer & Emerson, 1964) as having an effect on mother–child interaction, the self-concept of the mother, and on parental stress (Beckman, 1983; Beckman-Bell, 1980; Harris & McHale, 1989). Parents of children with disabilities must deal with the aspects of childcare often in unusual circumstances and for an extended period of time (Battle, 1974; Beckman-Bell, 1980; Fotheringham & Creal, 1974; Harris & McHale, 1989). Indeed, Beckman-Bell (1980), in a study examining the relationship between characteristics of infants with developmental disabilities and maternal stress, found that caregiving demands alone accounted for 66% of the variance in perceived parent and family problems.

In Harris and McHale's (1989) study, mothers who participated the most in activities with their child who has a disability, whether leisure or caregiving activities, rated their family problems as more intense. They were concerned with the present and future well-being of their child, as well as with the excessive time demands associated with caregiving. It follows that such caregiving demands might also influence sibling relationships.

However, several researchers found no differences in sibling and parental adjustment related to the severity of the disability (Breslau, 1982; Kolin, Scherzer, New, & Garfield, 1971). Tew and Laurence (1973) found that siblings often react more poorly toward siblings with mild disabilities than toward those with more severe disabilities, perhaps because the child with a mild disability does not act like he or she "looks" like he or she should act. The siblings may also feel that the child with a disability is receiving more parental time and attention for no justifiable reason (see differential treatment sections).

Age of Child   The age of the child with a disability also seems to influence the adjustment of the siblings. Researchers (Farber, 1964; McHale & Gamble, 1987; Miller, 1969) have found that as individuals with disabilities grow older, their siblings experience more difficulties. This may be due to the fact that the child becomes increasingly difficult to manage and care for, while the differences between the siblings become more noticeable (Bristol, 1979; Wikler, 1983). Parents report that the family's isolation grows as the child matures physically, but not mentally or socially (Lobato, 1990).

In a study of individuals with mental retardation living in family care homes, Stoneman and Crapps (1990) assessed the relationship of parents and siblings with their relative who lived in the home. Although only about half of the clients had any contact with their families, the providers noted that parent and sibling relationships were closer when the individuals with disabilities were older and more able. Siblings visited from increasingly greater distances as their siblings with disabilities aged. Home care providers also reported a significantly lower amount of stress for the client when siblings visited more frequently.

It is interesting to note that siblings continued to visit after their parents were no longer alive; in fact, clients over the age of 60 actually had a slightly higher ratio of visits by siblings than did other age groups. The authors suggest that this is consistent with Seltzer's (1985) view that persons who have a sibling with mental retardation assume the primary support role after the parents are not able to function as such.

Zeitlin (1986), in a study of 35 adults with mental retardation, found that the vast majority of their siblings remained in contact. Most of the contact consisted of hierarchical siblings, especially sisters, providing assistance to their brother or sister with mental retardation. Not unexpectedly, Zeitlin found that the adult siblings' concern for their brothers or sisters followed the expressed wishes of the parents. It is interesting to note that these adults expressed a desire to have a reciprocal relationship with their siblings.

SIBLING INTERACTIONS

While much research on siblings of children with disabilities has focused on the adjustment of the child without a disability and on therapeutic interventions to facilitate that adjustment, researchers are also beginning to explore other aspects of the process of sibling relationships—*interactions*. As Senapti and Hayes (1988) point out, the focus has been on the "products of relationships" rather than on the interaction itself (p. 109). It certainly makes sense that the actual interactions should be the focus, especially since many of the factors described earlier (age-spacing, gender, severity of disability, etc.) are not factors a parent or service provider may have any particular control over.

Researchers are studying these interactions in the same way that they are examining sibling dyads when no child with a disability is present. For instance, Mash and Mercer (1979) and Peltz (1977) focused their research on students diagnosed with behavior disorders. While those with disabilities clearly had heterogeneous social behaviors, they did display more appropriate play behaviors and less activity changes when among their siblings without disabilities than when they played alone or with peers who had disabilities. Five broad areas of research in interactions with sibling dyads that include a child with a disability are those of context/role considerations, extent and quality of sibling interaction, differential treatment by parents, stress/coping styles, and adult interactions. Each of these emerging areas are outlined below.

Context/Role Considerations

Stoneman, Brody, Davis, and Crapps (1987, 1989) at the University of Georgia have argued for the importance of contextual considerations in the study of sibling relationships. They have looked specifically at the roles siblings take and activities in which siblings are engaged, as described in their research studies that follow.

Stoneman et al. (1987, 1989) collected observational data on sibling interactions. The 1987 study looked at same-sex sibling interactions in natural in-home contexts. Whether or not there was a sibling with mental retardation in the pair, they found that there was a high level of interaction. The types of activities siblings engaged in were related to the gender of the siblings and to whether or not the younger sibling had mental retardation. In sibling pairs where there was a younger child who had mental retardation, the pairs of boys were likely to be playing with toys while the female pairs engaged in non-competitive physical activities like swinging or tumble play. Comparison pairs were more likely to be playing games or watching television. Older brothers and sisters with a younger sibling who had mental retardation were more likely than comparison siblings to be engaged in asymmetrical roles—managing, teaching, and helping.

Stoneman et al.'s 1989 study looked at sibling interactions in standardized observational contexts (snacking, toy playing, watching television) in an effort to further determine role asymmetry, egalitarianism, and the affective quality of sibling relationships. This study also found heightened role asymmetries between older siblings when their younger brothers or sisters had mental retardation. Older siblings took greater responsibility for teaching, helping, and directing than did the comparison group. Differing amounts of interaction and various patterns of relationships were noted depending on the activity contexts.

Abramovitch, Stanhope, Pepler, and Corter (1987) compared sibling pairs having a child with Down syndrome to pairs having a child with no known disability and found results similar to those of Stoneman and her colleagues. In the groups who had a sibling with a disability, the children without disabilities assumed the dominant, leadership roles even when they were the younger sibling. These siblings also displayed significantly more nurturing and affectionate behaviors toward their siblings than did the children whose siblings did not have a disability.

Stoneman et al. (1987) also found a link between competency and role asymmetry in sibling pairs. It seemed that the less competent in language and adaptive skills the disabled siblings were, the greater was the role asymmetry in the pair. Stoneman et al.'s study found that language and adaptive skills of the children with mental retardation positively predicted the amount of time spent playing with older siblings, as well as the possibility of less role asymmetry. In the 1989 study, the level of role asymmetry increased with the age of the child with mental retardation. They note that these findings support Farber's (1960) contention that when siblings are younger, sibling interactions tend to be more egalitarian. As they grow older, however, the children without disabilities assume increasingly dominant positions when their sibling has a disability, whereas in families with two children without disabilities, sibling relationships become more egalitarian with age (Cicirelli, 1982). As Dunn (1983) noted, there is less reciprocity in the relationship when a sibling with a disability is present. Stoneman and her colleagues suggest that the greater role asymmetry with age eventually paves the way for the advocacy role that many persons of siblings with disabilities assume as adults.

Sibling Activities/Interactions

McHale and Harris (1992), in an effort to look at the extent and nature of sibling interactions rather than their affective quality, found that children (ages 8–14) with younger siblings, particularly girls, spent more time in caregiving activities with their siblings who had a disability. In contrast, children who have siblings without disabilities spent more time performing chores together. They did not find any differences among families in the total time spent with a brother or sister who had a disability versus a brother or sister who did not have a disability, but did find that girls perform more caregiving activities and boys more play activities. The researchers also found that more time in caregiving was significantly related to reports of anxiety symptoms; however, no other significant correlations between activities and the quality of the relationship were found. Perhaps, the slightly higher ratings of anxiety and lower self-esteem may be the price that children who have a sibling with a disability pay for a more mature self and broader outlook (McHale & Gamble, 1989; McHale & Harris, 1992).

McHale and Harris (1992) also looked at the affective tone of sibling interactions and report differences in what siblings perceive as contributing to the relationship. These findings were similar to Begun's (1989) study, which compared females' evaluations of their relationship with a sibling who had a disability with a sibling who did not. The experiences with siblings who had a disability were characterized as involving less intimacy, similarity, admiration, and competition, as well as more dominance by the sister without the disability. The sisters also reported less reciprocity from the brother or sister with a disability than from the siblings with no disability, while at the same time engaging in more nurturance with those with disabilities.

It is important to view this in the context of several other studies that have also noted more nurturant type behaviors and less reciprocity in sibling relationships that involve a child with a disability. Several authors (McHale et al., 1986; Ogle, 1982; Schaefer & Edgerton, 1981) found that parents rated sibling dyads higher (and, thus, more positively and kindly) on the Sibling Inventory of Behavior (Schaefer & Edgerton, 1979) when the dyad contained a child with a disability than when both children in a dyad did not have disabilities. Miller (1974), likewise, found that children tended to engage in activities of a more instrumental nature (helping, teaching) when their siblings were disabled, and in activities of a more expressive nature (self-fulfillment, mutual satisfaction) with their siblings who did not have disabilities.

Thus, it seems that children who may feel stress or have problems with a sibling who has a disability will not "take out" such
feelings on that sibling. If anything, the research shows that children
are kinder and more positive toward their siblings with disabilities.
This is in concordance with the teaching, helping roles observed by
Stoneman and her colleagues earlier in this chapter.

Gamble and McHale (1989), in correlational analyses, showed
that children's affective reactions to sibling stressors were related
more systematically to well-being and relationship ratings than were
the actual frequency of stressors. Therefore, siblings' reactions and
coping strategies were important in determining self-ratings of well-
being (McHale & Harris, 1992).

Differential Treatment

A common concern for children and adults is the way they are treated
by their parents in comparison to the way their siblings are treated.

Children begin at an early age to monitor their parents' behavior toward themselves and their siblings and to detect differences in the ways they are treated (Dunn & Stocker, 1989). As noted by Dunn, Stocker, and Plomin (1990) and McHale and Pawletko (1992), in addition to the actual differences in the ways parents treat their children, the *realization* by the sibling that he or she is being treated differently may also have effects on their well-being and development. Parents should be keenly aware of children's perceptions of parental fairness and its effects on sibling adjustment.

As discussed by McHale and Pawletko (1992), a related set of studies by Brody et al. (1987), Bryant and Crockenberg (1980), and Stocker et al. (1989), have focused on differential treatment and its effect on the sibling relationship. Bryant and Crockenberg (1980) concluded that siblings do compare parental interest and attention, and that evidence of preferential treatment toward one child can result in ill will and emotional conflict in the sibling relationship. Brody et al. (1987) and Stocker et al. (1989) found similar findings implying that preferential treatment may have negative implications in a child's relationships with his or her sibling, while simultaneously having positive consequences for the child's own adjustment.

McHale and Harris (1992) and McHale and Pawletko (1992) report on the differential treatment of siblings in four dimensions. These four dimensions are maternal involvement in activities with the older versus the younger child, household responsibilities assigned to the older versus the younger child, disciplinary responses employed by the mother in response to conflict, and the older child's satisfaction with parental differential treatment. They found greater levels of differential treatment in families with a child who has a disability. Mothers spent more time with younger siblings overall, but the differences were greater when the sibling had a disability. In terms of disciplinary strategies, mothers used more positive (love) strategies, such as reasoning, compromise with older siblings, and more power (assertive) strategies with younger siblings when the siblings had a disability.

McHale and Pawletko (1992), in an attempt to understand the context of sibling relationships and adjustment, examined differential treatment of siblings (maternal involvement, discipline, children's chores) in two contexts—families with and families without a child with a disability. Home interviews and maternal reports of 62 children, ages 8–14 years, indicated greater levels of differential treatment in families who had a child with a disability. Children who had a sibling with a disability and who were relatively more involved in younger sibling activities (help, play, outings) or who performed relatively more chores, experienced the highest levels of depression and anxiety. Children whose siblings did not have disabilities and who were the least involved in their activities reported the fewest symptoms of anxiety and depression. When looking at sibling *relationship* measures, highly involved older children who had siblings without disabilities were the most vulnerable.

It is hard to summarize the complex findings described above; therefore, caution is warranted. The picture is more complicated than earlier work suggests (McHale & Harris, 1992). As McHale and Harris (1992) note, it seems that children who have a sibling with a disability spend at least the same amount of time with their mothers and receive generally the same types of discipline as those with comparison siblings. One difference between the groups is that those having a sibling with a disability did perform a greater amount of household tasks.

Satisfaction Levels While McHale and her colleagues did find greater levels of differential treatment in families having a child with a disability, they found no group differences in children's satisfaction with the differential treatment (McHale & Gamble, 1989). Satisfaction with differential treatment correlated only with differential maternal involvement—the more satisfied children were, the less time they spent (relative to younger siblings) with their mothers. Additionally, children's satisfaction with differential treatment was systematically related to their well-being and their evaluations of the sibling relationship. McHale and her colleagues urge more research in the area of differential treatment. They suggest that a child might feel good about better treatment for him- or herself, yet also feel guilty or even begin to feel negative because his or her sibling is receiving the poorer treatment. McHale and Pawletko (1992) conclude that differential treatment of siblings is a complicated phenomenon that depends on: 1) the domain of differential treatment being considered (e.g., mother–child activities versus disciplinary activities); 2) the potential "consequences" of differential treatment under consideration (well-being versus relationship measures); and 3) the family context. McHale and Pawletko (1992) suggest that while some forms of differential treatment may imply clear favoritism on the mother's part, other forms, such as higher involvement in care or play, may be viewed as an imposition by older children. Thus, children may evaluate different forms of treatment in various ways.

McHale and Pawletko (1992) caution that research to date has only been correlational in nature and that we cannot yet conclude that differential treatment causes well-being and sibling relationship differences rather than vice versa. They point out that previous studies have focused on either adjustment or characteristics of the sibling relationship as potential "outcomes" of differential treatment. Their study considered the possibility that receiving more favorable maternal treatment might be positively correlated with individual well-being (Dunn et al., 1990), but negatively related to the quality of the sibling relationship as indicated by Bryant and Crockenberg (1980), Brody et al. (1987), and Stocker et al. (1989).

McHale and Pawletko (1992) found that in mother–child activities, relatively less involved children reported better adjustment and more positive sibling relationships. They found less consistency, however, when looking at differential household chores and discipline. In children who receive more positive love (reasoning, compromise) and have siblings who are disabled, a higher level of anxiety coincides with the "guilt" these children have expressed at receiving more favorable treatment. Such feelings can also motivate the child toward more kindness and concern in the sibling relationship.

While McHale and Pawletko's (1992) study provides evidence that children with siblings who have disabilities *do* experience greater differential treatment than other siblings, McHale and Pawletko (1992) caution that such discrepancies arise not because the children are "neglected," but because their younger siblings with disabilities are treated so differently than are other children their same age. It is important to be aware that discrepant emotional reactions can arise. While a child may be able to understand and justify the differential treatment, he may still harbor feelings of neglect or isolation.

Stress/Coping Styles

Some researchers are beginning to look at stress factors and siblings' coping styles in an effort to understand adjustment in children who have a sibling with a disability. Gamble and McHale (1989) gathered ratings of the nature of stress and coping styles in 62 children, ages 7–14 years, half with a sister or brother who had a mental disability and half with a sibling without a disability. They found no significant group or gender differences for the overall frequency of stressful events or for the amount of anger felt between the two groups. However, the comparison group did report that their siblings "teased or bugged" them more often, and children who had siblings with a disability showed significantly higher affect ratings in response to their sibling getting hurt or sick.

Children, in general, reported responding to stressful events in different ways, and these various reactions and coping strategies were important in determining self-ratings of well-being (Gamble & McHale, 1989; McHale & Harris, 1992). Children who had a sibling with a disability and girls who had a sibling without a disability used coping responses characterized as "other-directed cognitions" (e.g., my brother is a creep) more frequently. Boys who had siblings without disabilities tended to use "self-directed" strategies more often (try to calm down, or think about ways to solve the problem). These strategies were positively related to adjustment and relationship reports. Perhaps as Gamble and McHale (1989) note, the siblings of children with disabilities react less directly because their siblings may not understand and/or their parents are less tolerant of such behavior. Girls, of course, may have similar sanctions placed on their behaviors.

Both stressor frequency and the use of cognitive coping strategies accounted for significant portions of the variance in sibling relationship measures. Self-directed strategies (e.g., doing something fun to forget about it) were positively associated with relationship measures while other-directed cognitions were negatively related.

Adult Interactions

Seltzer, Begun, Seltzer, and Krauss (1991) conducted a study to provide information about the nature of sibling and intergenerational relationships for adults with mental retardation. The most involved sibling was typically older than and of the same gender as the adult with mental retardation, lived near the family home, and had at least weekly contact in person or by phone. The adults with disabilities in this study lived at home and, it is interesting to note, maternal well-being was associated with the siblings' active involvement in the life of the adult with mental retardation.

Families with high levels of sibling involvement tended to be more expressive and cohesive, more oriented toward achievement and independence, and more likely to participate in active recreational activities than did families with lower levels of sibling involvement. However, they did find an imbalance in the exchange of affect between the sibling and the adult with mental retardation. The siblings were giving more than twice the support they received in return from their brother or sister. The authors also note that at this stage, siblings tended to give more affective support (showing concern for welfare) than instrumental support (helping with daily tasks or self-care activities).

Similarly, Begun (1989), in a study of adult and adolescent females and their siblings with mental retardation, found a lack of balanced reciprocity in the relationship with the females giving more instrumentally and affectively than the siblings. She also found that siblings who did not live together had less conflictual relationships.

SUPPORT FOR FAMILIES

Undoubtedly, recent efforts to provide community support to families who have a member with a disability will have a substantial impact on lessening the stress faced by parents and siblings. Gamble and McHale (1989) and Stoneman and Crapps (1990) discuss specific cognitive and social skills/strategies that could be taught to siblings to maximize the interactional process and/or their own adjustment. Stoneman and Crapps (1990) caution that these should be developed with sensitivity and in moderation. Community services may help to minimize and, in some cases, alleviate problems experienced by siblings, but only when they are comprehensive in nature and flexible enough to meet the varying and ever-changing needs of families and their individual members.

The development and implementation of a full continuum of community-based services has been the goal of many parents, siblings, and professionals working together to improve the quality of life for persons with disabilities and their families. This full continuum may include the following family-oriented services:

Respite care
Home health service
Transportation programs
Sibling counseling and training
Parent counseling and training
Recreational programs
Community living programs (e.g., supported living)

Financial assistance
Social work
Advocacy services

Later chapters in this book more closely examine the issue of support services for families.

SUMMARY & FUTURE DIRECTIONS

The review of the literature in this chapter should clarify the complexity and importance of families, and the significance of sibling relationships to the family system and to individual family members.

Early studies of siblings without disabilities focused on demographic characteristics, such as birth order, in relation to personality characteristics. The focus of recent investigations has shifted, however, to observational studies of the interactions between siblings. A similar trend in the literature involving siblings of children with disabilities has evolved.

The literature, involving a sibling of a child who has a disability, looked first at sibling-status variables that contribute to the psychosocial adjustment of the sibling without a disability. Siblings without disabilities were affected by the presence of a child with a disability in both positive and negative ways. It seems that there is a continuum of positive and negative outcomes for siblings, and that their position on this continuum is related to a number of variables that have been discussed in detail. A sibling's status on such a continuum can change over time.

Such research does, of course, have its limitations. Hannah and Midlarsky (1985) note that many of the early studies reporting negative effects not only failed to use comparison groups, but also used various methods of observation from sources other than the siblings themselves. As mentioned earlier, these variables are often hard to control or change, therefore, the use of research in the area of sibling interactional processes may be especially fruitful to practitioners and parents alike.

It seems that variables such as context, roles, and parental differential treatment are important considerations in looking at these processes. Children know by an early age that their parents treat them differently from their brothers and sisters. In families having a child with a disability, differential treatment is sometimes exaggerated. Whatever their feelings as a result of being treated differently, it seems that for the most part, siblings do not vent their frustrations on their brothers or sisters with disabilities. If anything, siblings are kinder to their brothers and sisters than they are to other siblings, often taking a teacher or helper role. Their relationship seems to become even less "equal" as the children grow older.

What this relationship means for the child with a disability remains to be seen. Would it be more helpful for that child to learn the "give-and-take" of the real world from the siblings? And what does it eventually mean for the sibling without a disability? As Bell (1968) reminds us, interaction is a two-way process. McHale and Gamble (1987) caution that play experiences with a sibling who has a disability may be a constant attempt to entertain or teach new skills rather than a pleasurable give-and-take relationship. The siblings may feel eventual resentment at constantly having to assume the teacher or helper role and may avoid contact or not initiate interactions after a while (McHale & Harris, 1992). As can be seen, children's coping styles are an important variable needing further exploration (Gamble & McHale, 1989).

Future research must continue to explore the domain of differential treatment. We need to assess children's perceptions of differential treatment and how this perception varies with certain children (McHale & Harris, 1992). We need to know when children understand why they are treated differently, and how the seeming legitimacy of a child having a disability mitigates the differential treatment (McHale & Pawletko, 1992).

Future research must also consider the development of sibling relationships and interactions throughout their lifetimes and in natural environments (Gallagher & Powell, 1989). We also need to know more about the role of the father and extended family members since most of the research in sibling relationships, which has used parent ratings or looked at parent qualities, has involved only the mother's perspective. McHale and Harris (1992) also suggest longitudinal designs to measure the potential growth and positive benefits of growing up with a child who has a disability as these might not be exhibited until adolescence or even adulthood. Stoneman (personal communication, 1991) feels that it is time for an ethnographic/qualitative perspective on sibling interactions.

The effects of brothers and sisters on a child with a disability must also be explored, as well as the effects that parental differential treatment might have on that child. Dunn (1983), Gamble and McHale (1989), and Simeonsson and Bailey (1986) suggest that the temperament or personality of the siblings, the physical capabilities, and the functional behavior of the child with a disability are also important factors to consider in sibling relationships. In fact, Stoneman et al. (1988) suggest that future comparison groups should be matched on adaptive skills rather than on just the chronological age of the siblings. McLinden-Mott and Braeger (1988) suggest further research to develop sensitive measurement instruments that can account for caregiving demands as well as self-esteem.

There are, of course, broader family issues that should also be examined. Stoneman et al. (1988) suggest research on the special demands placed on the sibling without a disability when two or more children in the same family have a disability. Likewise, single mothers of children with disabilities experience more general stress and financial difficulties than do married mothers (Bristol, Reichle, & Thomas 1987). Bristol et al. (1987) and Fewell and Vadasy (1986) remind us that to meet the changing demographics and needs of the American family, new and flexible service options must be developed.

When a brother or sister has a disability, will the effects on siblings be negative or positive? The complexity of this question prohibits answering quickly or easily. Research that draws a single conclusion presents too simplistic a solution for the resolution of such a compound issue. On the basis of what we know in the 1990s, perhaps the best answer is, "It depends." It depends on a number of contributing factors, including parental attitudes and expectations, as well as parental differential treatment, family size, family resources, religion, severity of the child's disability, and the pattern of interactions between the siblings. With the use of the new family-oriented services, professionals' understanding of the unique need of families, especially of siblings, is increasing. It is hoped that these new community-based programs will help to ensure that the experience of having a brother or sister with a disability will be positive for all family members.

4

Special Concerns
&
Unique Needs

You, too, are a valuable, developing individual human being. You, too, need to be recognized, to be loved, and to develop into the best person you can be. Your brother or sister with the handicap needs to experience the most robust, risky, rough-but-kind interactions with you that he or she can tolerate—as close to normal sibling relationships as possible (p. 75).
Robert Perske, 1981

Sometimes the most meaningful stories are told out of context, prompted by an informal comment, a passing thought, or the sudden recognition that the listener may, indeed, be interested. Mike told his story along the shores of a Tennessee lake after he learned that the person fishing next to him was a special educator. The recreational pursuit of fishing seemed unimportant in comparison to the emotion of Mike's story.

Mike grew up in a small town in middle Tennessee in the 1940s. When he was 8, his younger sister was born with Down syndrome. As was typical in those times, she did not attend school and received limited services. However, she lived at home rather than at one of Tennessee's institutions, an arrangement that was not so common at the time. Mike was embarrassed about his younger sister. He did not understand her disability. Why was she always ill and unable to speak very well? He was so ashamed that, at times, he would claim she was a distant cousin or an abandoned child. At times, he was angry at her; at other times, he was sad, happy, or frightened. He was confused about his sister and his responsibilities toward her.

Mike had a close childhood friend, John. The two had been friends since they entered school, and they remained friends as adults. Although they were very close, Mike never invited John to his house. He was afraid that his friend would learn about his sister. Since Mike, himself, did not understand his sister, he certainly could not expect John to understand. Mike kept John far away from his family. He was afraid of losing a friendship because of his sister.

Oddly enough, John never invited Mike to his house either. It was not until both men were adults that Mike learned (by accident) that John's brother had cerebral palsy.

At the conclusion of his story, Mike said it all—"We could have shared this, but we were both too afraid and too confused."

What would the lives of these friends have been like if they had shared their secrets with each other? These two men grew up together, but in some important ways, they grew up alone. Their friendship and mutual experiences could have provided a source of support for the special problems and needs common to siblings of individuals with disabilities. Instead, they kept their concerns to themselves, never daring to share an integral part of their lives with each other. Certainly, Mike's story is unusual not only in its ending but also, against present standards, in the lack of services available to his sister. However, in other aspects, his story is like those of so many others.

All siblings who have sisters and brothers with disabilities express a number of special concerns they have about themselves, their

families, the community, and the future. Their emotions are mixed (some positive, some negative), and their questions, although sometimes unvoiced, are many. They have problems with parents and with talking to their friends about their brothers or sisters. Some siblings have extraordinary responsibilities for the child with a disability. These responsibilities produce a number of specific worries and needs. Like Mike, some siblings do not know how or with whom to share their feelings, problems, and needs. Other siblings need basic information about their brothers or sisters or training to learn how to best help the exceptional child.

This chapter focuses on the special concerns and unique needs of siblings. It provides a foundation for succeeding chapters, which will detail methods to meet the special needs of siblings who have brothers and sisters with disabilities.

SIBLINGS' SPECIAL CONCERNS

Siblings who have brothers and sisters with disabilities are, first and foremost, people. They share the same concerns and problems most other siblings experience as children and adults. Like all people, they encounter varying degrees of problems.

Since the 1960s, individuals who have brothers and sisters with disabilities have been the subject of an increasing amount of research. A comprehensive study on the special needs of siblings was reported by Itzkowitz (1989). In her work, she used surveys to interview 679 siblings, who ranged in age from 7 to 83 years, with a mean age of 31. These siblings had brothers and sisters with varying disabilities, and represented a cross-section of socioeconomic status and all areas of the United States. This group reported having specific needs for information, professional support, family support, education, and community services. Itzkowitz notes that, based upon her findings, it is important for professionals to recognize these needs and that such needs will vary according to the age of the sibling. Younger siblings need support primarily from the family unit. As siblings grow older, the need for respite services, counseling, and school services becomes more important.

Itzkowitz's research, the studies reviewed in Chapter 3, and our own extensive interviews with siblings demonstrate that siblings tend to share a number of special concerns. These concerns are independent of the type of disability affecting their brother or sister, the family size, the sex of the sibling, or the birth order of the sibling. Siblings typically discuss concerns about:

1. The child with a disability
2. Their parents

3. Themselves
4. Their friends
5. The community, in particular, school
6. Adulthood

The Child with a Disability

Naturally, siblings have a number of special concerns about their brother or sister with a disability and his or her particular condition. Their concerns focus on the cause of the disability, the child's feelings and thoughts, prognosis for a cure or improvement, the services the child needs, how they can help the child, where the child lives, and what the future holds for the child. These seven major areas of concern give rise to questions like those in the following list, which siblings may ask openly or sometimes hesitate to ask. It is important to help siblings address these concerns.

Concern	Question
Cause of the disability	Why does my sister have a disability?
	What caused the disability?
	Will future brothers and sisters also have disabilities?
	Whose fault is it?
The child's feelings	Is my brother in pain?
	Does he have the same feelings I do?
	What does he think about?
	Does he know me?
	Does he love me and my parents?
	Why does he behave so strangely?
Prognosis	Can my sister be cured?
	Will she improve?
	Can she grow out of this?
	Can treatment really help?
Needed services	What special help will he need?
	Who are these professionals who work with him?
	What do they do with him?
How to help	What am I supposed to do with my sister?
	What can I expect from her?

Concern	Question
	Can I help teach her?
	How can I interact with her?
	Should I protect her?
Where the child lives	Why does my brother live at home?
	Wouldn't a group home be better for him?
	Why doesn't he live at home?
	Aren't institutions bad for persons with disabilities?
The future	What will happen to my sister in the future?
	Will she always be with us?
	Will she go to school?
	Will she have a job?
	Will she get married and have a family?
	Will she ever live on her own?

Their Parents

When siblings talk about their family, whether informally, formally, privately, or in groups, much of the discussion centers on their parents. Siblings tend to have concerns about parental expectations, communicating with parents, their parents' feelings, their parents' time, helping their parents, and their participation in child-rearing.

Concern	Question
Parental expectations	What do my parents expect of me?
	Why are my parents so hard on me?
	Why do they expect so much?
	Why do they overprotect me?
	Are my parents using me to compensate for my sibling's shortcomings?
	Why do they let my brother "get away" with so much?
	Will they treat me normally?
Communicating with parents	How can I discuss my feelings about my sister with my parents?

Concern	Question
	How should I handle disagreements with them?
	Can we openly talk about my sister, her problems, and what we are going to do about them?
Their parents' feelings	How do my parents feel about my brother?
	Are they afraid, sad, happy, lonely, confused or excited like I am?
	Do they love me as much as my brother?
	Why do they fight so much about my brother?
	Do my parents know why this has happened to our family?
Their parents' time	Why must all of their time be given to my sister?
	Why won't they spend more time with me?
	Why must we always do something that involves my sister?
	Why can't I have some private time with them?
Helping their parents	What can I do to help Mom and Dad?
Participation in child-rearing	Should I express my views on raising my brother?
	Why do they always ask me to babysit?
	Why am I always responsible?
	Do they want me to control his behavior?

Themselves

Privately, usually when discussing a related topic, some siblings begin to share special concerns they have about themselves. They are concerned with their feelings, their health, and their relationship to the sibling.

Concern	Question
Their feelings	Why do I have such mixed feelings about my sister?
	Do I really love her or really hate her?
	Why does she make me so happy and also so angry?
	Am I jealous of the attention she receives?
	How can I deal with my mixed feelings?
Their health	Will I "catch" the disability?
	Is there something wrong with me?
Their relationship to the sibling	How can I get along better with my brother?
	Will we have a normal brother–sister relationship?
	Why am I smarter and stronger than my older brother?
	How can I be a better, more loving sister?

Their Friends

Almost all siblings discuss their relationships with their friends and the special problems encountered as a result of the disability. Siblings are concerned with informing their friends about the child with a disability, as well as teasing, accepting the child, and how dating will be affected.

Concern	Question
Informing their friends	How can I tell my best friend about my brother?
	Should I invite the friend over to meet my brother?
	Will my friends understand?
	Will they think I'm disabled, too?
	Will they tell everyone at school?
Teasing	What should I do when my friends tease my sister?

Concern	Question
	Why are they so mean to her?
	Why do they tease me about my sister?
	What should I say to them?
	What should I do when other kids are making fun of persons with disabilities?
Their friends' acceptance	Should I invite my brother to play with us?
	Can my friends accept my brother?
	Will they like him?
	Will they be afraid of him?
Dating	What will my boyfriend think of my sister?
	Will my sister frighten my girlfriend away?
	Will my boyfriend think there is something wrong me?
	What if my sister makes a scene when my girlfriend comes over?
	How much should I tell my boyfriend about my sister?

The Community

Naturally, siblings are preoccupied about concerns involving the child and the community. In particular, siblings have special concerns regarding school, community acceptance, and community living.

Concern	Question
School	What happens in special education classes?
	What does my sister learn?
	Do my teachers treat me differently?
	Will kids at school treat my sister okay?
	Will I be compared with my sister?
	Will I be responsible for my sister's problems and her behavior?

Concern	Question
	Why do teachers always call me when there is a problem?
	Why don't they tell me if there is a problem?
	Do I have to associate with my sister at school?
	Aren't private schools better for children with disabilities?
Community acceptance	Will my brother be accepted in public?
	Why do people stare at us?
	What should I tell strangers?
	What if my brother has a seizure on the playground or in the store?
	Will people take advantage of him?
	Will he be exploited or cheated by others?
	Will anyone outside of the family be my brother's friend?
Community living	What is a group home?
	Isn't an institution a better place for people with disabilities?
	Will the neighbors accept my sister?
	Will my brother get and hold a job?

Adulthood

As siblings get older, their special concerns focus on the unique problems associated with adulthood. These concerns typically involve guardianship, their own family, and the nature of their continuing involvement.

Concern	Question
Guardianship	Will I be responsible for my brother when my parents die?
	What will be expected of me?
	Will I be financially responsible for my brother?
	Will my brother have to live with me?

Concern	Question
	Who will be a guardian if I am unable or unwilling?
Their own family	Will my spouse accept my sister?
	Does the presence of a disability affect my chances for having healthy children?
	Do I need genetic counseling?
	How do I provide a proper balance in my responsibilities to my sibling and to my spouse and children?
	How will my children be affected by their aunt who has a disability?
	Can I be fair to both my family and my sibling?
	What will happen if my sister comes to live with us?
Continuing involvement	How should I continue to be involved with my brother?
	Should I visit his group home?
	Should I advocate on his behalf?
	Should I join a parents' and/or siblings' group?
	Am I selfish if I don't want to see my brother anymore?

SIBLINGS' UNIQUE NEEDS

The special concerns expressed by most siblings provide a way of gauging the nature and intensity of a sibling's individual needs, special problems, and worries. Of course, each sibling's needs vary; not every sibling encounters the same problems or the same degree of problems, and family responses (as discussed in Chapter 3) will differ. Some siblings have few, if any, special needs; others have many. These needs demand respect and understanding. Information, counseling, and training must be available for siblings as well as their parents.

Respect

Like all people, siblings who have brothers and sisters with disabilities have a need to be recognized and respected as individuals.

They should be known for their own accomplishments, their own characteristics, their own feelings, and their own joys. Siblings have a need to not be compared to the other child. They need to stand on their own and develop an identity outside of their family and especially outside of their brothers and sisters. Siblings have a major need to be respected as individuals by their parents. They need to not be pushed too hard in an attempt to overcompensate for lost parental hopes, nor overprotected because the parent applies blanket restrictions to all of the children. These needs are not unlike the needs experienced by all siblings; however, they may be intensified by the presence of the child with a disability and the family structure that has developed to accommodate that child.

Understanding

Siblings who have sisters and brothers with disabilities need understanding. Unlike other siblings, their lives may be altered by the added pressures and problems associated with living with a child with a disability. They need to know that their special concerns are recognized and respected as legitimate. They need affirmation that others (especially adults) understand their problems and are willing to help.

Information

Siblings have a unique need for honest, direct, and comprehensible information in order to answer questions about their brothers or sisters, their entire family, themselves, school, special services, guardianship, treatment, and so forth. Siblings need different information at various stages of their lives. They need a system to gather such information in an easy-to-access manner; a system that is responsive to their personal questions rather than to predetermined, generic questions. Siblings need an information system that is longitudinal rather than episodic in nature, one that adapts to their changing needs and is readily available throughout their lives.

Counseling

Some siblings need to share their feelings with trained counselors to enable them to understand and accept their feelings. Others need a mechanism to help them deal effectively with their behavior and to change their behavior. These siblings need counseling services. Some siblings need formal and individualized counseling, while others require a more informal approach with a social service professional. Some siblings need to be involved with other siblings so that they can share their feelings and learn from one another.

Training

Training represents yet another broad category of needs. Many siblings have a strong desire to help their parents with the child who has a disability. In order to serve as an effective helper, the sibling often needs special training. Some siblings seek education to learn how to teach specific skills to their sister or brother; others want to learn how to manage the child's behavior; still others want to learn how to plan and interact with the child.

An analysis of these special needs implies the development and implementation of a diversified service system that offers training, guidance, and support to siblings with brothers and sisters who have disabilities. Siblings may need different services at various stages in their lives. Not all siblings will require outside services, but those who do should have access to services that will meet their varying needs.

SUMMARY

As this chapter has illustrated, siblings who have brothers and sisters with disabilities experience a number of special concerns and, consequently, have special needs. Although it is impossible to generalize one set of concerns to all siblings, many siblings worry about the child with a disability, their parents, themselves, their friends, the community, and adulthood. These concerns lead to a set of specific needs in regard to respect, understanding, information, counseling, and training. Although the concerns and needs presented in this chapter are not an exhaustive list of all possible worries and requirements, they reflect the scope and range of the concerns and needs experienced by most siblings who have brothers and sisters with disabilities.

The chapters in Section II specifically address ways in which the needs of siblings can be met. These chapters suggest ways to provide information to siblings, counsel siblings, facilitate social interaction between the child with a disability and the sibling, train the sibling to teach the child, develop positive community programs, and help adult siblings deal with their concerns.

II

Strategies
To Help Siblings

5

Providing
Information

*I have often seen children develop gross misconceptions when
preventive measures are not provided. They will put together bits
and pieces of conversations they have overheard and, not knowing
what is happening, compose their own scheme of things by filling in
the gaps . . . (p. 2).*
Lorrie Starr, 1984

Karen eagerly enrolled in her first college course in special
education. For the past few years, she had set her sights on helping children
with learning problems. As a part of the requirements for this course, Karen
visited several community programs for adults with disabilities. It wasn't
until after she visited a local group home that her life changed forever.

At the group home, Karen noticed one of the residents looked remarkably like herself and her brothers and sisters. The woman's name was Kathy,
and she had the same blond hair, freckles, blue eyes, the same nose, and the
same dimples when she smiled. Even more surprising, Karen and Kathy
shared the same last name. Karen learned that Kathy was institutionalized at
birth, and the teachers at the group home told her that she just recently
moved to the community. Her parents, who wanted her to stay in the institution, protested the move.

Karen called home and learned from her mother what she had already
begun to suspect. Kathy was her older sister. When Kathy was born in 1955,
her parents were advised to immediately institutionalize her and turn her
care over to professionals. When the other children were born, there seemed
to be no easy way to discuss Kathy, her problems, or why she was not living
at home. Karen's parents felt it would be better not to share this information,
deciding the situation was better kept a secret. Never did they think that
Kathy would be in the same community and cross paths with one of her
natural siblings.

The next day, Karen knocked on one of her professor's doors. She
needed someone who could give her straight talk; she needed someone who

would understand what had happened to her; and she needed to understand why her parents had never told her about her older sister. Karen needed to know what to do next. Overnight, she felt her self-identity had changed. She needed to redefine her role as a sister, and she needed the necessary information. Together, Karen and her instructor discussed a course of action. She would start by frankly discussing Kathy with her parents, spending time with Kathy, and reading about persons with disabilities.

In the months that followed, Karen and Kathy spent many hours together. Their mother and father spent time with both of them, and particularly took time with Karen, attempting to explain why they had taken the actions they did. The next few months were emotionally difficult for Karen and her parents. They learned to talk openly and honestly with each other about Kathy. By listening to and respecting each other's needs and emotions, they were all able to grow and come to terms with their feelings and their new-found relationships.

Karen's story, although unique, vividly illustrates the need for information commonly encountered by siblings who have brothers and sisters with disabilities. As noted in Chapter 4, siblings are anxious about the cause of and prognosis for the disability, the feelings of their brother or sister with a disability, what services will be needed, and how their relationship with this brother or sister will be affected. Unlike the straightforward approach Karen was able to take in her situation, most requests for information are less direct and are woven in the daily fabric of family life: "Mom, why can't Kevin talk yet?" "What does cerebral palsy mean?" "Does it hurt to be blind?" "Why won't he play with me?" "Will I get sick, too?" Some children, however, have trouble expressing these questions or may not get the answers they need.

THE NEED FOR INFORMATION

"Should I ask my father?" "What will he say?" "Will he be hurt if I talk about Mike's problem?" "Does Mom know what Johnny's problem is?" "Should I ask?" Some families live in silence. Silent questions seldom get answers. Without answers, many children fabricate their own stories and explanations for various disabilities. Often, their own explanations and interpretations are far from the truth. Some families prefer silence to the possible risks of communication. They, however, have neither experienced the value of candid discussion nor felt the benefits of searching together for answers to shared questions.

Why do some siblings never ask? Burton (1975), in reviewing the lack of questioning on the part of children who have siblings with cystic fibrosis, postulates that the children's silence may reflect their desire to protect their parents from the pain of the disability. He suggests that some children do not question because of fears that the

parents may break down or may reject the questioning child. These siblings need information, but they keep their questions and thoughts to themselves.

Many other siblings are poorly informed about a brother's or sister's disability (Chintz, 1981; Crnic & Leconte, 1986; McKeever, 1983). This lack of information is often the result of parents who either will not recognize or accept the child's condition or who simply do not actively provide information to siblings. In some family situations, a disability may be denied by parents. Parents who have not come to grips with a disability and acknowledged its existence will provide little support to siblings. Denial is usually clearly communicated, stifling questions and comments from family members. Parental denial typically blocks the flow of information and leaves siblings' questions unvoiced and unanswered once again. Denial, therefore, results in silence.

Lobato (1990) notes that for some siblings, especially very young siblings, their understanding of the disability represents a unique combination of what they have been told, what they've overhead and observed, as well as what they have conjured up on their own. In a study of families with children who have cystic fibrosis, Burton (1975) found that 53% of parents did not discuss the disability with the siblings. Of the 47% who did, information that was shared was simplistic and, thus, the explanations were minimal. Several researchers suggest that information needs to be repeated frequently as some children do not retain much information about the specifics of disabilities (Burbach & Peterson, 1986; Potter & Roberts, 1984).

Parents experience a range of mixed feelings about their children with disabilities (Featherstone, 1980). The topic of disability may be confusing and is usually painful. Sharing information with their other children can be a source of stress for parents. It appears that, in general, sharing information about the disability can be problematic (Seligman, 1983). It is important to help parents move beyond their personal feelings of confusion and grief, and on to an acceptance of the disability and a readiness to begin working as a family to adjust to their special circumstances.

Siblings' needs for information are much like those of their parents. Just as parents feel a need to gather a variety of information to help them adjust, so, too, will their children. Recently, Wilson et al. (1989) found that of siblings they surveyed, 87% expressed interest in participating in a sibling group to learn more information and coping strategies. Itzkowitz (1989) also found that a significant majority of siblings expressed a desire to receive information in a structured format. A lack of information or misinformation about a disability can lead to unwarranted worries or fears. For both parents and siblings, the need for information will change as the child with a disability grows older. Confronting the different periods of transition in a child's life, as noted in Chapter 2, will call for new kinds of information.

Featherstone (1980) notes, however, that although siblings have needs that parallel their parents', these needs are not exactly the same because, obviously, siblings are not parents. Siblings interact with and react to their brothers and sisters in ways different from those of their parents. Their sense of identity is usually more closely tied to siblings. Siblings, unlike parents, have limited life experiences to help put a disability into perspective and may never know life without the brother or sister who has a disability. The sibling relationship, unlike the parental relationship, is usually lifelong.

As discussed in Chapter 4, siblings typically need specific information about:

The child with a disability (in particular, aspects of the disability, prognosis, and implications)
Their parents
The services the sibling will require
The future

Additionally, siblings need information about themselves. They need to know about their role, their responsibilities, their feelings, and how relationships with their friends may be affected.

Like their parents, siblings do not need episodic information. Instead, they need to receive information throughout their lives. They need information that changes as they change. Young children have informational needs that are vastly different from those of adolescents. Recognizing their changing needs will help parents and professionals provide varying and more sophisticated information resources as the siblings grow up. As they mature, their ongoing need for more information on different topics and for more detail underscores the fact that the delivery of answers to questions must be viewed as a longitudinal need.

TALKING WITH SIBLINGS— THE KEYS TO EFFECTIVE COMMUNICATION

Providing clear, concise information to siblings is more easily said than done. *Effective* communication between the sibling and parent or professional is the key. Effective communication can be enhanced by attending to the following 12 points:

1. *Actively listen to siblings.* The first step in providing information is to listen actively to the sibling. Active listening implies that the listener put other projects and tasks aside while the sibling talks. An active listener questions the sibling to make sure he or she understands the message. An active listener also repeats or paraphrases the communication to let the sibling know he or she has correctly heard what was said or asked.

2. *Take your time.* It may be difficult for siblings to ask questions, especially questions they view as embarrassing or painful. The sibling should have plenty of time to talk, ask questions, and interpret information. Likewise, parents and professionals should not feel they need to share all their information at one time. Gradual assimilation will most likely help ensure that the sibling retains the information. It is hard to learn everything in one sitting or with one explanation. Parents and professionals should be patient with questions as well as answers.

3. *Serve as a model.* Parents and professionals should act as models by openly asking questions and seeking information themselves. Parents and professionals should demonstrate that asking questions and seeking information is a healthy and a valued behavior. Additionally, parents and professionals can model effective communication by honestly expressing their feelings and thoughts.

Parents and professionals can also serve as models in terms of the acceptance of and interactions with the child who has a disability. Models continually communicate information more strongly through their actions than their words.

4. *Be knowledgeable.* Parents should become informed about knowledge concerning the disability and seek information from those who have a substantial knowledge base. Parents and professionals should always strive to increase what they know about specific disabilities, not only for their own benefit, but also so that they can serve as a source of information for siblings and for the child with a disability.

5. *Be sincere and honest.* Even when parents have developed a thorough knowledge base, it is likely that siblings will pose questions that can not be easily answered. Answers should always be accurate. If the answer to a particular question is unknown or complex, the parent or professional should say so. Simplistic answers to complex questions or untruthful responses will only hamper future communication. If an answer is not known, it may be best for both the sibling and parent or professional to undertake some joint research to seek the answer. A trip together to the library will clearly communicate an interest in questioning.

6. *Provide understandable answers.* Providing too much information to a youngster or inadequate or overly simplistic information to adolescents or adults will hinder effective communication. Consideration must be given to the age of the sibling and the specific question being asked. (Does the sibling want a quick yes or no? Or, does he or she want detail?) A wise approach may be to provide some information and then to ask, "Do you understand? Can I tell you more?" Remember, too, to use age-appropriate language and examples when answering questions. When a 4-year-old asks, "What's retarded mean?" a simple response such as, "It means Mike learns slower. It will take him longer. Like learning your numbers. It took him longer to learn but he can do it now," might provide the needed information and set the stage for additional understanding. When a 10-year-old asks the same question, a more detailed response is usually needed. For example, "When someone says a person is retarded it means he has a disability that affects his brain. Your brother Mike has mental retardation because part of his brain is hurt. People who have mental retardation take a longer time to learn things. Remember how quickly you learned all the names of the birds for your science project? It's going to take Mike much longer to learn all those names. He still likes birds the way you

do; he just will have trouble remembering their names. Does that make sense?"

7. *Have an open attitude.* Parents and professionals should expect questions, all sorts of questions, from siblings. They should have an open attitude in terms of accepting questions on all topics related to the disability. No question is insignificant. Each should be answered with care and understanding.

8. *Provide balanced information.* Information can be presented in many ways. Concentration on the negative aspects will present a skewed picture of a disability and its related implications. A balanced approach, in which both the positive and negative aspects of a disability are openly discussed, is always preferred. Siblings need to have both sides, not information that is overly biased in one direction. This is especially important, given the new information that reveals how children with disabilities are responsible for many positive contributions to the family constellation (Summers, Behr, & Turnbull, 1989). While it may be natural for a brother or sister to stress the negative aspects of the sibling, parents and other adults have a responsibility to stress the positive contributions of the child with the disability. Such information will help siblings develop a balanced and, it is hoped, a positive outlook regarding their relationship with their brother or sister.

9. *Capitalize on nonverbal communication.* Facial expressions, body movements, how a person sits, or where he or she stands all communicate interest and respect to siblings. Parents and professionals should be aware of their nonverbal communication when talking with siblings. Siblings, like all other people, recognize those who respect their concerns and inquiries via the nonverbal communication expressed.

10. *Facilitate questions.* Some siblings will not ask questions aloud. Parents and professionals can facilitate questions by:
    a. Posing questions themselves ("I wonder what will happen when Bill leaves school?")
    b. Directing questions to siblings ("Have you ever thought about what it would be like to be blind?")
    c. Using natural events, television shows, videotapes, and movies, or books and magazine articles that depict disabilities or family problems to start a discussion about specific sibling issues ("The girl in this book has a hearing aid like Susan" or "Do you think we could try this with Todd?")

All of these situations can help facilitate discussions in which information may be shared. These opportunities help to provide a context for the information and may also motivate both parents and siblings to share information with each other.

11. *Anticipate questions.* At certain times in the life of a person with a disability, family members may have more need for information than at other times. For example, when the child with a disability first attends school, approaches puberty, or leaves home, questions may be more intense. Anticipating these times of uncertainty and providing special information will be most helpful (e.g., "John is going to work at the grocery store. Have you ever thought about John going to work when he gets older? John has to start now to learn good work skills if he is going to be successfully employed later on. Do you want to talk about what John will do at his job?").

12. *Follow up earlier communication.* Parents and professionals should not expect that the sibling will understand the answers to complex questions with one explanation. To ensure that the sibling understands and to deal with related questions, it is wise to follow up conversations (e.g., "Craig, I told you about Tommy's supported employment last week. Did you think of any other questions about his job or what Tommy will do there?"). Follow-up provides an opportunity to clarify information and leads naturally to additional questions.

INNOVATIVE APPROACHES
TO INFORMATION SHARING

In response to the increasing awareness of the needs of siblings for clear, concise information and to moderate some of the problems related to siblings' lack of information or misinformation, a number of professionals have initiated informational programs for siblings. These innovative programs have primarily focused on siblings of children who are receiving special services in school or hospital settings. As a result of these collective efforts, a number of aspects critical to the successful establishment of informational programs can be seen.

Programs & Workshops

An early project was initiated by Kaplan and Colombatto (1966) to provide information and activities to siblings who have brothers and sisters with mental retardation. In a pilot project during the summer, young siblings (ages 2½–5 years) participated in a series of enrichment activities and field trips. Since the siblings were too young to participate in discussion groups, the activities provided an informal context for the siblings to bring up problems and to share their thoughts and misconceptions. Teachers in this project were trained to listen for such statements and to provide understandable, age-appropriate information to the siblings. Comfortably discussing mental retardation with siblings and providing them with ample opportunity to ask questions about the disability benefited the young siblings participating in the program.

Murphy, Pueschel, Duffy, and Brady (1976) pioneered informational workshops for siblings of children with Down syndrome who were being seen at the Developmental Evaluation Clinic of Boston's Children's Hospital. During parental interviews, staff inquired about sibling relationships and encouraged parents to bring siblings to the clinic. When the siblings arrived, they observed clinic activities and met with professional staff members who answered their questions. To more fully meet the needs of siblings, a series of Saturday workshops was designed to provide more comprehensive information to siblings. In these Saturday workshops, siblings were divided into three age groups (6–9, 10–12, and 13–18) and participated in a number of discussions, presentations, and demonstrations. These included meetings with:

1. A physician to discuss chromosomes and characteristics of Down syndrome
2. A physical therapist to discuss muscle tone and activities that help children with Down syndrome develop their motor skills
3. A psychologist to discuss learning characteristics of children with Down syndrome

Additionally, siblings observed teaching demonstrations and had the opportunity to look at chromosomes through a microscope.

Within the context of these workshops, siblings met other siblings, saw other children with Down syndrome, and shared their feelings and problems with professionals. Murphy and her colleagues (1976) reported that siblings often discussed telling their friends about Down syndrome, institutionalization, and problems related to the future. Within the context of the informational workshop, siblings had the opportunity to learn from one another as well as from professionals.

Feigon (1981) developed sibling information-sharing groups that were started at the Dysfunctioning Child Center at Michael Reese Hospital in Chicago. These groups of siblings (ages 10–18) met for 12 weekly sessions. The groups were structured to provide both information and a support system to the siblings. Each group received information about the disability and discussed their family, their feelings, and their social needs and responsibilities. Specific information on working with the child was provided as requested by group members. Feigon suggests that programs of this type be voluntary and heterogeneous (not limited to a specific disability). Given the nature of the group, it is necessary to provide flexibility in terms of length of meetings, structure, and content.

Lobato (1981) conducted a systematic training program for young siblings (ages 4–7) of children with a wide range of disabilities (e.g., Down syndrome, cerebral palsy, epilepsy, and heart defects). This program was designed:

1. To teach the siblings factual information about developmental disabilities.
2. To increase the siblings' recognition of the personal strengths and positive characteristics of their sibling with a disability and other family members.
3. To teach the siblings to constructively express their reactions to stressful family situations.

The training consisted of having the siblings attend small-group (three siblings) training sessions for 1½ hours for 6 weeks. During the training sessions, the leader presented information about developmental disabilities with the siblings, role-played, and discussed feelings and problems related to their family situations. Evaluation of these informational training sessions revealed that the siblings were able to accurately define developmental disabilities. Most of the siblings increased their positive self-reference statements and made positive verbalizations regarding their brother or sister with a disability and other family members. Additionally, Lobato found that for some participants, social interactions at home were positively influenced.

Benson (1982) has described a series of workshops for siblings (ages 8–15) of children with developmental disabilities. The workshops were developed to help siblings learn about disabilities and to facilitate sharing of experiences among siblings. Each workshop was implemented over a weekend. During the first day, siblings were engaged in sessions in which the basic nature and causes of developmental disabilities were explained. Additionally, siblings took part in structured discussions that focused on the experiences of their families. During the second day of the workshop, the siblings were provided an opportunity to participate in recreational activities with each other, their parents, and their siblings with disabilities. This workshop structure had an overall positive effect on the siblings. They increased their knowledge about disabilities and developed more positive attitudes toward persons with disabilities.

Byrnes and Love (1983) directed a series of sibling day-workshops sponsored by the South Central Regional Center for Services to Deaf-Blind Children in Dallas, Texas. These workshops focused on information sharing via age-appropriate recreational activities. The specific objectives of these workshops were:

1. To "de-mystify" their brother/sister's educational program
2. To more fully understand their brother/sister's handicap
3. To better understand the restrictions and frustrations imposed by having a handicapping condition
4. To become more knowledgeable about community resources for their brother/sister (p. 4)

Byrnes and Love (1983) provided a detailed activity analysis for each of the workshop's objectives. To address the first objective the siblings:

1. Toured the school
2. Met with professionals to learn about special services
3. Observed their brother or sister in the classroom and discussed specific educational programs
4. Experimented with special equipment
5. Observed other children with different disabilities

The second objective focused on providing specific factual information. To meet this objective, siblings:

1. Participated in group discussions on the cause of the disability
2. Discussed genetic aspects of specific disabilities
3. Learned the meaning of unfamiliar technical terms
4. Discussed the roles of professionals

The third objective of these workshops attempted to provide an understanding of the problems associated with a disabling condition. Here, the siblings:

1. Met and talked with people with various disabilities
2. Simulated disabilities
3. Used a variety of adaptive and prosthetic equipment
4. Role-played situational barriers to mobility

The workshop also concentrated on providing information about community resources. To accomplish this fourth objective, siblings:

1. Discussed community-based support groups
2. Toured community-based programs for adults with disabilities
3. Discussed community placements for their brothers and sisters

Based on their work, Byrnes and Love (1983) feel that no *direct* counseling or therapeutic activities should be introduced in the workshop agenda. Through the planned activities, they found that siblings often spontaneously share their feelings and problems. These natural expressions should be dealt with by group leaders with the help of the other siblings who may have the same feelings or experience similar problems.

Fairfield (1983) has described two information workshops conducted by the staff at the Pediatric Genetics Department at The Johns Hopkins Hospital in Baltimore. The workshops were conducted simultaneously. One workshop was for siblings; the other, for parents. In the parent workshop, parents listened to a panel of adult siblings who had grown up with a brother or sister with a disability. The panelists discussed their feelings, ways in which they dealt with their friends, their relationships with their siblings, and how their lives were positively and negatively affected. The structure of the information workshop for siblings was primarily recreational, which facilitated informal sharing of information and problem solving. The siblings (ages 6–12) participated in a number of group activities, games, and art projects to enable them to meet one another. The activities led to a discussion of their problems and needs, which were addressed by the professional group leaders.

Willenz-Issacs (1983) designed an information project for siblings of hearing impaired children attending the Kendall Demonstration School at Gallaudet College in Washington, D.C. Since deafness impairs communication between family members, the focus of the workshop was communication. After interviewing a number of adults who are siblings of persons with hearing impairments, the staff designed the workshop to meet several objectives. "We wanted to let brothers and sisters of Kendall students know how important they are, to give them information, and to help them gain some perspective on their relationships with their siblings" (p. 2).

Parents and their deaf children went to a special movie, while the siblings attended the workshop. After an introductory activity, the siblings received a detailed tour of the school, listened to a simulation of what a person with a hearing impairment might hear, and experimented with an audiology booth. During the workshop, the adult leaders presented a skit depicting play between children with hearing impairments and their siblings. The skit focused on problems related to play and asked the siblings to suggest various resolutions, which were then acted out. Finally, the older siblings attended a discussion group, while younger siblings participated in art activities.

An innovative program initiated at the University of Washington has provided a number of resources to assist siblings who have brothers and sisters with disabilities. This program, Supporting Extended Family Members (SEFAM), was designed to provide ecological support to families with children and adults with disabilities. Meyer, Vadasy and Fewell (1985) have detailed the components of a "Sibshop." This information workshop consists of two simultaneously run sessions—one for siblings and one for parents. The goals of the Sibshop are to provide siblings with an opportunity to:

1. Meet other siblings in a relaxed, recreational setting.
2. Discuss common joys and concerns with other siblings.
3. Learn how others handle situations commonly experienced by siblings of children with disabilities.
4. Learn more about the implications of their brothers' or sisters' disability.
5. Learn about common sibling concerns.

The session for siblings consists of small-group discussions run by professionals who encourage questions about and provide information on disabilities. Within the group, siblings are encouraged to talk about themselves, to share their interests, and to discuss aspects of living with a brother or sister who has a disability. Additionally, the group leaders model ways to play with siblings and discuss problems related to interacting with brothers and sisters.

One of the best strategies developed and used in Sibshop is the fictional "Aunt Blabby." Aunt Blabby is an advice columnist who receives letters from siblings on critical issues. For example, Meyer and his colleagues present the following as part of the workshop:

Dear Aunt Blabby,

I have a problem that I'm sort of ashamed of. My brother, who has cerebral palsy, embarrasses me. Don't get me wrong—in a lot of ways he's a neat guy. He can really do a lot for himself, considering his handicap. My problem is that I get embarrassed when people stare at him in the shopping mall, or when he drools. What can I do about this problem?

Embarrassed

The siblings serve as the "experts" and develop responses to the Aunt Blabby letters. In this way the siblings share information and strategies in a proactive, problem-solving atmosphere. Through this creative approach, siblings have an opportunity to learn that they experience many of the same challenges and joys as other siblings.

While the siblings are engaged in the Sibshop, parents have an opportunity to increase their understanding of the unique needs of siblings by interacting with a panel of older siblings (ages 15–32). Panel members talk about themselves, their parents, and their brother or sister with a disability. They discuss aspects of being a sibling that they found both rewarding and distressing. The parents have an opportunity to ask the panelists questions and to seek advice.

At the conclusion of the workshops, parents and siblings come together for social events. In a follow-up evaluation of the project, the

families reported that parents and siblings talked together more as a result of information shared during the workshop (Meyer, 1983).

Another innovative approach by the SEFAM group involves a camp-out for siblings in state parks. Besides recreational activities, siblings engage in small-group discussions on topics such as how to ask parents questions and how to tell friends about their brother or sister with a disability. Within the camp-out context, siblings shared information while relaxing and developing interpersonal relationships.

Starr (1984) has described still another way to deal with siblings' varying needs for information. In her approach, play sessions are provided for siblings of chronically ill or recently deceased children. During these play sessions, a professional provides straightforward information to siblings as they act out their questions, fears, and misconceptions. Starr notes that it is important that information be provided repeatedly over a long period of time to ensure the child's comprehension and assimilation of the new facts.

Lobato (1985) reported on the development and evaluation of a training program to address the needs of preschool-age siblings for information and emotional support. She developed flexible workshops to accommodate the needs of families, which met for 1.5 hours a week for a 6-week period. The workshop focused on developing an understanding of developmental disabilities, recognizing their strengths and those of other family members, and learning ways to express their feelings. Lobato employed teaching strategies such as modeling, coaching, and role-playing puppets, and read children's literature throughout the workshops. As a result of these workshops, she found that the preschoolers became more accurate in their definitions of various disabilities. Of particular note, most of these youngsters increased their positive statements about themselves and their families including their brothers or sisters with disabilities.

Lobato (1990) presents detailed information and suggestions for developing information workshops for young children. In her work, Lobato has developed and tested workshops specially designed for the developmental characteristics of young children. Unique to her approach are the preliminary parent meeting and home visit in which the workshop leaders involve the parents in the discussion of critical issues and problems faced by the family. Given the young child's limited ability to generalize, Lobato's workshops pay special attention to helping the young child achieve new information and skills. They also teach them to apply these skills in everyday situations. This attention to generalization should be an ingredient in any workshop for siblings. In addition to presenting detailed information, Lobato also presents evaluation strategies that can be used in the sessions. Her approach is highly recommended for those designing information workshops for young children.

Burton (1991) developed a unique workshop for siblings called KIDPOWER, designed for children between the ages of 8 and 12. It focuses on the strengths that siblings possess and the positive impact that they can have on their friends and the general community. Developed at the University of Idaho, KIDPOWER focuses on:

- Creating a social support network
- Sharing experiences
- Developing behavior management skills
- Learning about disabilities
- Integrating children with disabilities into community programs

Accompanied by several workbooks, children are encouraged to draw pictures and write about their needs, while learning about people with disabilities. KIDPOWER focuses on positive contributions of brothers and sisters with disabilities and seeks to instill in children a sense of optimism toward the experience of being part of a special family.

Summers, Bridge, and Summers (1991) report their work with siblings in structured support group sessions. The focus of their groups is to have siblings shift from "other-directed cognitions" (e.g., thinking one's sister is a burden to the family) to "self-directed cognitions" (e.g., developing proactive strategies to address problems).

They detail the goals of a six-session approach to sibling support groups:

Session 1   Allow children to become acquainted and feel comfortable with each other.

Session 2   Discuss what it is like to live with a disability.

Session 3   Learn specifics about disabilities.

Session 4   Explore feelings that the individuals have regarding their brother or sister with the disability.

Session 5   Observe the child who has the disability in a treatment setting.

Session 6   Remind the children of what they have learned and help them feel comfortable.

Special Groups

In addition to workshops, special groups to address the needs of siblings who have brothers or sisters with disabilities are being formed. The Autism Society of America (ASA) supports a subgroup SHARE: Siblings Helping Persons with Autism through Resources and Energy. This subgroup is devoted to using the unique talents and perspectives of siblings to serve the well-being of persons with autism. SHARE publishes a regular column in the ASA *Advocate,* which features information for siblings written by siblings. SHARE also produces its own publications, resource directories, and bibliographies. (See Appendix B for SHARE's address.)

In 1981, a group of professionals, parents, and siblings formed the Sibling Information Network. The goals of the network are to provide a mechanism for mutual support and information sharing to individuals concerned about the well-being of people who have brothers or sisters with disabilities. The network publishes a newsletter, which contains a rich collection of articles, personal contacts, bibliographies, and announcements pertaining to siblings. The formation of the Sibling Information Network has enabled a sharing of ideas, problems, information, and innovative approaches, and has assisted in the development of a number of projects focused on providing information to siblings. (The network's address is included in Appendix B.)

ESTABLISHING PROGRAMS
TO PROVIDE INFORMATION

From the innovative efforts described in the previous section, a number of components of information-sharing programs for siblings can be identified. The guidelines below are specifically intended for professionals developing information workshops for siblings.

Workshop Goals

Naturally, the goals and objectives of individual workshops vary according to the needs of the siblings. Generally, however, workshops should focus on the following nine goals:

1. To teach specific information about the nature and cause of the disability
2. To teach siblings current philosophy directing services for persons with disabilities
3. To share information about services and materials needed by persons with disabilities
4. To provide information on the roles of professionals who work with persons with disabilities
5. To demonstrate teaching or other intervention techniques used with persons with disabilities
6. To identify community resources that provide services to persons with disabilities and their families
7. To facilitate the sharing of ideas, problems, solutions, and information among siblings
8. To help siblings develop a positive self-image via recognition of their unique contribution to their brothers and sisters with disabilities
9. To facilitate better interaction among family members

Program Content

The content of such workshops should focus on providing information rather than on providing counseling or therapy. As a natural outcome of information sharing, siblings typically discuss their feelings, problems, and attitudes toward their brother or sister. Within the context of information sharing, these feelings and problems can be addressed in a positive way. (Counseling approaches are reviewed in Chapter 6.) Opportunities should also be supplied for socializing and group leisure activities, particularly for weekend workshops. The entire program should not be too intense or too rigidly structured.

The specific content of workshops will vary according to the goals adopted, the disability addressed, the age of the siblings, and the time allocated. It is, therefore, impossible to provide a comprehensive list of all the topics that can be addressed in informational workshops. The following list provides an outline of generic topics that could be included in a series of sessions for siblings. Since the material is generic, it can be adapted for specific disabilities and different age groups. Above all, be sure that a workshop's content is based on the most up-to-date information. Providing information that is out of date will only serve to hamper siblings in their understanding of the disability and their adjustment to having a member in the family who has a disability.

1. **Developmental disabilities**
   a. Characteristics of the specific disability including physical, medical, learning, and social aspects
   b. Causes of the disability
   c. General prognosis for the disability
   d. Prevalence of the disorder
   e. Definitions of medical and technical terms
2. **Program philosophies**
   a. Normalization
   b. Deinstitutionalization
   c. Public school integration and full inclusion
   d. Community-based services
   e. Legal and human rights of persons with disabilities
3. **Services**
   a. Educational services
   b. Medical services
   c. Social services
   d. Financial services
   e. Adaptive equipment needs and use
   f. Legal services
4. **Professionals**
   a. The role of and services provided by educators, physicians, physical therapists, social workers, nurses, mobility specialists, occupational therapists, psychologists, audiologists, speech pathologists, and so forth
   b. Therapy models and service locations
   c. Special equipment used by professionals
5. **Intervention techniques**
   a. Special education teaching
   b. Special communication tactics
   c. Mobility procedures
   d. Physical and occupational therapy
   e. Techniques to assist with adaptive skills (e.g., dressing, eating)
   f. Aspects of special therapies (e.g., music and play therapy)
6. **Community resources**
   a. Group homes and supported living
   b. Vocational programs, especially supported employment
   c. Social Security
   d. Family support programs

  e. Respite care services
  f. Advocacy services
  g. Community recreational programs

7. **Interpersonal sharing**
  a. Problems and feelings encountered by siblings
  b. Advantages of being a sibling
  c. Disadvantages of being a sibling
  d. Interacting with siblings

8. **Contributions**
  a. Ways to help siblings at home
  b. Helping siblings in the community

9. **Family communication**
  a. Needs of parents
  b. Asking parents questions
  c. Discussing ideas with parents

10. **Friends**
  a. Telling friends about siblings
  b. Dealing with teasing
  c. Teaching friends about disabilities
  d. Playing with friends and siblings

11. **The future**
  a. Guardianship
  b. Financial planning
  c. Estate planning
  d. Advocacy
  e. Living arrangements

  Activities The best information workshops provide a number of varied activities for siblings. Just providing lectures will hardly hold the attention of siblings. Table 5.1 lists a number of activities for siblings. Some of the activities are obviously especially suited for young children (e.g., puppet shows and skits), while others are particularly appropriate for older children (e.g., discussion groups).

Table 5.1. Suggested activities for information workshops for siblings

Tours of school programs	Discussion groups
Observations of the sibling at school	Panels to address specific topics
Observations of therapy sessions	Role-playing
Interviews with professionals	Films, records, and other media
Using special equipment and materials	Stories
Simulating various disabling conditions	Puppet shows and skits
	Presentations by professionals

Table 5.2. Suggested recreational activities for information workshops for siblings

Barbecues	Overnight camp-outs
Arts and crafts activities	Luncheons
Team sports (basketball, bowling, volleyball, softball, etc.)	Parties
	Swimming
Relay races	Group games
Field trips	Dances

Recreation A number of successful information workshops have provided structured opportunities for siblings to interact with each other by engaging in recreational activities. Table 5.2 presents a number of recreational activities that can be used within the context of a workshop. Again, some of the activities are better suited for young children, while others are more appropriate for adolescents or young adults.

Parental Involvement

Some parents will be apprehensive about their child's participation in a workshop. Most parents will want to be assured that the information presented is in agreement with their own information, understanding, and values related to the child with the disability. To help parents reach a decision and become involved, details regarding the goals, content, and structure of the workshop should be sent to parents well in advance of the scheduled sessions. Opportunities for parents to talk with workshop leaders should be provided.

Siblings need a time to be by themselves, to discuss problems and seek information without parental influence. Many workshops include a special component for parents. These sessions can provide helpful information to parents about siblings and help them discuss issues related to siblings. Panels of adult siblings who talk with parents powerfully convey the unique needs of siblings. At the conclusion of the major portion of the workshop, parent and sibling groups should come together for a mutual sharing of information gained or for more informal recreational activities.

Age Grouping

Workshops should be organized to meet the varying needs of the different age levels of siblings. Five basic age groups are recommended:

1. Preschool: 3–5 years
2. School-age: 6–9 years
3. Preadolescent: 10–13 years

4. Adolescent: 14–18 years
5. Adult: 18+ years

Arranging groups of similar age siblings will facilitate discussion and help the participants focus on common needs.

Group Leaders

Group leaders can be professionals, older siblings, parents, or interested adults. Leaders should be knowledgeable about the topic to be addressed, able to facilitate discussion, and able to present information in an enjoyable manner. Two leaders per group are highly recommended.

Group Size

Depending on the goals of the information workshop, size is a critical variable. Typically, the most productive groups do not exceed 20 or have fewer than 5 siblings. Ideal groups have between 10 and 12 members.

Workshop Location

If possible, it is best to provide workshops in locations where the sibling with a disability receives services. In this way, the participating siblings can observe the surroundings and equipment firsthand. By conducting the workshop in the school or clinic, the program will have more significance to the children, as they will come in direct contact with the environment experienced daily by their brother or sister who has a disability.

Longitudinal Programs

Successful information programs provide longitudinal opportunities for siblings to gather information. As their needs change and siblings mature and assimilate new knowledge, new and more sophisticated questions arise. Comprehensive information programs will be able to meet these varying needs. One-time, episodic information sharing, although a vast improvement over no service provision, will not satisfy the siblings' ongoing needs for information.

Follow-Up

An essential component of information workshops is follow-up. Program leaders should actively contact participants to assess the degree to which siblings understood the information presented and can use the information. These follow-up contacts also provide opportunities to clarify misconceptions and to provide additional information and resources as needed.

Evaluation

Information workshops should be evaluated by siblings and parents. The evaluation might include:

1. Content-related questions to assess comprehension
2. Analysis of the strengths and weaknesses of the program
3. Additional information needs
4. Suggestions for future workshops

A sample evaluation is reproduced in Figure 5.1.

**The Sibling Information Workshop
for Adolescents**

Post-Evaluation

Session # ____   Date: _____

1. Age: ____
2. Why did you come to the workshop? _____
    _____
3. The best part of today's meeting was: _____
    _____
    _____
4. The worst part of today's meeting was: _____
    _____
5. Name one thing you learned today: _____
    _____
6. How will this help you and/or your sibling? _____
    _____
    _____
7. Is there something you want to know that we did not address? _____
    _____
    _____
8. Was the workshop leader: a) helpful?   ____
                             b) interesting? ____
                             c) boring?   ____
9. Do you plan to come back again? _____
10. How can we make these workshops better? _____
    _____
    _____
    _____

Figure 5.1. Sample evaluation form for sibling workshops.

PROVIDING INFORMATION
THROUGH BOOKS & OTHER SOURCES

A rather informal, although powerful, way to provide important information to siblings is through reading material. Numerous books have been written to help explain disabilities to children and adolescents. In particular, a number of books are devoted to the special needs of siblings.

One of the best books that provides information on disabilities in a straightforward, easy-to-understand manner is *Living with a Brother or Sister with Special Needs: A Book for Sibs* (1985) by Donald Meyer, Patricia Vadasy, and Rebecca Fewell. Written for adolescents, this book explains many different disabilities and deals with a full range of common feelings experienced by siblings. Services and therapies typically provided to children with disabilities are also described in order to help siblings understand and appreciate the need for these services.

Appendix A lists and reviews available literature that siblings may find helpful. Most of these titles are available in local libraries. Schools and clinics that have sibling programs should maintain a collection of these books to lend to families. This is an inexpensive, yet effective, way to provide information to siblings.

Other information sources may include television programs and films, videotapes or movies, and even commercials and printed advertisements. Recent television shows have featured children, adolescents, and adults with varying disabilities. For the most part, these presentations have addressed some of the problems and needs of people with disabilities in a sensitive manner. These story lines may help to stimulate discussion about similar situations in the sibling's family as well as offer factual information. Other audiovisual materials and documentaries specifically based on various disabilities may be available through school libraries or some social service agencies.

SUMMARY

Individuals, young or old, who have a sibling with a disability have unanimously expressed a need for information. This need is for information that is factual and objective, as well as for information regarding more subjective and emotional issues. Some siblings never voice their questions; therefore, they never become informed. Silence reigns on all sides of the family. Questions that go unasked often receive "answers" invented by the child. These fabrications lead to misconceptions that can last into adulthood.

It is essential that questions and honest communication are encouraged in order to eliminate fears and misconceptions. Parents and professionals should be aware of effective communication skills, such as listening actively, being accepted and respectful of all questions, knowing how to facilitate questions and discussion, and answering any questions suitably and honestly.

Many innovative approaches to disseminate information to groups of siblings have been designed. Usually, these programs are associated with schools or clinics serving children with disabilities. Several models for a variety of ages, preschool through adolescence, have been developed across the country. Some programs offer similar opportunities for parents to become more aware of the special needs of siblings.

Numerous organizational aspects must be considered when planning such information workshops or sessions. Workshop and program content, including varied activities and socializing opportunities, should be carefully outlined. Other factors to consider in developing a program include parental involvement, age grouping, group size, leadership, location, follow-up, and evaluation.

Another efficient and effective means for sharing information with siblings is through books. Books, both nonfiction and fiction, are available for all ages to describe specific disabilities and/or offer insight into the lives of individuals with disabilities, their families, and their siblings. Television programs, videotapes, films, and other audiovisual materials may also be accessible in a community and provide another avenue to information sharing.

6

Counseling
Siblings

Like their parents, sisters and brothers have good reasons to feel
afraid, angry, guilty, and isolated. . . . Specifically, brothers and
sisters talk about embarrassment, identification, and confusion more
than adults do (p. 144).
Helen Featherstone, 1980

Siblings who have brothers and sisters with disabilities react in a variety of ways to their individual situations. Grossman (1972) found that for some siblings, the experience is surprisingly positive; yet for others, it is intensely negative. As Grossman reports, some siblings bitterly resent their situation, feel guilty about the rage they harbor toward their sibling and their parents, and fear that they, themselves, might be defective in some way. Siblings with strong negative feelings need special help in understanding and handling their feelings and in dealing with their problems in a constructive manner. That special help may include counseling.

Consider the following cases:

In 1981, Lisa wrote to the Sibling Information Network to request some help and to share her recent turmoil. She wrote her letter from a psychiatric hospital in New England. At the young age of 16, Lisa decided to commit suicide by ingesting a bottle of aspirin. After swallowing the pills, she called her mother for help. Recovered physically, she is now attempting to recover emotionally. Her letter states her case plainly: "No one ever has time for me. My Mom and Dad are so concerned about Bill and his problems, I am ignored. Don't they know that I hurt inside; don't they know that I need help? I don't like my brother. I wish he were dead. At times I want to kill myself. I really need help. Can you help me? Will you talk to me?"

>Lisa's brother, Bill, has a learning disability. He has great trouble reading and comprehending written symbols. Lisa's parents, in their efforts to assist Bill, helped form a parents' group for others who have children with learning disabilities. Lisa's mother has been busy with the organization at least three nights per week and spends considerable time providing Bill with enrichment activities to help compensate for his learning disability. Lisa's parents are distraught over her attempted suicide. As Lisa describes her reasons for this drastic call for help, her parents acutely feel the pain she is experiencing. They feel guilty and confused. Lisa and her parents know the stress that can occur when a family member has a disability.

Lisa's case is certainly not characteristic of all siblings with brothers and sisters who have disabilities. It is, however, a powerful reminder that siblings often experience intense feelings when they have a brother or sister with special needs. Lisa's initial letter was received with surprise because such intense emotion is not usually expected in a family having a member with a learning disability. She reminds us that no matter how mild the disability, family dynamics may intensify these emotions. Unfortunately, Lisa had nowhere to turn for help. In desperation she resorted to a guaranteed, although nearly fatal, method of drawing her parents' attention to her feelings and needs. It can only be speculated what sort of more positive scenario might have evolved if Lisa had had access to someone who could help her before she reached the critical point.

>Kevin wrote a letter to the Sibling Information Network requesting similar assistance: "I am 14 years old and my brother, Gary, (12 years old) is retarded. He has Down syndrome and goes to a special school. I really want to talk or write to other kids who have retarded brothers. There is no one here I can talk to about my brother. Sometimes I just need to express my feelings with someone who can understand and know what I am talking about. Can you help me?"

Kevin's letter, like so many others, clearly indicates that siblings need an open channel of communication to express their feelings, particularly to people who will take the time to listen and understand.

In a moving essay, Zatlow (1982) described her feelings toward her brother, Douglas, a young adult with autism. She notes that "we [siblings] all adapt as best we can but sometimes the penalty for our constant accommodation is considerable" (p. 2). For Zatlow, the responsibility of helping to raise her brother was an arduous struggle at great emotional expense. Zatlow mentions specific concerns she had about her brother's future and her possible role as his guardian if she were to inherit the responsibility of caring for him. She urges the development of alternatives for families so that siblings will not be denied their own lives and will be given an opportunity to develop their own separate identity.

Kelly (1982), writing about his experiences as a brother of a child with Down syndrome, has also provided some insight into a sibling's feelings:

> Terry was always one of us, and Mom and Dad never understated the fact, even though his other brothers knew he was different. Little did I suspect that I would grow to hate the difference before I learned to respect it.
>
> "Maybe we're lucky in a way to have been blessed with a special needs child," I'd hear my parents say to themselves. Often, we would be forced to contain our personal problems and focus attention on a *truly* needy kid. . . . Terry and I were in it together. We'd play together. Sometimes I'd fantasize rather than analyze what it was like to be him. In fact, I'd wonder and fantasize so hard that I'd wish I were him and he me. It hurt. "Why can't he be like me?" and "I'd do anything so he could know what it was like to be normal." What I believe I was doing then was assuming a sympathetic nature that was blind to love.

Kelly's experience of not revealing his personal problems and his fantasies is certainly not unusual to siblings with brothers and sisters who have disabilities. Indeed, these feelings are commonly experienced by siblings.

SIBLINGS & THEIR FEELINGS

As discussed in Chapter 4, brothers and sisters who have siblings with disabilities experience a full range of feelings related to the sibling, the parents, the entire family, themselves, other people, and the world in general. They feel excitement, anger, joy, frustration, sadness, guilt, loneliness, fear, and jealousy; these feelings vary in intensity and meaning and may occur in response to isolated events or to the overall family situation.

Of course, such feelings are not unique to siblings who have brothers or sisters with disabilities. Many siblings experience similar emotions toward brothers and sisters who have no disabilities (Bank & Kahn, 1982b; Lamb & Sutton-Smith, 1982; Sutton-Smith & Rosenberg, 1970). Sibling jealousy and rivalry, in particular, are commonly experienced by most siblings (McDermott, 1980). However common these feelings may be, when left unresolved or suppressed, they may cause substantial life problems and most certainly will interfere with the development of positive sibling relationships.

Some of the intense feelings that may be experienced by siblings of children with disabilities are:

Fear

Siblings may be afraid of "catching" the disability (Binger, 1973; Burbach & Peterson, 1986; Trevino, 1979).

Siblings may be overly concerned and frightened about possible futures for their brother or sister, their parents, and themselves (Seligman, 1983).

Siblings may fear that the child with the disability is exposed to exploitation and abuse in treatment programs.

Many siblings fear the reaction of their friends, especially future or present spouses, when they learn about their brother or sister.

Siblings may be afraid to have their own children, for fear that they, too, will be born with disabilities (Klein, 1972).

Loneliness

Siblings may feel isolated from peers and, in some cases, may be rejected by their friends (Meyer, Vadasy, & Fewell, 1985).

Siblings may feel isolated from other family members.

Siblings may feel different from other children and may feel their family experiences are not shared by other families.

Anger

Siblings of children with disabilities experience greater degrees of anger than other siblings (Seligman, 1983).

Typically, siblings feel anger toward the child with the disability, their parents, society, and God (Featherstone, 1980).

Anger may be the result of feeling ignored and unappreciated.

Anger may be directed toward peers who treat the child cruelly.

Resentment

Siblings may feel resentment as parents spend excessive amounts of time with the child who has the disability.

Siblings may resent curtailment of social activities as a result of the presence of the brother or sister.

Siblings may feel resentment at the unfairness of the family situation and the different expectations parents hold for their children.

Embarrassment

Most siblings, at some time, feel embarrassed about their brothers and sisters with disabilities.

Siblings may feel embarrassed when the child with the disability behaves inappropriately in public, causing attention to be directed toward the family.

Siblings often express embarrassment when introducing the child to peers, boyfriends/girlfriends, and so forth.

Extensive adaptive equipment may cause embarrassment.

Confusion

Siblings may feel confused about their role as sibling and "surrogate parent."

Siblings experience confusion over treatment priorities for the child with a disability and lack of concern for their own needs.

Confusion may be heightened when parents disagree about rearing the child, treat the child differently, or are not at the same stage of acceptance of the disability.

Jealousy

Siblings may be jealous of the attention the child with the disability receives.

Jealousy is commonly focused on the unfairness or unevenness of parental attention.

Pressure

Some parents apply excessive amounts of pressure on the siblings to achieve in order to help them compensate for their own disappointments (Schild, 1976).

Siblings may be pressured to care for the child with the disability, which results in the taking on of responsibilities that are beyond what is normally expected in sibling relationships (Farber, 1959; Grossman, 1972).

Older female siblings typically experience greater demands to help care for the child with the disability (Breslau, Weitzman, & Messenger, 1981; Cleveland & Miller, 1977; Farber, 1959).

Siblings in large families experience less pressure than siblings in small families (Grossman, 1972).

Siblings from less financially stable families may experience more pressure due to their inability to afford outside assistance to aid in the child's care.

Siblings of chronically ill children are often burdened with extensive physical care activities (Travis, 1976).

Guilt

Siblings may feel guilty about their emotions of anger, jealousy, and hostility (San Martino & Newman, 1974).

Guilt feelings may be repressed when negative thoughts and feelings have been punished.

Excessive guilt may be manifest in overly helpful acts directed toward the child with the disability (Seligman, 1983).

Frustration

Attempting to establish a normal sibling relationship with a brother or sister who has a disability may lead to great levels of frustration (Featherstone, 1980).

Not all siblings experience such intense negative feelings. A number of researchers have found that some siblings have predominantly positive feelings toward their experiences with their brothers and sisters who have disabilities (Graliker et al., 1962; Grossman, 1972; Simeonsson & Bailey, 1986). Some of these positive attitudes are reflected in several of the excerpts in Chapter 1, as well as in Chapter 3 in relation to the family system. Families are so complex that it is difficult to identify feelings common to siblings who have brothers and sisters with disabilities, and perhaps impossible to pinpoint why positive or negative feelings take hold. In their extensive review of the literature, Simeonsson and Bailey (1986) note that the research does not present a very clear picture of the adjustment of siblings in families where one child has a disability. It appears, however, that the development of negative feelings may be the result of a number of factors including:

1. Severity of the disability
2. Age of the child who has the disability
3. Age-spacing between the child with the disability and the other siblings
4. Birth order
5. Size of the family

6. Pressures exerted by the parents and professionals who are dealing with the child with the disability
7. Financial status of the family and amount of financial resources needed to help the child with the disability
8. Residence of the sibling who has the disability
9. Sex of the child who has the disability
10. External services needed by the child who has the disability
11. Physical and social adjustments the family has made to accommodate the child
12. External resources available to help family members
13. Amount and type of responsibility placed on the siblings for the care and treatment of the child with the disability
14. Extent to which the child with the disability manipulates or mistreats the other siblings
15. Extent to which the parents have adjusted to the disability
16. Parental feelings toward the child with the disability
17. Temperament of both children
18. The perception and experience of being treated differently from the other siblings by one's parents
19. The actual interactions among siblings

When negative feelings develop, they need to be dealt with in an open and honest fashion. Suppressed or repressed negative feelings can result in significant adjustment problems and may impede the establishment and maintenance of other social relationships. Murphy and Corte (1989) note that brothers and sisters who harbor unexpressed emotions can be "at-risk" for developing problems. They describe several ways siblings may respond to this lack of expression. Some siblings may regress and act as young children, often mimicking the child with the disability. The children may become more vulnerable to illness and cling to their symptoms for extended periods of time. Other siblings may act out with fighting, tantrums, lying, cheating, stealing, or other acts of defiance. Still other siblings may adopt the "model child syndrome" as a way of compensating for the brother or sister. When siblings have such negative feelings, or act out those feelings, they are in need of support to help them understand, accept, and handle their thoughts and emotions in proactive ways. One source of support is counseling.

WHAT IS COUNSELING?

The term *counseling* is used freely in everyday language. Counseling services are available on a range of diverse topics, such as marriage reconciliation, taxes and mortgages, weight loss, or the purchase of an automobile. Counseling means giving advice, encouragement, information, or some sort of general assistance to an individual or group. Counseling also denotes a particular helping relationship between a person and a skilled professional aimed at remediating specific problems. Through this helping relationship, individuals have an opportunity to examine their values, feelings, attitudes, and beliefs, as well as the way in which these are reflected in their behavior (Munson, 1971). Counseling implies a learning process in which persons develop an understanding of themselves and learn specific skills to deal effectively with their problems and concerns.

Counseling siblings of persons with disabilities, as in all counseling, implies the establishment of a helping relationship between the sibling and a competent counselor. This relationship is founded on respect for the sibling and his or her problems and needs. An honest, caring relationship between the counselor and the sibling is basic to the counseling process.

Goals for Siblings

When siblings have adjustment problems related to their brother or sister, counseling services should be provided (Post-Kramer & Nickolai, 1985; Slade, 1988). This counseling must be focused on the attainment of specific goals. First, the sibling should come to a deeper and broader understanding of personal feelings and problems. As siblings participate in the counseling process, they should realize the cause of their feelings and problems. Second, siblings should develop skills and attitudes that enable them to cope with their problems and feelings in a constructive manner. They should exit the counseling relationship with a specific course of action that will help prevent potential problems from escalating to troublesome levels in the future. Third, counseling should enable siblings to pursue their life goals as fully functioning members of society. Counseling should lead to personal growth and fulfillment that will enhance both individual and overall family functioning. Fourth, counseling should allow the sibling to strengthen the relationship with the brother or sister who has the disability. As the sibling experiences personal growth and develops new skills, he or she should learn to relate in more positive ways to the brother or sister with the disability as well as to other family members.

Counseling & Psychotherapy

At this point, it may be helpful to distinguish between psychotherapy and counseling. Both psychotherapy and counseling are essentially concerned with the same treatment goals (e.g., self-exploration, self-understanding, and behavior change), and both hinge on the relationship between the professional and the person seeking help. However, there are important differences between the two treatments. Pietrofesa, Hoffman, and Splete (1984) note that psychotherapy differs from counseling in the following ways:

1. deals with the more "serious" problems of the "mentally ill";
2. places more emphasis on the past than on the present;
3. emphasizes insight more than change;
4. requires the therapist to conceal rather than reveal personal values and feelings; and
5. requires the therapist to act as an "expert" rather than as a sharing partner with the client. (pp. 6–7)

Brammer and Shostrom (1982) explain that psychotherapy is more concerned with severe life problems and involves a greater level of intensity and time involvement than counseling. According to George and Christiani (1981):

> the goals of psychotherapy are more likely to involve a quite complete change of basic character structure; the goals of counseling are apt to be more limited, more directed toward aiding growth, more concerned with the immediate situation and more aimed at helping the individual function adequately in appropriate roles. (p. 8)

Bank and Kahn (1982b) have described the use of psychotherapy with siblings, primarily siblings of brothers and sisters without disabilities. The goal of their therapy was to uncover the nature of the bond between the siblings—whether it was close or distant and how it developed. These therapists have established a psychotherapy process to handle *severe* life problems experienced by adult siblings. Their approach is clearly beyond the scope and purpose of this book. The majority of siblings will *not* need psychotherapy to handle their feelings and concerns or to learn new ways to solve their problems. Less intense, more informal counseling is recommended for most siblings who have brothers and sisters with disabilities.

WHO ARE COUNSELORS?

Counselors are usually thought of as psychiatrists and psychologists who are highly skilled in behavioral and medical sciences. There is, however, a growing acceptance of counselors from a broader population who may have only minimal training in counseling techniques (Brammer, 1977; Stewart, 1986). These more informal counselors may include peer counselors at the high school and college-age level, crisis-line telephone counselors, teachers, and family members.

Since counseling is the establishment of a helping relationship between two people, the counselor must possess skills to develop and maintain that relationship. Typically, counselors receive professional training to develop specific skills that fulfill the goals of counseling. It is important for counselors to be fully aware of their skills and the limits of their competence so they will not attempt to overstep their boundaries. Occasionally, counselors may be asked to help with serious emotional problems, such as severe depression, which require treatment from highly skilled professionals. Competent counselors are quick to identify other professionals with advanced skills and refer these persons to them. Social workers, psychologists (clinical, counseling, and school), psychiatrists, nurses, and educators may be employed as counselors of siblings. The necessary ingredients for successful counseling do not come from holding a certain title, but by the attainment of specific competencies and skills.

Effective counselors of siblings share a number of characteristics, including the following:

1. *Maturity*   Counselors should demonstrate mature thoughts and actions, personal stability, and security.
2. *Interest in people*   Counselors must like people; they must be able to care for others and be sensitive to the human needs of those they seek to help.
3. *Honesty*   Counselors must be authentic and not hide behind a facade or a professional mask. The counselor must be open and willing to share thoughts with others.
4. *Rapport*   Counselors must be able to establish comfortable relationships with other persons. These relationships should be established in natural ways, neither forced nor contrived.
5. *Empathy*   Counselors must understand siblings. They should be able to adopt the sibling's perspective and, thus, come to a fuller understanding of the sibling's problems, concerns, and feelings.
6. *Acceptance*   Counselors must accept siblings in a nonjudgmental manner. Counselors must also be able to accept and understand themselves.
7. *Trust*   Counselors must trust and have confidence in siblings.
8. *Involvement*   Counselors must demonstrate their involvement through their communication with the sibling. They must be attentive to what siblings say and do.
9. *Ethics*   Counselors should demonstrate the highest degree of ethical behavior. Counselors must maintain strict confidence and should never initiate treatment beyond the scope of their expertise.
10. *Knowledge*   Counselors of siblings must be knowledgeable of the full array of social services and community resources available as well as cognizant of state-of-the-art philosophies concerning human development, behavioral principles, and disab-

ling conditions. Successful counselors are fully aware of current research related to siblings as well as innovative service programs aimed at meeting their needs.

THE COUNSELING PROCESS

Effective counseling does not happen by chance; it is a deliberate activity involving several steps or stages. Effective counselors enable siblings to develop new perspectives and skills in a systematic and secure manner. Whether counseling occurs individually or in small groups, the counseling process is generally the same. This basic counseling process involves seven steps, which are described in the following pages after a discussion of the importance and structure of the first meeting between the counselor and the sibling.

The First Meeting

There is general agreement in the counseling field that the first meeting between the counselor and the person seeking help is critical to the overall success of the future sessions and, thus, should be carefully planned. During the first meeting, the foundation for later trust, respect, and acceptance will be established.

Brammer (1973) notes that most people entering a counseling relationship do so with certain misgivings. It is not easy to meet new people, share problems with strangers, and express feelings. For some people, their problems seem so overwhelming or so unique that the thought of sharing them produces a great deal of anxiety and concern. Like all people, siblings who are starting a relationship with a counselor do so with apprehension, uncertainty, insecurity, and, in some cases, defensiveness. These initial anxious feelings are influenced by the factors surrounding the first meeting. For instance, are the siblings attending the sessions voluntarily, or have they been required to attend by a parent, teacher, or counselor?

The first task for the counselor, then, is to help the sibling relax. The first meeting should be structured to alleviate the sibling's negative feelings about the new relationship. This requires communicating with the sibling in a manner as "genuinely, caringly, and concretely as possible" (Egan, 1975, p. 75).

Establishing good rapport and building the basis for a future relationship is paramount (Meier, 1989). The first meeting should be neither rushed nor too long. In small-group situations, counselors should limit the information presented to essentials and provide the opportunity for the siblings to express themselves. Siblings should be encouraged to voice their concerns and their feelings, and to talk about their reasons for attending the counseling sessions. Successful counselors provide stimulation to encourage siblings to talk and to avoid talking too much themselves.

Other critical objectives of the first meeting are:

1. To clarify the concerns of the siblings and what they hope to accomplish
2. To identify the siblings' needs
3. To explore unstated feelings, attitudes, and beliefs
4. To investigate the siblings' base of knowledge regarding particular or general disabilities
5. To explain the nature, structure, outcomes, and limitation of the counseling process

The first contact between the siblings and the counselor should be very personal. Attending to administrative details may hamper the establishment of good initial rapport. Greetings, small talk, and an expression of appreciation for their attendance should always precede any administrative procedures.

During the first meeting of a group session, it is helpful to ask the siblings to complete an introductory card and a sentence completion form, like those shown in Figures 6.1 and 6.2. These forms were prepared for adolescents and help to focus the first meeting on the sibling's concerns, feelings, problems, and needs that will be addressed throughout the counseling process. The written nature of

My name is: _____

Address: _____

_____

Telephone: _____

School: _____ Grade: ____

Favorite subject: _____

Least favorite subject: _____

My brother/sister's name is: _____

What type of disability does he/she have? _____

_____

What do you hope to accomplish here? _____

_____

_____

Figure 6.1. Introductory card for sibling groups.

Name: _____ Date: _____

1. I am most happy when _____
   _____

2. Life is easiest when _____
   _____

3. The most important thing in my life right now is _____
   _____

4. If only _____
   _____

5. On Saturdays I usually _____
   _____

6. Life is hardest when _____
   _____

7. It's not easy to _____
   _____

8. Sometimes I really need _____
   _____

9. When I get older _____
   _____

10. It makes me angry _____
    _____

11. Sometimes I feel sad when _____
    _____

12. The best thing about my family is _____
    _____

Figure 6.2. Sentence completion form.

this activity may help the sibling concentrate on his or her thoughts without the pressure of keeping up a conversation or making eloquent statements. Allowing 15 or 20 minutes for this activity will be well worth the time. Of course, if this activity will in any way interfere with establishing a friendly, open relationship with the siblings, it should not be considered. Siblings who have reading or writing problems, for instance, should not be asked to complete such forms because the added pressure and anxiety might impede the establishment of rapport.

After the siblings complete an introductory card and sentence completion form, a first meeting with a small group of siblings might begin as follows:

> Well, I'm really glad that we were able to get together like this. It's great that we can be together to talk with each other. Let's go around and introduce ourselves and maybe state where you go to school and your grade. (*Introductions.*)
>
> I want to start by telling you something about our group sessions and what we can achieve here. If we are successful, you will each leave the sessions with a better, deeper understanding of yourself, of your feelings, and of your behavior. I hope each of you sees this as an opportunity to do something special for yourself. Today and every time we get together, you should feel free to talk and express your thoughts and feelings. Everything we tell each other must be kept confidential. That means I won't tell anyone what you say and you must not share the thoughts and feelings of the others with anyone. That includes parents, boyfriends, and girlfriends.
>
> During these sessions, my role will be to help you clarify and understand some of your feelings. I will also help you plan some course of action to help you with a particular problem or concern you have. We might even practice solving some problems that all of you experience.
>
> Your job is to openly and honestly express your feelings, react to the others in a caring and helpful way, and practice the various suggestions made. If this is going to work for all of us, each of us must work at it.
>
> We will be meeting for 2 hours, once a week, on Tuesdays, 4 to 6, in my office. Right now, our schedule calls for six sessions. The number of sessions can be changed as we see fit.
>
> Are there any questions? (*Pause for 1 minute.*). Okay, if there are no questions, let's start by trying to set some goals for ourselves. Why did we come together? . . .

At the end of the first meeting, the session should be summarized briefly. Siblings should leave the first meeting with a review of the counseling process, the counseling goals established, and a general understanding of the role of the counselor and the responsibilities of the siblings throughout the counseling relationship.

Seven Steps in Counseling Siblings

Seven steps are typically used in counseling siblings who have brothers and sisters with disabilities. Although these steps are sequentially arranged, the boundaries between them overlap and, indeed, some of them are ongoing.

Step 1—Establish a Relationship This step begins as soon as the sibling and the counselor first meet and will continue until the relationship is terminated. Throughout this step, the counselor should communicate a sincere respect for the sibling and an attitude of acceptance toward him or her. The sibling should be treated as a valuable person. The nature of this relationship is defined and limited

to the goals of counseling. The relationship will be enhanced as the counselor demonstrates skills in relating to others and in providing needed assistance.

Step 2—*Understand the Sibling's Feelings and Needs*
This step determines what feelings the sibling has toward himself or herself, and toward his or her siblings, friends, parents, and so forth, as well as discusses any needs the sibling has that are not being met. At this stage, the counselor is concerned with the sibling's perception of his or her difficulties and his or her feelings about them (Stewart, 1986). The counselor and sibling examine the problems and feelings from many different vantage points so that the best course of action can be planned. Stewart (1986) notes:

> Understanding alone is not sufficient. The counselor must verbally ex-
> press understanding to the client. It is during this phase that empathy, or
> the ability to perceive the client's thoughts and feelings and to communi-
> cate this understanding, assumes special significance. Learning to devel-
> op empathy with the client takes both time and practice. It is learning to
> hear the client and to convey that you heard. (p. 58)

Step 3—Explore Options During this stage, counselors should suggest a number of possible ways to alter or solve the siblings' problems. In this way, the counselor urges the sibling to make progress toward the counseling goal. The counselor must not make the decision as to which alternative is best but rather suggest many viable options. The parameters of each option in terms of time, effort, cost, risk, sacrifice, and so forth, should be discussed during this step. The sibling's analysis of the implications of each option must be carefully reviewed.

Step 4—Plan a Strategy As Brammer (1973) notes, "There comes a point when the person seeking help must 'decide or act and stop talking about himself, his problems or his possible plans'" (p. 66). As the sibling analyzes the various options presented earlier, he or she will gradually begin to adopt a suitable strategy. The sibling should be encouraged to *select* a strategy, rather than just accept the advice of the counselor. Implementation and eventual success of the strategy will require personal commitment. The counselor should assist the sibling in analyzing the strategy from several perspectives to ensure that most problems and outcomes are anticipated. At this time, the resources needed to carry out the strategy should be identified and located. A written plan of action, generated by the sibling and reviewed by the counselor, may help to structure and determine what will be done to meet the goals of the counseling sessions.

Step 5—Practice New Skills Throughout the counseling process, the sibling has been developing new insights about his or her behavior, feelings, and concerns. The sibling should be reaching a new level of understanding and acceptance. As previously mentioned, the sibling should have a strategy planned to help achieve the counseling goals. The counselor must help the sibling practice the strategy and the new skills before they are actually implemented outside of the counseling environment. In this way, the sibling can receive support as the skills develop and the counselor ensures that the initial efforts to apply new skills have the greatest likelihood of success.

Role-playing is a useful tactic to help siblings practice their newly learned skills. The counselor and sibling establish a realistic situation and practice various roles and behaviors to deal with the problem presented. It is helpful for the sibling to see the counselor role-play as the sibling using the new skills and to then ask the sibling to do the same. To ensure that the new skills are generalized to many situations, several role-play sessions are recommended.

Step 6—Terminate the Sessions Typically, the counseling relationship is short term. As the sibling achieves the goals established in the first few sessions, both the sibling and counselor should prepare to terminate the counseling relationship. The decision to terminate must be a mutual one, although the sibling should assume the major responsibility for this (Stewart, 1986). It is important that the sibling leave the relationship feeling that the counseling has been constructive. A review of the sessions, initial problems, chosen strategies, and new skills is highly recommended. If the counseling has been successful, the sibling will leave with a positive attitude and with specific skills that can be used to deal effectively with problems he or she may encounter. In closing the relationship, the counselor should make sure the sibling still feels valuable by recognizing the achievements and skills mastered by the sibling.

Step 7—Follow-Up Follow-up is often neglected in the counseling process, but is almost always needed. It is not likely that siblings will be able to maintain changes in their feelings, attitudes, and behavior unless they receive periodic support. Follow-up should be viewed as a "booster shot" to help the sibling carry through with what was accomplished in the counseling sessions. Telephone calls, brief visits, or written notes by the counselor will not only help to remind the sibling of the accomplishments achieved earlier, but will also communicate an honest concern for the sibling. Asking the sibling to drop a note or to call monthly to keep in touch and let the counselor know how he or she is feeling may be helpful. Follow-up should be a part of all sibling counseling.

GROUP COUNSELING

Group counseling appears to be a preferred approach when working with siblings who have brothers and sisters with disabilities (e.g., Feigon, 1981; Kaplan, 1969; Schreiber & Feeley, 1965; Slade, 1988; Summers et al., 1991). Over the past 4 decades, group counseling has become a popular method of providing systematic help to people. *Group counseling*, according to Pietrofesa et al. (1984), is:

> contact between a counselor and a group of clients, each of whom is in a state of discomfort, wishes to ease that discomfort, and is willing to do that in the social setting of a group. (p. 371)

Ideally, the group situation provides an opportunity for the sibling to interact with other siblings who face similar problems and experience similar feelings, and to give and receive help from them as well as from the counselor. Stewart (1986) notes that group counseling typically renders its greatest outcome by demonstrating that others have similar difficulties and problems.

Structured Group Counseling for Siblings

The most predominant counseling approach documented in the literature entails structured group discussions. These groups operate on the premise that siblings need an opportunity to express their feelings and thoughts with other siblings who have similar experiences.

Schreiber and Feeley (1965) have reported on the successful implementation of a structured (or guided) group experience for siblings (ages 13–17) of children with mental retardation who were living at home. This sibling group was formed as one part of a broader effort to strengthen overall family life. It focused on the following goals:

1. To assist siblings to identify their reactions to their brothers or sisters who have disabilities
2. To help individual siblings examine and determine strategies for understanding and dealing with their siblings, parents, and peers, as well as problems related to living with a brother or sister who has a disability
3. To discover siblings' strengths and weaknesses

This group met every 2 weeks over an 8-month period and was led by a social worker. At the conclusion of this group experience, Schreiber and Feeley (1965) noted that it was not the severity of the disability that seemed to affect the adolescents' lives or happiness as much as it was the way the adolescents felt about themselves and their sibling. The participants in this group requested specific information on what they could do to help their families and the sibling with a disability. These researchers concluded that when parents have dealt constructively with problems regarding the child with a disability, the sibling tends to develop greater maturity, tolerance, patience, and responsibility than is typical for children of similar age. They assert that the sibling of a child with a disability needs reassurance, support, and specific information regarding the disabling condition.

Kaplan (1969) has expanded upon Schreiber and Feeley's work by establishing several discussion groups for adolescents who have a sibling with a disability living at a residential school. These groups met weekly, primarily to discuss problems and experiences related to having a brother or sister with a disability. In summarizing, Kaplan concluded that many siblings wish to avoid being associated with their brother or sister. The siblings in these groups specifically requested help regarding:

1. Discipline and behavior management
2. Informing their friends about their sibling
3. Discussing problems with other family members

This type of guided group experience has been actively endorsed as a way to help siblings share their experiences and, at the same time, to reach new levels of understanding (Caldwell & Guze, 1960; Kowalski, 1980; Sullivan, 1979; Wing, 1972). DeMyer (1979) asserts that many siblings need a structured forum to ask questions, to express their feelings, and to discover strategies that will help them solve their problems. The guided group approach seems to be a powerful treatment technique to help siblings.

Feigon (1981) has described the formation of sibling groups for adolescents who had brothers and sisters with varying disabilities. The groups, which began in 1973, met weekly for 12 sessions and were set up in discussion group style. Feigon analyzed the content of these group sessions and identified four common themes. The first theme centered on the family and the sibling's responsibility to the child with a disability. Within this topic, siblings discussed issues such as embarrassment, anger, resentment, loyalty, and commitment. The second theme, intrapsychic feelings, attempted to help the adolescents focus on his or her own feelings. Many siblings expressed concerns about their own health and achievements. The third theme, interpersonal information, focused on sharing information regarding disabling conditions, genetic concerns, and behavior management, and on introducing the child to friends. The fourth theme revolved around the social needs of the adolescents. In this context, the siblings discussed general topics, such as high school, friends, and special events.

Feigon (1981) has noted that such groups have two major functions. One function is purely informational. The siblings want specific information and the group sessions provide a forum for its receipt. Second, the group provides a therapeutic and supportive experience in which the siblings can address their individual needs. By focusing on their needs, group members "seemed to promote a greater understanding of themselves in relation to their sibling" (Feigon, 1981, p. 2).

A group of siblings, with the help of their group leader, recently described their sibling group (Borders, Borders, Borders, Watts, & Watts, 1982). They founded their group at United Cerebral Palsy of Greater Louisville, Kentucky, with the aim of meeting other siblings who have brothers and sisters with disabilities. "We wanted to talk about our siblings who are disabled and learn more about their disability, what it means for them, and what it means for us" (p. 2).

This group met every other week for 1½ hours over a several-month period. The group used role-playing to learn how to react to stressful situations. These siblings noted, "Through acting out, we are able to discuss everyone's viewpoint and begin to understand why people act or think the way they do" (p. 2). During their guided group experience, these siblings were able to share and discuss a number of feelings, including anger, happiness, jealousy, worry, and excitement. These siblings encouraged other siblings to join similar groups noting, "You will like your sibling more, and you will like yourself more" (p. 2).

Slade (1988) notes that, with school settings, group counseling is often utilized because of the common experiences shared by siblings. Slade describes two basic group approaches: 1) informational (learning about disabilities), and 2) affective (discussing feelings about brothers and sisters, parents, and the family). Within the group, Slade recommends the use of role-playing, as well as children's literature, to initiate discussion of critical issues.

Advantages & Limitations of Group Counseling

Group counseling, like any tactic to help people systematically solve their problems, has both advantages and limitations. Group counseling cannot be considered a cure-all treatment (Schneider-Corey & Corey, 1987). Careful consideration of the advantages and limitations of this type of treatment will help set initial parameters for what can be expected through group counseling, help anticipate what might be potential problems for a particular group, and provide a stronger base for choosing a counseling approach.

Advantages

Group counseling is efficient. Counselors can provide service to more siblings (George & Christiani, 1981).

Siblings provide a support system for each other.

Use of a group allows siblings to use a real-life setting to experiment with and to practice new behavioral strategies during the counseling sessions.

Siblings receive acceptance and validation of their feelings from others, not just the counselor.

Siblings learn interpersonal communication skills beyond those that can be developed in one-to-one relationships.

Groups allow siblings to put their own problems into perspective and to understand how similar and unique they are compared to others.

Siblings may be more receptive to suggestions made by other siblings than by a professional. According to Pietrofesa et al. (1984), learning about the commonality of problems, life events, and situations often allows the development of solutions to have more credence.

In groups, siblings can both receive and provide help.

Limitations

Some siblings' personalities do not lend themselves to the demands of the group setting. A quiet and shy sibling may simply get "lost in the crowd"; a domineering sibling may manipulate the group and impede the group process.

Some siblings may have problems and needs that require in-depth attention. Group counseling implies a diluted relationship between the client and a professional (Shertzer & Stone, 1980).

Sibling groups may concentrate on the mechanics of the group process, which detracts from individual concerns.

In groups, cliques can develop. This excludes some members and, thus, divides the group (Pietrofesa et al. 1984).

Some siblings may find it difficult to trust other members and, thus, not fully express feelings, thoughts, and concerns.

Group counseling requires advanced professional skill; sometimes, leadership may be weak and ineffective due to poor counselor training in group techniques (Schneider-Corey & Corey, 1987).

Special Considerations for Groups

Implementing successful therapeutic groups for siblings who have brothers and sisters with disabilities requires attention to a number of considerations. These include manner of participation, group size, age, gender, disability of the sibling, educational and socioeconomic level, meeting location, duration of the group and length of time for individual gatherings, and group leadership.

Participation Siblings must volunteer to come to group sessions. Those who are coerced or required to attend will most likely not benefit from the experience and may disrupt or hamper the group process.

Group Size It is generally recommended that groups range from six to eight members (George & Christiani, 1981). Of course, size depends on the goals that the group hopes to realize. Some goals require more, while others require fewer, members.

Age Homogeneity in terms of age is more critical for children and adolescents than for adults. The age of the participants should be kept relatively similar for children and within a 2- or 3-year age range for adolescents. Siblings of different ages have different problems and concerns that are best shared by those of a similar age.

Gender It may, at times, be desirable to consider single-sex groups; however, our experience with mixed sexes has been quite positive. Gazda (1978) suggests homogeneous groups, particularly preadolescents who may be reluctant to talk in mixed groups.

Disability of the Sibling Siblings who have brothers or sisters with disabilities share many of the same concerns. It may be helpful, though, to organize sibling groups around the severity and/or nature of the disability experienced by the child. Groups could be organized around a particular disability (e.g., blindness, cerebral palsy, deafness, mental retardation, emotional disturbance, or autism) or in a more generic nature (e.g., mild, moderate, and severe disabilities). Additionally, group composition may focus on where the person with the disability resides (e.g., natural homes, group homes, or residential schools).

Educational and Socioeconomic Level Pietrofesa et al. (1984) caution that attention should be given to clients' educational and socioeconomic levels when establishing groups. These factors should be considered so that they will not hinder the group's progress and interfere with communication and learning.

Location It is essential that the location selected for group meetings provides a comfortable, calm atmosphere. The area should be free from disruptions (telephone calls, messages, visitors, etc.) and should offer privacy. If group members know that the people in the next room can hear what is being said, it is doubtful that they will be open and express true feelings. Comfortable chairs around a table for adolescents and adults is a useful format. Children often seem to prefer to meet in a small circle on chairs or on the floor.

Group Duration and Meeting Time Groups can meet over a relatively brief period of time or for longer terms. We have found that our most successful groups tend to meet weekly for 5–7 weeks for preadolescents, weekly for 8- to 10-week sessions for adolescents, and bi-weekly for 8–10 sessions for adults. Naturally, the length of each session will vary according to the group's needs. Usually a group will meet for 1½ hours for adolescents and adults and 40–50 minutes for children. A time frame should be established at the onset of the meeting, with the provision that the session may be ended early but should not be lengthened.

Leadership The counselor leading the group needs advanced helping skills if the group is to successfully meet its goals. Most importantly, the leader needs to model effective communication skills and be able to demonstrate respect and empathy for each group member. The group leader must be able to encourage participation, clarify communication, and provide a source of information for the group members. Group leaders must be skilled in group dynamics and must be able to participate in communications while also observing what is happening. George and Christiani (1981) note that effective group leaders are skilled in listening, feedback, clarifying statements, linking the commonalities of the group, questioning to generate discussion, and summarizing group communications.

FINAL CONSIDERATIONS

Throughout this chapter, we have discussed the important role that counseling can play in helping siblings to recognize, understand, and deal with their feelings and problems. Final considerations that must be reviewed concern counseling younger children, discussions with parents, and referral.

Counseling Young Children

The counseling process seems best suited to adolescents and adults who strive to find and develop their own identities and solve critical life problems. Adolescents and adults typically have the verbal and cognitive skills to benefit from the counseling process. However, younger children may also experience a number of emotions and have problems that are similar to their older counterparts. Children who have brothers and sisters with disabilities may benefit from

counseling, provided that the counselor uses the special skills and understanding necessary for this age group.

Basically, the counseling process with young children is similar to the generic counseling skills outlined previously, except that these special clients have limited verbal and cognitive skills. Young children are limited in their behavioral repertoires and often have limited freedom of choice. Patterson and Eisenberg (1983) provided the following recommendations for counseling young children:

> Children need help labeling their feelings and will benefit from hearing their feelings restated by the counselor.
>
> The child must be taken seriously and given undivided attention during counseling.
>
> The counselor should not expect a great deal of conversation.
>
> Use of graphic materials and play may foster communication during the counseling session.
>
> During play, the counselor should observe and reflect upon the emotions revealed in the play, as well as encourage the child to add verbal expression.
>
> Unstructured play materials, such as puppets and dolls, are recommended; structured games are not.
>
> The counselor should initially engage the child in conversation about daily life events as a means of building trust and rapport.

Discussions with Parents

Counselors working with children or adolescents face a dilemma regarding their parents. How much should the counselor share with parents without violating the siblings' trust and confidence? The counselor may recognize that the parents also approach the counseling process with some apprehension. Feigon (1981), in describing a sibling group, noted that many of the families were suspicious of what their child would be told by the counselor, and many parents wanted to control the information that would be shared about the sibling. Most parents want to provide the best environment for all of their children and may be looking toward the counselor as a source of information and support to help them deal effectively with their child.

Sensitive counselors approach the dilemma in a straightforward, honest manner. They should:

> Meet with parents prior to the counseling session and explain in detail the counseling process and its limits, as well as describe a typical counseling scenario.
>
> Involve parents of young children in helping to establish the counseling goal. However, such involvement may not be ap-

propriate for most adolescents who need to identify their own needs.

Ensure the family that strict confidentiality will be maintained regarding all communications.

Provide written follow-up reports to the parents. These reports should focus on the general outcome of the counseling without violating the child's trust.

Provide parents with written guidelines and suggestions for developing positive family communication and for strengthening the sibling bond.

Wasserman (1983) notes that when siblings are unwilling to participate in counseling, parents may be used to reach the sibling. For example, the counselor, through parent education programs, can teach parents techniques to facilitate communication between parent and child. Counselors can focus their attention on helping parents learn strategies to deal with siblings' concerns, feelings, and actions.

Networking

As noted in Chapter 5, one of the important goals of information-sharing is the opportunity for siblings to network with others. Siblings need to know that they are part of larger systems (immediate and extended family, friends, community, etc.) that can serve as a source of support. The counselor plays a critical role in helping the sibling establish networks of support by linking the individual with others and with services that can provide longitudinal support. Often extended family members (grandparents, aunts, and uncles) can be utilized in a network to support the sibling. Establishing the link among siblings and other resources may not only provide support to the sibling, but also to the other willing helpers in the community. Counselors should not overlook the powerful influence of these networks.

Referrals

Some siblings have problems that go beyond the counseling approach; they may be in need of psychotherapy or other more intense treatment. The counselor should refer those siblings to competent colleagues. In the case of children and adolescents, prior to referral, the counselor must discuss the reason for referral with the parents and provide them with resources to meet their child's needs.

SUMMARY

This chapter focuses on providing help to siblings who have brothers and sisters with disabilities to assist them in dealing with their feelings and problems more effectively. Siblings typically experience a full range of feelings, including anger, joy, sadness, excitement, frustration, jealousy, and fear. Siblings also have a number of unique problems related to their experiences with their brothers and sisters who have disabilities. Counseling is a common and direct way to help many siblings with their feelings and problems. Effective counseling enables the sibling to develop a number of skills to recognize and understand problems and to solve them in a constructive manner. The goal of counseling is to help siblings deal with their feelings and problems independently. Whether siblings are counseled individually or in groups, it is important that the counselor be someone who has the needed professional competencies to ensure an effective counseling process so that siblings reach their individual goals as quickly as possible. This chapter should help to remind skilled helpers of the parameters and guidelines for such successful counseling.

7

Social
Interaction

My name is Beth and I'm eleven. I have a retarded brother,
Steven. . . . It's easy to make Steven laugh, and when we play our
own special ballgame or I tickle him, he seems to have such fun.
Then I feel good (pp. 1, 21).
Harriet Langsam Sobol, 1977

Kevin's older brother, Ryan, has Hunter syndrome, a genetic disability that results in a metabolic disorder causing mental retardation and deafness. Ryan is 7 years old and attends a private school. Kevin has just entered kindergarten. When they are together, either in the playroom or in the backyard, they seldom interact. Ryan typically goes after one of Kevin's toys, which results in screams or a tugging match. Ryan usually loses. When Kevin wants Ryan to play a game, Kevin's initiations and instructions are not effective, and he usually gives up trying to play with Ryan after a few attempts. Watching these attempts, their parents are saddened by what might have been and feel the frustration of not knowing how to reverse the situation. Ryan plays by himself; Kevin wants a playmate.

Elizabeth, age 7, has a speech defect and a learning disability. She and her 10-year-old sister, Marie, seldom play cooperatively. They seem to be constantly quarreling over toys, dolls, posters, the stereo, television, friends, the pets—you name it. Their mother reports that they have not had a peaceful day in years. The girls are punished for the fighting, but it seems to have little effect on their behavior.

Mike's younger brother, John, has Down syndrome. Both boys are teenagers (ages 17 and 15, respectively). John likes to follow Mike around. He always asks to do everything Mike does, and if he doesn't get to go with Mike, he'll pout and occasionally cry. Mike responds with mixed emotions. On one hand, he wants to include his brother in some of his activities; on the other, he wants some relief from John's constant demands. Mike wants John to know that he loves him, yet, he does not know how to reasonably share his time and activities with his brother.

All three sets of siblings described above share common problems relating to brothers and sisters with disabling conditions. These problems focus on social interactions related to play and leisure time. Although such problems are universal in sibling relationships, siblings who have brothers and sisters with disabilities may experience unique problems related to social interaction. Some siblings with disabilities may be nonresponsive to a sibling's initiations. Other siblings may be aggressive, while others are withdrawn. Some may not comprehend play instructions. Others cannot manipulate toys and games. Some siblings may never be physically able to run, jump, or wrestle; others may need to be taught play skills. This chapter focuses on social interactions between siblings, with the primary emphasis on ways in which positive social interactions between siblings can be enhanced.

THE IMPORTANCE OF SOCIAL INTERACTION

The importance of social interaction in a child's overall development has been well documented (Dunn, 1983; Guralnick, 1976, 1978; Hartup, 1978, 1979; Kohl & Beckman, 1990; Shores, 1987; Strain & Fox, 1981). Social interactions among children provide a context in which other critical learning experiences take place. Reviews of the literature have continually pointed to the critical role that social interaction with peers plays in the overall development of a child. Several authors (Strain, Cooke, & Apolloni, 1976; Van Hasselt, Hersen, Whitehill, & Bellack, 1979) have discussed the demonstrated relationship between a child's level of social interaction and successful learning experiences, which lead to long-term social adjustment. Through social interaction with peers, the child has a basis for learning in the areas of sex-role development (Mischel, 1970), moral development (Hoffman, 1970), and motor and language development (Apolloni & Cooke, 1975, as well as the opportunity to develop self-esteem (Frank, 1988). Benefits from social interaction are reciprocal in nature. That is, both children benefit from the interaction. Children without disabilities also receive a number of benefits from their interaction with children who have disabilities (Peck, Donaldson, & Pezzoli, 1990). They develop a sense of self and learn to appreciate human differences as well as their own individuality. Many siblings report that through interaction with their brothers and sisters who have disabilities they have learned lifetime skills.

Through social interaction, siblings are provided the foundation for a strong long-lasting relationship. It is hoped that through social

interactions siblings will go beyond their family bonds and become lifelong friends. What parent does not want their children to grow in friendship with each other? Perske (1990) notes that many positive and powerful outcomes have been founded on friendships. Strully and Bartholomew-Lorimer (1988) detail the many reasons why people with disabilities need friends. Many individuals with disabilities will have a greater likelihood of community acceptance and participation when they are engaged in friendships which extend and enhance the human services system.

Stainback and Stainback (1987) detail strategies that have helped children with disabilities develop and sustain friendships. These strategies have tremendous implications for brothers and sisters. Even though we often think about friendships as being outside family relationships, when brothers and sisters become real friends, something special happens within the relationship. Siblings who have become friends share a unique intimacy, they enjoy each other's company and move beyond biological and legal bonds. Friendship between a sibling and a brother or sister with a disability also serves as an example to other children and the community. This example helps set the occasion for others to develop friendships with the person with the disability, thus building important social relationships outside the family. The person with disabilities who has many friends will be less dependent upon the human services system (Perske, 1990). Friendship between and among siblings is the real focus of our attention on social interaction.

Unfortunately, some children do not socially interact with their peers. These children are often referred to as being socially withdrawn or socially isolated. In Strain et al.'s (1976) view of childhood social adjustment, preschool children are developmentally "at risk" if they do not experience positive, reciprocal social encounters with their peers. They are at risk due to exclusion from an informal, albeit important, source of instruction and learning. Strain and his associates (1976) maintain that children who are socially withdrawn experience difficulties acquiring appropriate language skills, moral values, motor skills, and socially acceptable methods for expressing anger and sexual feelings. Strain and Fox (1981) concur in assessing the importance of social interaction and point out that children identified as socially withdrawn during their early school years are "represented disproportionally in groups of juvenile delinquents, school dropouts during adolescence, and adults who experience adjustment problems" (p. 168). It has also been reported that children who interact very little with peers exhibit greater problems in school achievement (Kohn & Rosman, 1972), in interpersonal social skills during adolescence and adulthood (Ausubel, 1958), and with delinquency (Roff, Sells, & Golden, 1972), and may have greater mental health problems as adults (Cowan, Pederson, Babigan, Izzo, & Trost, 1973).

Peer social interaction seems to be a necessary ingredient for learning various social skills. If children do not socially interact, it is unlikely that they will simply "outgrow" this predisposition. Strain and Fox (1981) also assert that the vast majority of evidence suggests that social withdrawal in young children can become a persistent and serious problem, and that an absence of peer interaction can contribute to behavioral maladjustment in adulthood.

SOCIAL INTERACTION BETWEEN BROTHERS AND SISTERS

When considering social withdrawal in young children, much of the professional literature deals with social interaction between a child and nonfamily members in environments outside of the home. As Hartup (1979) has pointed out, however, it is family social interaction that provides the foundation for a child's exploration of the social world so necessary for the child's social development. Siblings, in particular, provide the child with the major source of social interaction in his or her first few years of life (Kaplan & McHale, 1980).

Similar to interaction with peers, social interaction between siblings can provide a basis for later achievement and development (Sutton-Smith & Rosenberg, 1970).

In an effort to investigate the extent of social interaction between siblings, Abramovitch et al. (1979) conducted a naturalistic study of sibling interaction in the home environment. Abramovitch and her colleagues observed 34 pairs of same-sex siblings in their homes and looked at social interaction along the dimensions of age, sex, and age interval between the siblings. Due to the nature of this pilot study, the researchers only looked at firstborn and second-born children who were of preschool age. In one group of siblings, the age interval between the children was considered long (3.5–4 years) and in the other group, short (1–2 years). Abramovitch et al. observed and categorized the social interactions or lack of them by observing each pair of siblings for two 1-hour sessions. They concluded that children interact with their siblings in the home and, by so doing, acquire their first extensive social experience with other children. The male sibling pairs exhibited more aggressive play behaviors than did the female pairs. Younger siblings tended to observe and imitate their older brothers and sisters more, independent of the age interval between them. Abramovitch et al. (1986), in their ongoing longitudinal observations of siblings, observed that the older sibling consistently initiated more aggressive and prosocial behaviors, while the younger sibling displayed more imitative behaviors. Thus, the older sibling dominated the relationship even as both grew older.

Lamb (1978a), in another study, observed and categorized the social interactions of 24 dyads of siblings in a laboratory setting. These dyads were composed of an 18-month-old child and his or her preschool-age sibling. Lamb found that the older siblings were more likely to vocalize and offer toys to the other child, whereas the younger siblings were more likely to watch, approach, and imitate the older siblings. Lamb concluded that older siblings serve as a model for younger siblings and that their social interaction is critical in the socialization process.

Since one aspect of social interaction is educational (Cicirelli, 1976b), increased social interaction among children with disabilities and their siblings should have positive effects on the children's development. Increasing social interaction between a child with a disability and his or her siblings would provide greater opportunities for siblings to model various socially appropriate behaviors and, thus, to learn from each other. In cases where there is extensive, positive contact between the child and the sibling, the sibling may exert considerable influence on the behavior of the child with a disability, perhaps having even more influence than the parents do. When opportunities for social interaction are enhanced, both children benefit from the outcome.

Positive social interaction among children with disabilities and their siblings, however, seems to be a problem in some families. Many siblings have requested specific help in this area (Graliker et al., 1962; Schreiber & Feeley, 1965; Sullivan, 1979). Parents of children with disabilities also recognize the value of social interaction and often wish to optimize social interaction between their children. If the sibling and the child with a disability do not socialize well with each other, the loss of the benefits of such a relationship will be more detrimental for the child with the disability than for the other child. Because the child with a disability may have limited opportunities to interact with other children, social interaction with siblings often takes on increased importance. Efforts to facilitate this interaction will be important to the child's development.

A REVIEW OF METHODS TO
FACILITATE SOCIAL INTERACTION

There will be no easy solution, but recognizing that a problem with social interaction exists for siblings is the first step toward remediation. Questions can then be posed, and intervention begun. What are the causal factors behind sibling relationships? How can interaction be enhanced? An examination of studies of peer relationships can be helpful. Although few studies have dealt directly with siblings, some researchers have been vigorously pursuing methods to help facilitate social interaction among children with disabilities and their peers. Many of their tested techniques have met with success and appear applicable to family situations. The suggestions that follow are derived directly from this literature.

Work on the facilitation of interaction between children with and without disabilities provides a foundation for parents who wish to increase interactions between siblings. Allen, Hart, Buell, Harris, and Wolf (1964) worked with a 4-year-old "socially isolate" girl who demonstrated poor articulation and frequent imaginary health-related complaints. When the child's teacher was taught to ignore socially isolate behavior and attend to positive peer contacts, the child's social interaction increased rapidly. In a related study, Buell, Stoddard, Harris, and Baer (1968) observed a 3-year-old child who rarely interacted appropriately with peers. Since this child did not play appropriately with outdoor play equipment either, the researchers began to prompt and reinforce the child's use of these materials. As the child's play on the outdoor equipment increased, she began to touch, talk to, and associate with her peers. In this study, the child maintained these social interaction behaviors, even when the teacher's prompting and reinforcement were discontinued.

In a study conducted by Strain and Timm (1974), a withdrawn 4-year-old girl with language and behavior problems was taught to play with peers. Her peers seldom engaged in positive social interaction with each other. To increase positive social interaction, the experimenters used an intensive schedule of praise for all of the children when they interacted. As a result, the child and her peers exhibited accelerated levels of social play.

Strain, Shores, and Timm (1977) conducted a study in which they trained children to increase their social initiations to withdrawn preschool children. The training of these peers primarily consisted of several sessions in which the experimenter told the peers "to try their best to get the older children to play with them" (p. 291). Role-playing, in which an adult assumed the role of the withdrawn child, was also incorporated into the training program. The results of this study indicated that the peers were able to increase their social behaviors directed toward the withdrawn children, and as a result, the positive social behaviors of the withdrawn children were increased. Also, the increase in peer initiations resulted in an increase in the social initiations made by the withdrawn children. These researchers concluded that peers can be taught to increase positive social behaviors of withdrawn children.

Recent work conducted by several researchers (Shores, 1981) has led to the development of specific techniques that may enhance social interactions between disabled children and those without disabilities. In an initial study (Tremblay, Strain, Hendrickson, & Shores, 1981), a group of preschoolers was observed during free-play sessions to determine which behaviors exhibited by children would facilitate social interaction. The results indicated that five specific social behaviors had a good chance of setting the occasion for positive social interaction: sharing, physical assistance, affection, rough-and-tumble play, and verbal organization of play (e.g., "Let's have a tea party"). In other related studies, these researchers experimentally investigated the effectiveness of these behaviors with children having disabilities who did not interact with other children. In these studies, age-peers were trained to initiate the identified social behaviors to the withdrawn children. When the age-peers used the identified behaviors, marked increases in positive social behaviors in the withdrawn children were noted. All of the withdrawn children in these studies responded positively and consistently to verbal organizations of play, sharing, and physical assists. The researchers concluded that such behavior can be used to set the standard for future, positive social behavior by children.

Similar studies were conducted to investigate specific methods that adults could employ to directly teach social behaviors to withdrawn children. Imitation-based procedures, in which adults employed modeling, prompting, and praising to encourage social interaction, were found to be effective with children who had varying levels of disability (Shores, 1981). To help teachers utilize the results of this research, a curriculum called Social Competence Intervention Package for Preschool Youngsters, or SCIPPY (Day, Powell, & Stowitscheck, 1981), was developed and tested. Curriculum components of SCIPPY include specific instructional targets, teaching procedures, and specific activities designed to set the occasion for social interaction. Results of field tests have indicated that teachers could successfully increase positive social interaction between children with and without disabilities (Day et al., 1984).

More recently, Knapczyk (1989) conducted a study in which cooperative play among school-age children was increased. Knapczyk instructed peer mentors to participate in play activities and adapt them to the needs of the children with moderate mental retardation. After the instructional period, the peers assisted the children with their participation in school play activities. As a result, the social interactions between the child with the disability and other children increased and were maintained over several months.

In a further demonstration of how reciprocal social interactions can also be taught to children who have disabilities, Kohl and Beckman (1990) demonstrated how social interactions among preschoolers with moderate disabilities could be increased using direct instructional tactics. In this investigation, six preschoolers with mental retardation were instructed in reciprocal play via modeling, verbal prompting, social praise, and corrective feedback. The children were taught in dyads for 5-minute instructional periods. The prompting and social praise were gradually reduced until they were eliminated altogether.

These same training components were recently applied in a home setting, in which parents successfully taught their children with and without disabilities to play together (Powell, Salzberg, Rule, Levy, & Itzkowitz, 1983). In this study, a social-training package (Powell, 1982) was developed and tested with several families who had young children (ages 3–9). This training package required parents to systematically train their children to interact using specific materials and teaching methods (e.g., prompting and praising). After they learned how to teach social interactions, all of the parents were able to increase the positive interactions between the siblings during both structured and informal play sessions.

James and Egle (1986) conducted a study to investigate a direct teaching approach to facilitate social interaction between children with disabilities and their brothers and sisters. In their study, they increased social interactions by teaching the sibling without a disability to initiate and maintain play. These experimenters taught the siblings during 12- to 15-minute sessions using modeling, practice, and feedback. The direct instruction included the use of prompts to the sibling (e.g., "Put his/her hands on the car"), role playing, and positive social reinforcement. After the siblings were taught, the experimenters instructed the child with the disability how to initiate play with the brother or sister. James and Egle note that the direct prompting strategy was effective in increasing reciprocal interactions and that these interactions generalized to other settings and times. It is interesting to note that these siblings were able to maintain their interaction at a 6-month review. The remainder of this chapter highlights many of the aspects of this work as well as other specific suggestions for other age groups of siblings.

ENCOURAGING SIBLING SOCIAL INTERACTION

Most parents expect their children to naturally play together and enjoy each other's company. Experienced parents know that this is often unrealistic. Some siblings have trouble playing with one another. When one sibling has a disability, special efforts may be needed to teach the siblings to play together. Through some simple teaching techniques and a basic understanding of how children differ in their interactions at various ages, parents can effectively facilitate social interaction (Powell, Salzberg, Rule, Levy, & Itzkowitz, 1983).

Developmental Considerations

Lefrancois (1973) has noted that children engage in three general types of play behavior. *Sensorimotor play* involves the manipulation of toys or engaging in physical activity (running, jumping, crawling) simply for the sensations experienced. Infants typically engage only in sensorimotor play because they are unable to perform more sophisticated activities. *Imaginative play* includes a wide variety of fantasy games. Preschoolers and children in elementary school often engage in imaginative play. *Social play* involves interaction between two or more children. Typically, social play is governed by explicit or implicit rules that direct the children's activities.

Children do not naturally play together. They learn to interact cooperatively as they mature. The type of play interaction between siblings varies according to their age and ability. To provide a context for facilitating social interaction, it is important to consider some basic differences among four age groups of children.

Birth to Age 3   Infants and very young children (birth to age 3) seldom interact socially with their siblings. Most of their play is sensorimotor and their interactions are usually directed toward parents and other adults. Occasionally, they will play with siblings, but most of their play at this stage is "parallel" (Parten, 1932) in that they play side by side with no real interaction. In parallel play, the children do not share nor do they employ mutually accepted rules to govern their play. Parallel play is a transitional time for children, from isolated play to cooperative interactions. Simple structured games and activities (finger plays, dancing, hide and seek) help the transition from parallel play to more advanced play in the next stage.

Ages 3 to 6   As the child reaches preschool age (3–6), cooperative interactions increase. The child learns to be less selfish and begins to realize that mutual collaboration with other children can increase the enjoyment of play. During the preschool years, children learn to share, to organize fantasy games, to engage in rough-and-tumble activities, and to help one another. Also during this time, children first develop the language and communication skills needed to facilitate and maintain social interaction. Play at this stage is still simple, yet, some rules and protocol are required to maintain interactions. Cooperative play at this stage typically occurs in a series of short episodes as opposed to extended durations of play.

Ages 6 to 12   When the child reaches school age (6–12), cooperative interactions with siblings and other children become more sophisticated. During this time, children engage in many forms of social play that include cooperative and imaginative activities. Rule-governed play, in which the children agree on rules and protocol, is more frequent. Sports, commercial board games, video games, and rough-and-tumble activities, as well as fantasy games, provide a context for social interactions.

Ages 13 to 18   Cooperative interactions for adolescents (13–18) involve a wide variety of activities. During this period, team sports and other sporting activities (e.g., Frisbee) comprise a large portion of social interactions. Adolescents also interact in more subtle ways. They listen to music, watch television shows, and "hang out" together. At first glance, these activities seem to be simply parallel acts; however, they usually involve more sophisticated behaviors, including sharing and verbal interactions. More overt social interactions, like going out for ice cream, talking on the telephone, participating in sports, going to dances, or developing a hobby, are just some ways in which adolescents interact with their peers.

What Parents Can Do

Within the home, parents can influence the rate and nature of social interaction between siblings. By systematically "setting the stage," parents can encourage social interaction. Through social praise and attention, parents can teach their children to increase their cooperative play behaviors. Although it is not always easy, parents can effectively teach social interaction skills to their children.

Siblings can be encouraged to socially interact with each other by focusing on the following five techniques:

Establish Reasonable Expectations.   Parents should not expect siblings to interact all the time. As mentioned earlier, social interaction between siblings seldom occurs before age 3, unless the child is engaged in a structured activity. Older siblings will develop a network of friends outside of the family and should be given ample opportunity to interact with these friends. Interacting with a child with a disability may be hard work, especially if the disabilities are severe or the child is withdrawn. Parents should not expect immediate changes in interaction patterns. Long-lasting changes require time and consistency. In some cases, the disability puts a great deal of distance between siblings who may be close in age. In such cases, reasonable expectations may include acceptance of unequal interactions in which the child without a disability serves as a leader or tutor, rather than a peer, of the child. The more severe the disability, the more difficult it will be to facilitate equal interactions between siblings.

Have Realistic Expectations. Social interaction between siblings usually occurs in short episodes rather than over extended periods of time. When facilitating interaction through structured play, it is important to keep the play periods rather short. With this in mind, structured play sessions between siblings should incorporate the following guidelines:

Preschool—10–12 minutes
School-age—10–30 minutes
Adolescence—15–60 minutes

Naturally, these times will vary according to the children's abilities and the activity. Again, expecting the social interaction to continue for extended periods of time is simply not realistic. It is most helpful for parents to establish a schedule for regular social interactions. For young children, a daily social interaction period may be favorable. For older children and adolescents, interaction on a weekly basis is more reasonable. These scheduled social interactions should be kept brief.

Select Activities and Toys that Lead to Interaction. One direct method of facilitating social interaction between siblings is to select activities and toys that will encourage interaction (Brody & Stoneman, 1986; Brody et al., 1982; Brody et al., 1985; Hendrickson, Strain, Tremblay, & Shores, 1981; McEvoy et al., 1988; Stoneman et al., 1984, 1986). Some toys and activities tend to encourage social interaction more than others. Blocks, balls, or trucks, for instance, will naturally facilitate more opportunities for interaction than will crayons, puzzles, or stuffed animals. Activities that can be used by both siblings need to be selected. The parent should locate activities that will be mutually enjoyable and not heighten the child's disability. Some activities and games can be adapted so that both siblings can interact on an equal basis. Sample interactive activities for siblings are listed in Tables 7.1, 7.2, and 7.3.

Arrange the Appropriate Play Environment. When children are just beginning to learn to play together the play environment is an important consideration (McEvoy, Shores, Wehby, Johnson, & Fox, 1990; Stoneman et al., 1987, 1989). The play environment should be free from competing activities (e.g., the television should be turned off). The focus should be on a few activities; any other play materials should be put away. Naturally, the play environment should be structured to limit interruptions and intrusions from other children. As the children develop their play skills, the environmental arrangements become less critical and should approximate normal conditions.

Praise the Siblings for Interaction. When siblings interact with each other, they should be praised by their parents. Praise should

Table 7.1. Interactive play activities and toys for siblings of preschool age

____ Catching balls	____ Playing spaceship
____ Kicking balls	____ Playing store
____ Rolling balls back and forth	____ Dolls
____ Block play	____ Cars and trucks
____ Playing with tinker toys	____ Playing school
____ Beanbag activities	____ Wagons
____ Acting out stories, television shows, movies	____ Dancing
	____ Singing songs
____ Tee-ball	____ Marching band
____ Bowling pins (indoors)	____ Playing cowboys and Indians
____ Balloon play	____ Playing policeman, fireman, mailman, and so forth
____ Playing tea party	
____ Playing house	____ Marbles
____ Playing doctor/dentist	____ Toy telephones
____ Playing dress-up	____ Fixing simple snacks
____ Blowing bubbles	____ Pretending to be animals
	____ Using puppets

be given in a way that will not interrupt the play, yet will communicate pleasure; for example, "You boys are playing so well together, Mom is so proud! Keep it up and I'll be sure to tell Dad." Praise should always be given in a sincere manner and the specific interaction should be mentioned. "That's good" has less effect than "It's nice to see you sharing your toys" or "I'm glad you helped Tim play with the video game." Various ways to praise siblings for social interaction are listed in Table 7.4.

Praise can be overdone. Parents and teachers are advised to keep praise statements short and to the point. If the praise interrupts the play, it serves the opposite purpose. As the play interaction increases over time praise will need to be gradually withdrawn to more natural levels and opportunities; for example, during dinner, note that the children played well together that afternoon. In this way children still receive the message, but it is given in a more naturally occurring manner.

Table 7.2. Interactive play activities for siblings of school age

____ Basketball	____ Cards
____ Badminton	____ Table games
____ Ping-Pong	____ Dominoes
____ Video games (taking turns)	____ Checkers
____ Fixing snacks together	____ Catching balls
____ Dancing	____ Throwing Frisbees
____ Fantasy games (e.g., playing Star Wars)	____ Taking a walk together
	____ Playing tag

Table 7.3. Interactive leisure activities for adolescent siblings

____ Going shopping together	____ Watching a television show together
____ Going out to eat with each other	
____ Fixing a meal together	____ Going to the movies
____ Listening to music together	____ Working on hobby or arts-and-crafts activity together
____ Playing pinball (taking turns)	
____ Playing video games (taking turns)	____ Taking a walk together
	____ Playing table games (Monopoly, Clue, etc.)
____ Playing basketball, soccer, softball, and so forth	
	____ Playing cards together

Directly Teach Interaction. Some children, especially those with disabilities, need specific instruction to learn how to interact. Parents should adhere to the following guidelines:

1. Select an activity for both children that will be of interest to each of them. (The activity should call for interaction.)

Table 7.4. Twenty ways to praise social interactions between siblings

Preschool age
1. "Sharing again? That's super!"
2. "That's a good way to get Tom to play."
3. "I'm happy that you are helping your sister."
4. "It's great when you two get along."
5. Give both siblings a kiss.
6. At the end of the play session, give each sibling a sticker and say, "You play so nicely together."
7. "Wait till Daddy hears what good helpers I have!"
8. "You played with your brother. Good job!"

School age
9. "John, Sue: you're such a great pair when you play like that!"
10. "Mike, it's awfully nice of you to help your brother play."
11. Give both siblings a hug.
12. "Wow! Playing together again? I'm pleased."
13. "Did I ever tell you that you're the greatest helpers I have?"
14. "I like to watch you play together. It makes me feel so happy."
15. "I don't believe it. Sharing and helping each other again!"

Adolescence
16. Write the adolescent sibling a short note to thank him for interaction with his sister.
17. "Since you included your brother in your game of basketball, I'll let you stay up later tonight. Good job."
18. "Your mother and I are very proud of the way you help your brother."
19. "When you play with your sister, you're a great example to the other kids. Thanks."
20. Give the sibling a hug.

2. Set aside a short period of time for the children to learn the activities.
3. Tell and show the children what to do. (Simply telling the children what to do is the easiest way to teach play interaction. In some cases, parents may need to show the children how to interact by modeling interactive behavior. When modeling, the parent may demonstrate how to share, start an activity, or help the child complete a play action.)
4. Praise the children when they interact.
5. Correct the children for inappropriate play (e.g., negative behaviors, uncooperative play, isolate play). For example, the parent can say, "John come sit over here next to your sister and share the blocks."

These five techniques will help promote sibling interaction and may help to avert some of the typical interaction problems.

TYPICAL SOCIAL INTERACTION PROBLEMS

McDermott (1980) notes that it is a myth that brothers and sisters naturally and easily love one another. Young children are typically selfish and primarily concerned with themselves, not their siblings. This natural selfishness can easily escalate into intense problems for families and is an obvious concern for parents.

All parents want their children to be friends with each other. As noted earlier, it is through this close and intense friendship that siblings learn from one another. However, parental goals of developing strong sibling friendships can be thwarted if the family does not recognize and prepare for typical social interaction problems common among siblings. Overreacting toward or ignoring sibling interaction problems may only intensify them.

Most sibling interaction problems are the result of rivalry (Bryant, 1982; Faber & Mazlish, 1988; McDermott, 1980; Ross & Milgram, 1982). Like all families, families having children with disabilities also experience sibling rivalry and encounter a full range of social interaction problems. Most sibling rivalry problems are no cause for alarm. These common problems may be effectively handled with a little planning and deliberate parental intervention. In some cases, however, sibling interactions can be so negative, so intense, and so chronic that parents may need to work closely with professionals to reverse these patterns.

Sibling interaction problems, especially in families in which one child has a disability, are created by jealousy and competition. Jealousy between and among siblings is quite normal. Each sibling desires and seeks the parental attention given to the other. In situations in which parental attention may be unequal due to the severity of a child's handicap, the jealousy may, indeed, be great. It is hard to ask young children to understand why parents need to spend extra time with a child who has a disability. In their eyes, the child is just another sibling who is receiving special attention. Unfortunately, no matter how hard parents try to provide equal attention to all of their children, unequal distribution of attention may simply be a fact of life for a family with a child who has a disability.

Like it or not, all siblings compete with one another for parental attention and outside recognition (e.g., grades, trophies, or awards). Competition between siblings is not only natural but, in most cases, is also healthy. Competition helps to prepare children for the realities of life. However, when one child has a disabling condition, too much competition for outside recognition may be harmful. When a child has a severe disability, competition between the child and the sibling without a disability typically favors the latter. This will, of course, result in additional failures for the child with a disability. In such situations, the natural competition between and among siblings may need some parental limits and structure.

Too much jealousy, extensive competition, or unfair competition can cause intense sibling rivalry. Jealousy and competition between siblings is usually vented in the form of fighting. Name-calling, shouting matches, wrestling, refusing to share, or taking each other's toys are common fighting styles of siblings, including brothers and sisters who have disabilities. Although some fighting is to be expected between siblings, parents can and should actively try to limit, and to provide reasonable consequences for, such fighting.

Limiting Jealousy & Competition

Parents should not expect all jealousy and competition to be eliminated since these are basic elements of human interaction, but several techniques are helpful in limiting these common sibling emotions.

Balance the Responsibilities of Siblings. Do not elevate one sibling to a "surrogate parent." Although it may be easiest to allow the child without a disability to be in charge, this can cause problems, especially for siblings who are close in age. It is natural to expect the oldest child to provide more direction and leadership; however, all children should receive some experience in making decisions, having responsibility, and being in charge of certain situations. Parents need to select varying activities and situations in which all children, including those with disabilities, can be in charge. In a like manner, the authority a child has over another, especially when one child has a disability, will need to be carefully monitored. When children are given too much authority over others, they may use it to meet selfish aims, which, naturally, intensifies problems between siblings.

Recognize Siblings as Individuals. A natural tendency in most families is to compare one sibling's accomplishments to another's. This type of comparing has obvious negative implications for a child who has trouble performing at the same level with siblings. Each child should be recognized individually.

Recognize Each Child's Accomplishments. Each accomplishment, no matter how small or unique, needs parental attention. In some families, the parents may pour attention on the accomplishments of the child with a disability and barely recognize a sibling's good grades because they are simply expected. In many cases, it may be easy to overlook a sibling's achievements in favor of the accomplishments of the child with a disability because the parents, themselves, may work harder with the child to realize his or her accomplishments. Equity in terms of recognition allows siblings to feel valued for their unique contribution to the family system.

Provide Time for Each Sibling. In the ideal situation, each sibling has equal access to parents and receives equal attention from them. In reality, this is seldom the case. Children with disabilities

typically require more intense parental attention. To overcome some of the problems that result from this unequal distribution of parental attention, parents should set aside special time with each of the siblings, either individually or collectively. Setting up a weekly, or even daily, time period devoted solely to the other children will communicate parental desires to attend equally to each sibling.

Prepare Children for New Siblings.   The presence of a new brother or sister should never come as a surprise to children. Since their lives will forever be altered by a new arrival, even the youngest child needs some preparation. Parents should talk about the new baby with siblings. Discussions about the new baby's needs, how the family will change, and what to expect from the baby help the children to include the new sibling in their lives. At these times, parents should actively remind the children how precious and valuable they still are.

Talk about Positive Characteristics.   Michael and Linda were concerned about their children, Jason, age 11, and Chris, age 9. They seemed to talk only in negative terms about Tommy, their brother with autism. After dinner and before television on Friday evenings, the parents started a game called "What's so good about . . . ." In the game, each round began by selecting a name (Mom, Jason, Tommy, etc.). Each person wrote down a response to complete the phrase, "What so good about . . . ." If responses matched the persons would each get a point. Tommy was "coached" by either Mom or Dad. In this way, the children were able to generate lists of each other's positive qualities. After a few weeks, a Friday evening was devoted to an art project, which was taped to the refrigerator door. The project displayed all of the good qualities for everyone to see. Discussing and posting the qualities of each child not only helped the siblings and parents to focus on positive attributes, but also helped visiting family members and neighbors to be aware of these good attributes.

Handling Sibling Fighting: Parental Strategies

It is important for parents to know that most siblings outgrow fighting. As siblings mature, they move from the simple selfishness of childhood to competition in the early school years and, finally, to collaboration. However, parents need to actively teach their children to limit their fighting and to work cooperatively together. The following 10 strategies are helpful in dealing with fighting between siblings:

Serve as an Example.   Parents should strive to handle their own feelings of jealousy and competition in a cooperative manner and, thus, provide a model to the siblings. Although parents should not expect children to immediately imitate their adult behavior, good models should be evident early.

Set Limits for Siblings. Parents should establish a reasonable set of rules that govern interactions and should *stick to them*. Rules such as no throwing, no hurting, no swearing, or no name-calling help to clarify the bounds of interactions. Every family will have different rules, and it is a good idea to make these rules explicit. This will also help parents in their "referee" role when siblings fight.

Use Natural and Logical Consequences. When discipline is needed, parents should use a natural and logical consequence. For example, when Mike and Sue are fighting over which cartoon show to watch, the television should be turned off for 2 minutes to help them learn to reach a compromise.

Always Praise Cooperation. Parents can actively teach their children to be cooperative by praising them when they play together, share, or solve problems in a collaborative fashion. Praise lets the siblings know that they will receive increased parental attention via cooperative behavior.

Ignore Simple Arguments. Parents should not attempt to intervene during all fights between siblings. A good rule of thumb is to ignore arguments that do not violate established family rules. At the same time, siblings should never be allowed to physically or emotionally hurt each other.

Stay Neutral. If it is unclear who started a fight or what the fight is about, it is wise for parents not to take sides. If both children are fighting, they should be treated equally in terms of the consequences. Taking sides, especially if the side is always that of the child with a disability, will only intensify sibling rivalry.

Be Consistent. Teaching siblings to be cooperative instead of argumentative requires consistent and predictable parenting. If parents handle sibling problems inconsistently, siblings will be confused.

Use Discipline When Needed. Children need limits and consequences for their behavior. Discipline that is consistent and logical can control fighting between siblings. Several proven methods of discipline can be used to limit fighting:

1. *Loss of materials or a toy* This is simply the removal of the item with which the children are playing. The item should be returned when the children demonstrate that they can play together cooperatively.
2. *Loss of a privilege* Excessive fighting might also result in the children losing a privilege (television, dessert, etc.).
3. *Time out* Time out is short for time out from positive reinforcement. In this consequence children are removed from a reinforcing (rewarding) activity or area for a few minutes. Time out should *always* be used for short durations of time. Three to five minutes is usually the best.

When the children are quiet they should be allowed to return to the activity. Time out works best if, upon their return, the children are praised for cooperative activity or other activity incompatible with fighting. For example, "Now you are sharing your toys. That's what I like to see!"

Share the Consequences and Alternatives. A fair warning may help to stop a sibling fight before it escalates into a battle. For example, "I've asked you both to watch TV quietly. If I come in again, the TV will be shut off for 5 minutes" or, "It would be nice if you'd both stop fighting on your own. If you need me to help you stop, I'll do that by sending you each to the corner and taking away your snack. I'll do this in 2 minutes, so it's up to you."

Be Creative. When teenage siblings fight, parents need to have more sophisticated strategies since physically moving an adolescent to a corner would never be appropriate. At these ages, consequences that involve privileges are most appropriate and effective. Having the siblings write a brief contract for good behavior (DeRisi & Butz, 1975; Homme, 1970) may be helpful. As siblings get older, parents should openly talk with them about their fighting and suggest alternative strategies for dealing with problems.

A FINAL NOTE

All families, whether or not they have a child with a disability, occasionally experience problems between and among siblings. These problems are a natural part of development and should be expected. If parents expect siblings to automatically love and respect each other, they are setting themselves up for disappointment. In families where one child has a disability, this is also true. It is unreasonable to expect children to inherently understand another sibling's problems and limitations. Deliberate and consistent parental attention is needed to help siblings overcome interaction problems and develop cooperation and appreciation for each other's uniqueness.

8

Siblings
as Teachers

*Parents are not the only ones who shape us: brothers and sisters
do, too. We fight, care, share, shame, support, and we survive—
these interactions help us develop the proper balance of hardness
and softness as adults. So, believe it or not, brothers and sisters can
be good for one another (p. 74).*
Robert Perske, 1981

If there is consensus on any one issue regarding brothers
and sisters, it is that siblings are responsible for teaching a myriad of
skills to one another. Siblings, because of the nature and intensity of
their relationships, provide both information and opportunities for
learning various motor, social, and language skills (Dunn, 1983; Lamb
& Sutton-Smith, 1982; Sutton-Smith & Rosenberg, 1970). This "teaching-learning" relationship can be naturally enhanced or hindered,
depending on varying family circumstances. Families with a child
who has a disability may find it necessary and desirable to strengthen
this teaching–learning relationship (Itzkowitz, 1989).

Can you remember when you learned something from a sister or
brother? Do you remember teaching a particular skill? It might have
been breaking in a baseball mitt, making popcorn, tying a shoe,
throwing a football, using a hammer, or singing a song. Whatever the
task, the memories of sharing skills and information with siblings are
powerful and help to form strong and lasting bonds.

Consider Michael and Christopher:

Michael, age 9, has finally agreed to teach his younger brother,
Christopher, age 6, how to ride a two-wheeler. They approach the bicycle
with a great deal of excitement and anticipation. Michael has a chance to try

155

out his teaching skills, and Christopher will have another opportunity to benefit from his brother's advanced age and skill. Both boys struggle with the task, and after several tense moments, skinned knees, bruised elbows, and five shouting arguments, Christopher pedals the bicycle a wobbly 30 feet before coming to a crash landing. Christopher's eyes light up as he realizes he is on his way to adult bicycling; Michael beams with pride as he shares his brother's success. Both boys run off to tell their Mom.

Undoubtedly, Michael and Christopher will long remember this first day of bicycling. It may be a story they will share as adults and even into their later years. Perhaps the details will have blurred, but the feelings of teaching and learning will remain vivid.

However powerful this type of teaching–learning situation, it is not the most common situation. Most teaching–learning occurs in a much less formal, more natural manner. It is probable that neither sibling recognizes his or her participation in this educative process. This informal instruction takes place in common situations, such as wrestling on the floor, playing with dolls, arguing over a candy bar, having lunch together, or even watching television. No one plans such learning; it just takes place. These informal, albeit powerful, teaching-learning situations are referred to as *incidental learning*.

To benefit from incidental learning, the learner must have at least three prerequisite skills. First, he or she must be able to interact.

Second, the learner must be able to attend to the "teacher" (in this case, other siblings), and finally, he or she must be able to imitate in some fashion. Unfortunately, many children with disabilities are excluded from the benefits of incidental learning because they lack these prerequisites. These children will need a more formal approach if they are to benefit from the teaching–learning sibling relationship. A more formal approach implies a situation in which one sibling deliberately teaches the other. Michael's and Christopher's experience with the bicycle is an example of *formal teaching*.

The learning problems often exhibited by children with disabilities demand that the sibling "teachers" have special skills to ensure that the instruction will be successful. Developing these special teaching skills may be a focus of programs aimed at helping siblings with brothers and sisters who have disabilities. These formal teaching programs typically focus on instructing the child so that he can learn new skills and/or help the sibling to manage and control inappropriate behavior. Teaching siblings to be effective teachers requires a systematic plan. This chapter explores the various ways in which the teaching-learning relationship between siblings can be strengthened.

FORMAL TEACHING PROGRAMS

Since the early 1980s, considerable effort has been devoted to developing and evaluating ways to include siblings in a formal teaching-learning process. These intervention programs tend to focus on training siblings to effectively teach their brothers and sisters specific skills and how to behave in more appropriate ways. This type of intervention program has a number of unique advantages and some potential disadvantages.

Advantages

Many siblings of children with disabilities want to help their brothers and sisters but simply do not know how (Sullivan, 1979). When they try to play with them or teach them, their efforts are rebuked or ignored, or tend to fail in other ways. This is hardly a surprising outcome because many of the learning problems exhibited by children with disabilities perplex even the most skilled professionals. The chief objective of programs to develop siblings' teaching skills, then, is to provide the siblings with specific methods that allow them to help their brothers and sisters.

Advantageous to both siblings, this type of training can help brothers and sisters develop more intense and more positive social relationships. Weinrott (1974) found that siblings who participated in a formal training program greatly improved the quality of their interactions with their sisters and brothers who have disabilities. These siblings began to spend more time with the child and initiated activities to teach the child new skills. Likewise, Schreibman, O'Neill, and Koegel (1983) found that after siblings completed a formal teaching program, they began to make more positive comments about their brothers and sisters with autism. Before the program, they might have commented, "She causes problems a lot, but I guess we have to put up with her," but after intervention, their observations were more inclined to shift to, "She behaves a lot better when we work with her right" (Schriebman et al., 1983, p. 136). The improved quality of these siblings' interactions might have been a direct result of teaching them how to better instruct their brothers and sisters.

Another potential benefit of intervention programs involves the extension of training to involve the child with a disability. By including siblings in the training, the efforts of professionals and parents are greatly enhanced. Having the sibling instruct the child in particular skills may help relieve some of the responsibility the child places on the parents and other family members. Increased instructional time may also lead to greater generalization of learned skills by the child. This occurs because of additional instruction in home- and community-based environments with new instructors (siblings). Teaching siblings to present information and skills in a systematic fashion will help to ensure that the child with a disability receives necessary instruction in many natural environments.

It has been found that formal teaching interactions between siblings will facilitate development of the sibling relationship. Weinrott (1974) demonstrated that siblings trained as teachers shifted from providing custodial care to their brothers and sisters with disabilities to engaging in more educationally related interactions. It seems reasonable that siblings who are trained to teach would spend more time instructing the child in various life skills rather than performing those tasks for their sibling.

Another advantage of this approach rests with the possible ripple effect such treatment may provide. Siblings who have been trained as teachers often pass along their skills to other siblings (Weinrott, 1974). Several siblings who have acted as teachers report that they enjoyed the participation in that it allowed them to be involved with their brother or sister in a positive way (James & Egle, 1986; Swenson-Pierce, Kohl, & Egle, 1987). Providing younger siblings with a positive model for interaction will certainly influence their subsequent interactions with the child who has a disability and may help prevent the development of sibling-related problems.

Finally, siblings who learn to systematically teach their brothers and sisters with disabilities may develop a deeper understanding of the learning and social problems faced by the child. These siblings may begin to appreciate parental and professional frustrations with the child's disability. Siblings who learn to teach may develop more reasonable and realistic expectations for the child. It appears that parents are more inclined to discuss problems related to the child after siblings attend formal training programs (Weinrott, 1974). Facilitating greater understanding and sharing of family problems is definitely a potential benefit of a formal teaching treatment program.

Disadvantages

Establishing a formal teaching relationship between siblings may not always be desirable. If one of the two siblings does *not* want to participate in the program, he or she should not be forced or coerced to do so. Forcing either sibling to join a teaching program, no matter how well-intentioned, will only lead to greater problems between the siblings. Both children must want to participate in order for the program to be successful.

A second potential problem can result from the attention given to the siblings' unequal status. It may not be desirable to identify the child without the disability as "teacher" and the child with the disability as "student." In situations where the child with the disability is always on the receiving end, he or she may become resentful of the sibling. Likewise, if the sibling is always expected to be a caregiver or "surrogate parent," there might be additional problems. Skillful parents must balance this "give-and-take" to provide as balanced a situation between the siblings as possible.

Another potential problem may involve possible sibling exploitation of the child with the disability. Parents need to monitor the application of the siblings' teaching skills to ensure that the sibling does not teach inappropriate behaviors or use the child to perform jobs or chores that they, themselves, should be doing. If Tom Sawyer had employed systematic teaching skills, he may have found ways to get out of more than just whitewashing a fence!

Why Teach Siblings To Teach?

As the discussion above illustrates, the advantages of formal teaching programs can be significant. Provided the potential problems are averted, instructing siblings in teaching methods can be beneficial not only for the brother or sister with a disability, but for all family members. The following points summarize the goals of, or reasons for, a formal teaching program:

1. To foster and/or strengthen positive interaction between siblings in both formal and informal situations

2. To enhance the development of positive attitudes between siblings
3. To lessen the learning problems and skill deficits experienced by the child with a disability through increased instructional time with siblings who serve as "adjunct" instructors
4. To enhance the generalization of learned skills from school settings to home settings and from teachers to family members
5. To provide a model for untrained siblings and friends to interact with the child who has a disability

A REVIEW OF TRAINING EFFORTS

The idea of training siblings to formally teach their brothers and sisters with disabilities developed as a direct result of successful efforts to involve parents and age-peers in the education of children with disabilities. Reviews of the literature regarding the involvement of parents in teaching these children indicate that parents can be taught to successfully utilize systematic teaching methods (Boyd, 1980; Clements & Alexander, 1975; Johnson & Katz, 1973; Kaiser & Fox, 1986; O'Dell, 1974). Additionally, several research studies have indicated that age-peers can be taught to be effective tutors with children who have disabilities (Young, 1981; Young, Hecimovic, & Salzberg, 1983).

Given the successful outcomes with parents and age-peers, it seemed logical that siblings could also be involved in the systematic instruction process. Indeed, in the following studies, researchers worked successfully with siblings to teach useful skills to children with disabilities.

Study 1 One of the first documented attempts to instruct siblings on how to be teachers was conducted by Bennett (1973). In this study, a preschooler (age 54 months) was systematically trained to teach her younger sister with a hearing impairment (age 30 months) to use plural words. Specifically, the plural form of the word *fork* was the target of instruction. Although limited in its scope, this study demonstrated that when properly instructed, even a preschool-age sibling can be taught to be a systematic teacher.

Study 2 Weinrott (1974) developed a training program for 18 adolescent siblings of younger children with mental retardation. These adolescents attended a 6-week training program held in conjunction with a therapeutic summer camp attended by their sibling with mental retardation. Weinrott's training program consisted of the following activities:

1. Teaching the siblings basic systematic instruction skills, including reinforcement, defining behavior, task analysis, prompting, pacing, and fading

2. Having the siblings observe individualized teaching sessions conducted with campers
3. Applying learned skills during intensely supervised practice sessions
4. Viewing videotapes of their teaching efforts
5. Receiving detailed feedback from skilled adults in regard to their application of the teaching skills with learners who have disabilities

The siblings also attended workshops on reading readiness, speech, medical considerations, creative dramatics, and the sociology of mental retardation.

Throughout the camp program, the siblings were able to successfully apply systematic instruction skills during various teaching sessions. The siblings were also observed using their newly acquired teaching skills in informal settings, such as during mealtime and recreational events.

To evaluate this intensive training program, Weinrott asked the children's parents to complete a questionnaire several months after the training was completed. The questionnaire sought to measure the effects of the training program on general family interaction patterns. The parents reported that the siblings had "moderately" or "vastly" improved the quality of their social interaction with their brother or sister. Weinrott's analysis of this evaluation data indicated that the siblings' interaction shifted from primarily custodial care of the child with a disability to a focus on teaching the child adaptive behavior. In two-thirds of these families, parents reported that siblings were spending more time with the child with mental retardation than they had prior to the initiation of the training. Parents reported that they, themselves, were more willing to discuss problems related to the child after the sibling completed the training. Most of the parents also reported that, after the training, the siblings would comment on the parents' interactions with the child and that this feedback was helpful in maintaining consistency within the family. Parents also reported that the other children in the family who did not participate in the training learned the teaching skills from the trained sibling. Weinrott's program has helped to establish the value of training adolescent siblings to systematically instruct their brothers and sisters with disabilities.

Study 3 In 1975, Cash and Evans described a demonstration project in which three girls (ages 3–6) were taught to modify the behavior of their young siblings with mental retardation. These girls viewed a 6-minute training film, which presented aspects of systematic instruction such as modeling, prompting, giving verbal information, praising, and punishment. Cash and Evans evaluated their efforts by observing each girl's ability to teach her sibling before, during, and after the training. The siblings demonstrated more systematic teaching behaviors after the training film than they had before the film.

Study 4 In a similar study, Miller and Miller (1976) included the siblings of a child with a disability in a formal teaching program. Two sisters (ages 9 and 11) of a 4-year-old girl with behavior disorders were successfully taught various strategies to teach their sister to engage in simple play activities. These sisters were instructed in general behavior management techniques, such as praising appropriate behavior and ignoring inappropriate behavior. These siblings were then engaged in a speech teaching program. Using their teaching skills, they were able to increase the child's attempts to say words and to decrease inappropriate vocalizations.

Study 5 Colletti and Harris (1977) conducted a series of studies to determine the efficacy of involving siblings in home-based treatment of children with disabilities. In one study, a sister (age 10) was successfully taught to use reinforcement procedures to teach a simple skill to her 9-year-old sister who had autism. In a second study, two brothers (ages 11 and 12), who had a brother with severe neurological impairments, (age 9), were taught to provide the child with reinforcement for correct responses to several tasks. One sibling taught simple addition skills, while the other helped the brother with a disability to write the letters of the alphabet. Once these brothers and sisters learned to use reinforcement, they were able to successfully teach their sibling.

Study 6 A study in 1983 by Schreibman et al. demonstrated the effectiveness of teaching behavior modification skills to siblings who had brothers and sisters with autism. In this project, older siblings (ages 8–13) were paired with their brother or sister who had autism (ages 5–8) and were asked to teach a variety of skills (e.g., coin identification, number concepts, letter identification, and pronoun discrimination). After their initial teaching attempts, the siblings were shown videotapes that presented information on the use of reinforcement, shaping, chaining, and discrete learning trials. Additionally, the siblings received instruction on handling problem behaviors exhibited by the child. Finally, the siblings applied the newly learned skills by teaching a skill to their brother or sister, while receiving corrective feedback from the researchers.

In an evaluation of this effort, Schreibman and her associates found that, after training, all siblings increased their correct use of behavior modification skills. As a consequence of the siblings' increased skills, the children with autism showed steady improvement in the various learning tasks presented. As part of this study, siblings were also observed in less structured, generalized settings. In these settings (e.g., a living room with toys) the sibling and the child with autism were asked to play together, and the siblings' use of teaching skills was scored. The siblings demonstrated that they were able to use the newly acquired skills in these less formal settings.

Study 7 Lobato and Tlaker (1985) conducted a study to investigate whether or not a 21-year-old sibling could serve as a teacher to modify the behavior of her 13-year-old brother with severe mental retardation. The sister was instructed in the use of systematic instruction and applied behavior analysis during weekly training sessions. When the sibling began instruction, she taught her brother to brush his teeth and make his bed, tasks that the adolescent could not complete before instruction. Through the sister's use of systematic teaching tactics, her brother was able to master toothbrushing and bedmaking skills at acceptable levels.

Study 8 In a study by Swenson-Pierce et al. (1987), siblings (ages 10–13) were selected to teach their younger brothers and sisters who had moderate to severe levels of mental retardation. Siblings focused their teaching on domestic skills targeted by their parents as important. Skills taught included making a bed, preparing snacks, and making a sandwich. The siblings were taught to teach via a five-point instructional program:

1. Explanation of the sibling's role as a teacher
2. Instruction in prompting, time delay, and social praise
3. Instruction in task analysis
4. Role-playing of instructional tactics
5. Actual instruction with the child and feedback

In the last phase of instruction, the researchers provided feedback and suggestions to the siblings to enhance their instructional skills. As a result of this study, siblings demonstrated their ability to learn systematic instruction and the siblings with disabilities increased their competence in the instructed domestic skills. It is important to note that the siblings who participated indicated that "they enjoyed participating in the study and that it did not interfere significantly with their personal time" (p. 58). Two of the "teachers" reported that they would continue to use their new skills in other areas with their siblings.

Although much research is still needed in regard to the utilization of siblings as teachers, the studies presented here provide an adequate foundation for this type of intervention with siblings and children with disabilities. Each of the studies has systematically added to our knowledge base, so that successful instruction using the validated elements of these studies can now be prescribed. The next section of this chapter focuses on specific ways in which parents and professionals can use these research results to establish formal teaching programs for siblings.

ESTABLISHING A
SIBLING TEACHING PROGRAM

The decision to use a formal teaching program for siblings should not be regarded lightly. A successful program requires intensive planning and preparation. A poorly planned program will often be more harmful than helpful. As mentioned earlier, the siblings' willingness to participate in the teaching sessions is absolutely critical to success. If Sean does not want to teach his sister Amy (who has athetoid cerebral palsy), forcing the issue is inadvisable. Similarly, if Amy does not want to be taught by Sean in formal sessions, then other treatment options, such as informal teaching, should be discussed. Sibling willingness is a prerequisite to the commencement of formal training.

When considering this type of formal teaching program, professionals and parents need to address the following questions as a part of the planning process:

> What skills will the sibling need to be an effective teacher?
> How should the sibling learn these skills?
> How should actual teaching sessions be arranged?
> What support will the sibling need?

General Guidelines

Before these questions can be answered, some general guidelines should be followed. These guidelines are designed to ensure that the treatment will meet its goals.

Clarify Teaching Expectations. The parent or professional should list answers to the following questions: What do you hope to accomplish by using the sibling as a formal teacher? Are both children likely to benefit, or are your expectations one-sided? How will you know when the goal is attained? The answers to these questions will guide the development of the treatment program.

Do Not Force Either Child To Participate. Children should be willing volunteers. Neither child should be coerced to participate in any way. Teaching sessions should not interfere with favorite activities, such as athletics, scouting, music lessons, playing with friends, or watching favorite television shows. Remember that forcing a child to participate will undoubtedly cause more problems in the sibling relationship.

Arrange the Environment So that Success Is Ensured.
The tasks that the sibling will teach should be simple and straightforward. (Complex skills should be introduced later or reserved for professionals.) The sibling teacher should be proficient in the task to be taught; therefore, it is wise to have the sibling teach something that he or she already knows how to do well.

Keep the first few teaching sessions brief; limiting the first few sessions to 15 minutes is recommended.

Keep the teaching environment free from distractions. Turn off the television, radio, video games, and stereo. Do not serve snacks while the teaching is in progress. Do not have friends over or talk on the telephone.

Select a specific area for the teaching session. A special place in the house that can be used consistently helps to maintain the uniqueness of the teaching. Inconsistency, such as changing the location, may initially confuse the children and may not convey the message that this is an important activity.

Reward Both Children for Participation. It should be clear to both children that their behavior (teaching or being taught) is valued by parents and professionals. Each sibling may need separate rewards. Written letters of appreciation are held in esteem by sibling teachers. These written statements have lasting value; they can be saved and shared with parents and teachers. Parents and professionals should consider giving their own time and undivided attention as a reward for the siblings.

The Sibling Teacher Should Be Older than the Child.
Generally, at least a 2-year age differential between the sibling and child with the disability is recommended. A younger sibling teacher, especially one who is not an adolescent, may have trouble understanding the traditional role reversal. Using a younger sibling may also cause resentment on the part of the child with the disability.

What Skills Will the Sibling Need?

It is quite clear from past research and demonstration projects that the most effective skills used to teach siblings are derived from applied behavior analysis. These skills are sometimes referred to as systematic instruction. Complete reviews of these teaching skills and their use in instructing children with disabilities have been presented by Baker, Brightman, Heifetz, and Murphy (1976), Becker (1971), and Sulzer-Azaroff and Mayer (1977).

The value of using systematic instruction with learners who have special needs has been well documented (Snell, 1987; Whitman, Sciback, & Reid, 1983). All of the skills presented in applied behavior analysis have been empirically derived. In other words, the effective-

ness of these skills has been clearly demonstrated in teaching-learning situations and, thus, they can be quickly taught to both adults and children. A specialized degree or certification is not necessary in order to use applied behavior analysis skills effectively. Many of the behavior and learning problems exhibited by children with disabilities have been successfully corrected using these skills. Furthermore, systematic instruction is intended for use in natural environments, such as homes, communities, and schools, as opposed to traditional therapeutic treatment centers (e.g., hospitals and clinics).

The initial skills taught to sibling teachers should be straightforward and, obviously, pragmatic. With siblings, it is not necessary to discuss theories or to compare applied behavior analysis with other treatment tactics. The goal is not to make the sibling a professional, but an effective teacher.

Basic Skills The following *initial* skills should be taught to siblings:

1. *Reinforcement* Sibling teachers need to be proficient users of reinforcement. They need to use praise, and to learn to vary the praise in order to keep reinforcement fresh. They also need to know how to use reinforcement contingently and consistently. They should demonstrate that they can deliver reinforcement in a timely and meaningful fashion.
2. *Prompting* It is suggested that siblings engaged in formal teaching need to learn the following skills in producing behavior: *verbal*

prompting, modeling, cueing, and *physical guidance.* Additionally, siblings should be taught to use sequential prompting (see Lent & McLean, 1976) and to wait between prompts (see Snell & Gast, 1981; Snell and Zirpoli, 1987).

3. *Identification of behaviors* Describing behaviors in precise, observable terms appears to be required for effective instruction (see Mager, 1975). Siblings need to know how to identify the behaviors that they want their brothers and sisters to learn.

4. *Task analysis* Much of what will be taught needs to be broken down into small, achievable components. Siblings should first attempt easily learned behaviors. Task analysis that focuses on a performance skill (e.g., buttoning a shirt) as opposed to an academic skill (e.g., adding three digits) should be presented first (see Snell, 1987, for a discussion of task analysis).

5. *Chaining* Siblings should be taught to use either forward or backward chaining (see Snell & Zirpoli, 1987). Chaining helps to link simple behaviors (e.g., holding a spoon) into complex behavioral repertoires (e.g., self-feeding).

6. *Use of discrete learning trials* To help organize the teaching sessions, siblings should learn how to present material in discrete trials that follow an A-B-C pattern (antecedent-behavior-consequence). This pattern will, of course, be applied in all learning situations, including behavior management.

7. *Record keeping* The sibling should learn simple ways to keep track of the learner's progress. A simple checklist or chart may be helpful.

8. *Tactics to handle problem behavior* Siblings should learn to ignore or to remove rewards for inappropriate behavior. Aversive tactics, however, should never be used or taught to siblings.

Advanced Skills Once the above skills are mastered, more advanced skills for siblings can be presented. These skills should only be introduced if the sibling expresses an interest in further training. If siblings have not been enthusiastic, they should not be overwhelmed by higher-level techniques. Four advanced skills are:

1. *Schedules of reinforcement* Siblings should know how to use continuous, fixed, and variable schedules of reinforcement and how to alter continuous schedules to fixed or variable ones (see Snell, 1987).

2. *Prompt fading* Advanced sibling teachers should know how to gradually reduce the assistance, or how to fade the intrusive prompts they use for teaching (see Snell & Zirpoli, 1987).

3. *Generalization programming* Once siblings have demonstrated teaching skills in the formal teaching session, they should learn

tactics to teach the child with a disability to transfer newly acquired skills to other situations. Baer (1981) has provided an excellent review of these generalization teaching skills.

4. *Graphing* to help make record keeping more useful and more easily interpreted, the sibling should learn to graph data. Again, simple and straightforward methods are encouraged. Complex data and graphing systems (e.g., semilogarithmic graphs or trend analysis) should be avoided.

How Should the Sibling Learn These Skills?

Siblings can be taught to be teachers using a variety of approaches. Simple techniques (e.g., a book that describes teaching skills) to complex methods (e.g., a multiweek training course) have been used to prepare siblings for teaching their brothers and sisters. Unfortunately, determining the best method for training siblings to be teachers is not easily accomplished. The method used to train siblings depends on available resources, the goals of the treatment program, and the number of siblings participating.

Parents and professionals should consider a number of aspects regarding the training of siblings before such a program is initiated. These factors are briefly discussed below.

The Instructor It is essential that the persons directing and providing the training should have mastered advanced skills in applied behavior analysis. A special education teacher, psychologist, behavior therapist, or social worker may be best able to teach siblings the skills they will need to work with their brothers or sisters. It may also be possible to recruit professors from a local college or university to do the training. Many professors, especially those in colleges of education, are skilled in teacher education and are familiar with problems and solutions regarding the education of teachers. Of course, the instructor will need to be familiar with the intervention goals and will need to maintain an enthusiastic approach.

Group versus Individualized Instruction Training siblings in a group is usually more desirable than working with siblings individually. Besides being more cost and time efficient, group training enables siblings to interact with other peers who are learning the same skills. Group instruction also provides an excellent format for allowing the siblings to practice teaching skills with one another before they work with their brothers and sisters.

Written Directions It is always a good idea to provide the siblings with a brief written manual that describes the teaching skills. The use of written manuals has been found to be an effective method for training nonprofessionals in teaching tactics (Clark et al., 1977; Heifetz, 1977). The manual should be written in a manner that will be easily understood by siblings. It should also contain descriptions of the application of these teaching skills with children who have disabilities.

Modeling   Lecturing siblings on teaching tactics is not as effective as actually showing them how to teach. In a review of several methods used to teach unskilled persons applied behavior analysis skills, modeling was found to be the most effective training method (Green et al., 1976). Siblings should see examples of how reinforcement, prompting, record keeping, task analysis, and so forth, are used in the teaching process. Several of the demonstration projects described earlier in this chapter used videotapes to demonstrate proper teaching techniques to siblings.

Practice and Feedback   Hearing about, reading descriptions of, or observing examples of teaching skills is not enough to enable siblings to be effective teachers. They also need opportunities to practice the teaching skills under intense supervision. Practice provides siblings with detailed feedback, which may lessen the initial frustrations of the sibling. The sibling can begin by practicing with learners who do not have disabilities. Once the sibling is comfortable in using the teaching skills, practice feedback should occur with the child who has a disability. After the practice session, the instructor should provide detailed feedback on the success of the teaching skills. Videotaping the first few sessions may be helpful in allowing the sibling to judge his or her own performance and to note where improvements need to be made. Practice and feedback sessions are often overlooked, yet, they are essential to successful intervention.

Follow-Up   Initial mastery of the teaching tactics does not imply that the sibling will be able to carry out a teaching program over an extended period. To eliminate any potential problems, follow-up feedback sessions should be conducted on a regular basis. This means that the instructor will observe various teaching sessions and visit with the sibling. At the very least, telephone contact with the sibling should be maintained to answer questions and to help solve any problems encountered by the sibling. Training must be ongoing and long-term rather than a one-time effort.

How Should the Teaching Sessions Be Arranged?

First, the parent and/or professional, along with the sibling and the child with the disability, should specify the exact skills that will be taught. A menu of needed skills, like that shown in Figure 8.1, should be developed. The learning tasks should be kept very simple at first to ensure that both children will be successful. The initially targeted skills may not be the most important skills for the child with the disability to learn, but should be chosen to offer the best guarantee of

What _Nick_ **Needs to Learn**
name

1. _Names of coins (penny, dime, quarter)_

2. _Colors (red, yellow, blue, green)_

3. _Shapes_

4. _Buttoning shirt_

5. _Use of pronouns_

Teacher : _Kelly, Nick's sister_
name

What will be taught ?

Buttoning his shirt

Colors

Figure 8.1. Sample menu of needed skills.

success for both children. After the sibling demonstrates his or her skill as a teacher, more complex skills can be taught.

Next, a time for formal teaching needs to be established. The time selected should be convenient for each person involved and should not interfere with favorite activities. It is not necessary for formal training to occur every day. Three times a week is usually plenty; however, the frequency of the sessions should be decided upon by the siblings and their parents. Keep the teaching sessions relatively brief. A 15-minute limit is appropriate for the first few sessions. The time can be gradually increased. In most cases, it is recommended that no teaching session extend beyond 30 minutes.

Finally, a special area of the home (or school or clinic) should be designated for the teaching sessions. This will help establish continuity as well as put a special distinction on this activity. The area should be generally free from distractions and be appropriate to the learning task. For example, if the sibling is teaching the child with a disability to dress, this is best done in the bedroom; likewise, learning an academic task may be done in the kitchen or living room. In addition, the teaching materials used by the siblings will have more significance to both children if they are used only during the teaching sessions.

What Support Will the Sibling Need?

Like many other projects undertaken by brothers and sisters, teaching programs also need to be supported by parents in order to be successful. The type and intensity of support will be as varied as the siblings and children with disabilities participating. A suggested list

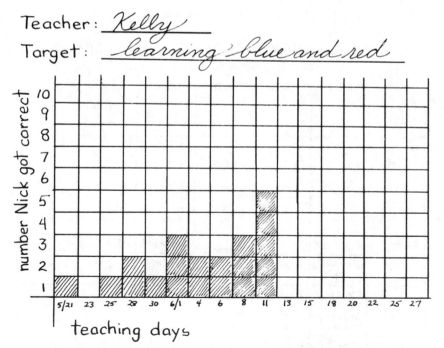

Figure 8.2. Progress chart for sibling teaching.

of considerations for deciding how the teaching program will be supported follows.

Continuing Feedback As mentioned earlier, continued feedback sessions are an integral part of the training process. These feedback sessions also serve to provide ongoing support to both siblings. A regular schedule of feedback should be arranged. The feedback should occur immediately following the teaching session in order to be most effective.

Providing Rewards Both the sibling teacher and the child should be rewarded regularly by the parents, teacher, counselor, or social worker who initiated the teaching sessions. Rewards will vary according to the age of the children, but they should focus on praise and written statements of accomplishments. Occasional special treats (going for a milkshake, seeing a movie, etc.) for the sibling teacher may also offer desirable attention from a parent or other adult.

Posting Results Posting a chart with the results of the completed teaching sessions in a prominent place (e.g., refrigerator door at home, bulletin board at school) is an effective way to solicit positive comments for the siblings. In all of our efforts to foster sibling training, posting results has been the easiest and most effective way to support the teaching sessions. Simple charts, similar to the ones displayed in Figures 8.2 and 8.3, have been successful.

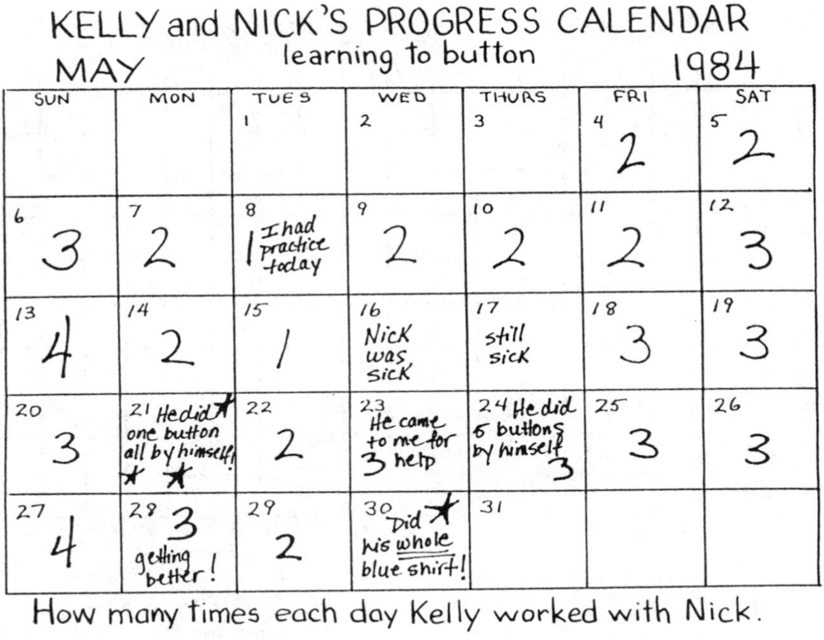

KELLY and NICK'S PROGRESS CALENDAR
MAY — learning to button — 1984

SUN	MON	TUES	WED	THURS	FRI	SAT
		1	2	3	4 — 2	5 — 2
6 — 3	7 — 2	8 — I had practice today	9 — 2	10 — 2	11 — 2	12 — 3
13 — 4	14 — 2	15 — 1	16 Nick was sick	17 still sick	18 — 3	19 — 3
20 — 3	21 He did one button all by himself ★ ★	22 — 2	23 He came to me for 3 help	24 He did 5 buttons by himself 3	25 — 3	26 — 3
27 — 4	28 — 3 getting better!	29 — 2	30 Did ★ his whole blue shirt!	31		

How many times each day Kelly worked with Nick.

Figure 8.3. Progress chart for sibling teaching.

The Daily Diary Another simple way to provide support is to encourage the sibling teacher to maintain a diary of the teaching. A special book in which the sibling can record notes and observations can be purchased as a reward for the older sibling. (One family purchased a tape recorder so that the sibling could record a personal account of the teaching activities.) In this way, the sibling is certain to receive special attention and recognition from others while also reflecting on the importance and value of the activity.

SHOULD SIBLINGS BE INVOLVED WITH DISCIPLINE & BEHAVIOR MANAGEMENT?

"Mommy! Wendy just threw the toy across the room! Tell her to stop it!"
"Mother, Tanya is making the noises again and it's gross!"
"Dad, Tony is using bad words. Can I spank him, like you do when I say those words?"

All children, whether they do or do not have disabilities, exhibit behavior problems at one time or another. Some children with disabilities exhibit rather frequent and intense behavior problems that cause serious anxiety for the family. It is not unusual for siblings who witness abhorrent behavior to run to parents for action or suggestions on what they should do. In many cases, parents are unable to give clear-cut answers because they did not witness the event. The role of the child without a disability in behavior management and discipline is, at best, controversial.

Like it or not, though, most siblings *are* engaged in teaching and behavior management. Their involvement, however, is usually haphazard. It is beneficial to recognize that siblings can serve as effective teachers in educating their brothers and sisters in proper behavior. To do this effectively, the sibling needs specific instruction and support similar to those used to teach the child new skills.

Much like teaching new skills to children with disabilities, siblings who are involved in behavior management also need to develop skills derived from applied behavior analysis. Primarily, siblings should be taught the following skills:

1. *Reinforcement* How to praise their brothers and sisters for good behavior
2. *Ignoring* How to ignore inappropriate behavior and how to remove rewards for misbehavior
3. *Behavioral context analysis* How to recognize the A-B-C pattern (antecedents-behavior-consequences) of misbehavior

4. *Recording incidents of misbehavior* How to keep track of progress and failures
5. *Handling behavioral emergencies* How to differentiate a behavioral emergency from common misbehavior and how to know what to do about it

These five broad categories of behavior management skills can be easily taught to most siblings by either parents or professionals who use these procedures in everyday settings. Obviously, the sibling who has participated in training aimed at teaching new skills to siblings with disabilities does not need much additional training. Other siblings need a more intensive program to learn to use these skills in a systematic fashion. Like the training discussed previously, ample time should be given the sibling to learn and practice these skills. Feedback and written directions should also be provided. Other guidelines are as follows:

1. If the sibling wants to help with behavior management, have him or her use the skills for a specific behavior (e.g., swearing) as opposed to *all* types of misbehavior.
2. Teach the sibling to attend to the child when the target behavior is *not* occurring and to ignore the child when the misbehavior is occurring.
3. Teach the sibling to keep a simple record of misbehavior and to share the data with parents on a frequent and regular basis.
4. Involve the sibling in discussions about discipline and the child with the disability. If the sibling makes viable suggestions, they should be tried and evaluated.
5. Reward the sibling often for ignoring misbehavior and for reinforcing the child's appropriate behavior. Behavior management programs are difficult to implement, even for highly skilled professionals, and children need a great deal of support.
6. Never allow the sibling to administer corporal punishment (e.g., spanking). The sibling should be restricted to ignoring and removing attention from the misbehavior.
7. If participation in behavior management is too stressful for the sibling, discontinue it. Suggest another strategy for the sibling so that the responsibility is removed. ("Kevin, you've done a great job helping us with Theresa's crying. When she does this again, come and get me, and you can watch your television show in the den.")
8. Teach the sibling to recognize behavioral emergencies (e.g., Tim breaks a window, Joe destroys his hearing aid, Lisa bites her finger) and to immediately report them to parents or other adults.

9. If more than one sibling is available to help, try rotating the behavior management responsibility among the children without disabilities.

10. Be reasonable in your expectations of the sibling. Do not suggest that he or she be involved in handling serious behavior problems. At no time should the sibling be held accountable for the misbehavior of the child with a disability.

Involving siblings in behavior management requires a systematic and planned effort. Success will be more difficult to detect than when siblings are teaching new skills to a brother or sister with a disability. However, if properly prepared, siblings can play a central role in teaching appropriate behavior. Their role should be limited and well supervised, and siblings should be rewarded for their extra effort.

CAPITALIZING ON
INFORMAL TEACHING

Thank goodness everything we learn is not a result of formal teaching! Much of what we know is learned in an informal manner. Most likely, in many situations, we are not even fully aware that we are learning and that someone else is teaching. This informal process, described earlier, is referred to as incidental learning. In this process, we learn by observing, encountering, and solving problems; interacting with others; reading; and listening.

Indeed, most of the learning between siblings occurs in a natural, incidental fashion. Neither sibling is fully aware that learning is taking place when they are building a castle out of blocks, wrestling on the floor, arguing over a television show, or sharing a snack together. The learning just seems to take place.

Despite the "incidental" nature of this type of learning, the "teacher" and "learner" are involved in a process that has several unique components. To benefit from incidental learning opportunities, the learner must be able to attend to subtle cues and responses of the teacher and to imitate the teacher. Imitation is a critical prerequisite to benefiting from incidental teaching. Effective incidental teachers, although unaware of the skills they utilize, do, in fact, incorporate aspects of systematic teaching. They model the desired behavior, allow the learner to practice the behavior, and provide feedback to the learner.

Consider the following examples.

> Rachel, age 5, and Paul, age 4, are sister and brother who enjoy playing tea party with their dolls.

> Rachel: Paul, bring the babies to the table. Good! Now we can make a cake.
> Paul: O.K. I'll mix it.
> Rachel: Put all the stuff in and stir it like this (*demonstrates*). Now you do it. Good! Now put it in the oven with me. Good!
> Paul: Let's feed the babies.
> Rachel: Okay. You can get the cups and I'll get the milk.
> Paul: Real milk?
> Rachel: No, just pretend, but it's like real milk.
> Paul: Okay.

> Nick, age 4, and Becky, age 2, dig around in their toy box to gather their musical toys together. Nick bangs on the xylophone; Becky bangs on it, too. Both children laugh. Nick takes Becky's finger and uses it to play the miniscule piano, which results in giggling and more laughing. The play continues as both children talk about loud and soft sounds, Daddy, Mommy, the kitty, and so forth.

Both sets of children are engaged in a teaching-learning process, albeit informally, through these simple and common interactions. The use of systematic instruction tactics can be seen in the directions given, the modeling provided, and the feedback delivered.

Some children, especially those with communication, sensory, motor, intellectual, and/or emotional problems, may have a harder time than most children in deriving the benefits of incidental learning. These children may have trouble attending to siblings or age-peers and may not be able to imitate in a natural fashion. They may not be responsive to a sibling's social contact and, thus, may discourage the sibling's informal interactions. Siblings can, however, be taught to enhance this incidental learning process between themselves and their brothers or sisters with disabilities.

Siblings who have been taught to formally teach their brothers and sisters should have little problem using these skills during the course of the day. Use of reinforcement and prompts is effective in many environments (grocery store, shopping mall, playground, bathroom, school bus, etc.). However, the sibling may need some extra help in learning to apply these skills effectively during such informal times.

To capitalize on the power of incidental teaching between siblings, parents and professionals should:

1. Remind sibling "teachers" to use their newly acquired skills (especially reinforcement, prompting, and ignoring) when they are with the child.
2. Reward the sibling when such teaching skills are applied outside of formal teaching situations ("Susan, I liked the way you ignored Beverly when she was misbehaving. You're certainly learning to be a good teacher!").
3. Teach the sibling to be persistent when initiating social overtures to the child. First attempts to solicit interactions often fail, and the sibling needs to learn to keep trying.
4. Suggest ways the sibling could use the formal teaching skills in informal ways ("Dan, when Jim shares his toys with Lucia, why don't you tell him what a good job he is doing?").
5. Encourage the sibling to spend more time with the child in mutually enjoyable activities ("Let's make some chocolate pudding, and you and Wendy can have a snack together").

FINAL CONSIDERATIONS

This chapter discussed how siblings can serve as teachers for their brothers and sisters. This type of teaching-learning interaction is one powerful way to help facilitate a positive sibling relationship. Other secondary benefits, such as increased skill acquisition and social recognition for both children, are also significant. The limitations and potential problems of such an approach to instruction, however, must not be overlooked. It simply is not for every sibling, and siblings should not be forced to participate in an intervention program. Properly instituted though, a sibling teaching program can be rewarding. The program to instruct siblings how to teach should be well-planned, and follow-up training and support should be amply provided to siblings. Teaching children with learning problems is difficult work, and the successful program will recognize this by providing guidance and support to the sibling "teachers."

Earlier in this book, some of the problems between siblings are discussed. One common problem is perceived "inequality" between the children—one brother or sister is somehow "better" than another. Using siblings as teacher may, in fact, heighten this problem. Parents and professionals need to work hard to minimize this possible side effect by attending to each child's contribution in an equal fashion. "Students" who resent their "teacher" and vice versa do not tend to learn very much from each other. The balance between siblings can be maintained by regularly and frequently recognizing each child's contributions and accomplishments.

In addition to formal teaching approaches, siblings can also work with their brother or sister by helping in behavior management or providing incidental teaching. As with planned teaching of new skills by siblings to a brother or sister with a disability, parents and professionals should be supportive of siblings' efforts in these more informal areas and should provide guidance and feedback on a regular basis.

9

Siblings
at School

*Elementary school brought normal changes in friends and activities.
We placed Deborah in an elementary school with an excellent,
integrated, orthopedically handicapped program (not our
neighborhood school) and, at the same time, transferred Elizabeth
to the same school. They ride the special education bus together to
school and then go to their separate classrooms. This has been a
very successful venture, for the school is "theirs" and they know
each other's friends and teachers but have their own classroom
functions. They share science and social studies each week and
enjoy doing that homework together (p. 3).*
Karen Freeman, 1984

Jonathan was in the fifth grade at Grassland School when his
sister Michelle enrolled in public school for the first time. Instead of entering
first grade, as Jonathan supposed she would, Michelle went to the newly
established special class. The first few days were anything but easy for either
of them. Michelle seemed to cry and scream all day, especially when
Jonathan was walking by the room.

Jonathan felt sorry that his sister was in a room with a sign that read
"Severe and Profound," which he felt not only labeled his sister, but also
himself. No one ever really saw the students in that mysterious class unless
they were coming to school or leaving at the end of the day. They never went
outside for recess and even ate lunch in the room.

The sign on Michelle's classroom door was a constant reminder to
Jonathan and to his friends that something was drastically wrong with
Michelle. His friends said that room was for the "real bad retards and
gimps." Because of the way the school was structured, his classmates would
only know his sister as a freak, not as a "neat kid" who could laugh and play
jokes.

Most days, Jonathan was teased by his friends. Was something wrong
with Jonathan because his sister was disabled? No one ever asked him for

information about Michelle. It seemed like the kids teased and made fun of all the students in the "Severe and Profound" room. Jonathan did not know how to handle the teasing. Should he ignore it? He didn't want to join the joking and teasing, but maybe that would be best. He found out that anger wasn't the answer when a pushing-and-shoving incident resulted in no recess for 2 days.

Then, Jonathan was called upon to be his sister's school aide. He was asked to take Michelle to her class every morning and to stop in and pick her up every afternoon. When Jonathan entered the room for the first time, he thought it looked like a hospital with all sorts of strange equipment, mats, wheelchairs, and even a special bathroom with a tub. His mother also asked him to carry Michelle's lunchbox and her notebook that carried messages from her teacher.

Soon, Michelle's teacher asked Jonathan if he would like to come to the class and help teach his sister. Jonathan was at a loss; he did not know what to say. Michelle's teacher mentioned that she visited with his teacher and Jonathan would be given release time to help out. How could he say no to that? He didn't want to help teach her, but was it expected of him? He wondered why he had to help escort her, carry her things, "stick up" for her, deal with the teasing, and now even teach her. He did these things at home and was beginning to feel there was no time for himself. Did he have to do everything just because his sister had a disability?

After the first 2 weeks of school, Jonathan tearfully told his mother he wanted Michelle to go to a different school!

Jonathan's response is hardly surprising. Jonathan really loved his sister, but the new demands placed upon him by both well-meaning teachers and his mother did not take into consideration his needs. Escorting his sister to and from the bus meant that he missed out on a quick game of basketball before class and that his friends went off without him after school. Everything about the new situation seemed structured against Jonathan from the very beginning.

Mary and Eileen had a different school experience altogether:

Eileen, like Michelle, had multiple disabilities. She had both cerebral palsy and moderate mental retardation. Mary was in the fourth grade when Eileen started attending public school. Eileen's program was truly integrated. No stigmatizing sign drew special attention to the room. The students ate in the cafeteria, shared the gym and playground, attended assemblies with the other students, and went to the library and art room, and Eileen even went to the microcomputer room. Mary saw her sister often, as did many of Mary's friends. Eileen's teacher developed a "peer–tutor" program to assist her students. These peer–tutors took Eileen to and from her bus and worked with her in the classroom, library, and art room. Eileen even helped in a schoolwide popcorn sale.

Mary was asked to help carry Eileen's medication to school every Monday and return the empty bottle every Friday. Occasionally, she would take money and special messages to Eileen's teacher, Mrs. Mayes. Mary was always happy to see Mrs. Mayes because she seemed to really care about her. She would always inquire about Mary's activities, interests, accomplishments, and schoolwork. She listened to Mary and would always give her a hug. Eileen's teacher did not put demands on Mary; yet, Mary was happy to help Mrs. Mayes in any way that she could.

Of course, there were some problems to be solved. Occasionally, some of the other children would tease the students with disabilities, including Eileen. Once in a while someone would say something to Mary that would hurt her feelings or make her angry; however, these were balanced by other students who were eager to help out. Mary saw other children her own age serve as peer–tutors and work hard for the privilege of being with the students who had disabilities. Mary observed her sister eating in the cafeteria with the other students. She observed Eileen listening to a story in the library, seated on the floor with a fourth-grader who helped keep her from falling over. Mary watched her sister participate in school activities and establish her own friends. She observed that many of the people and children at school cared about Eileen the way she did. Her sister was different and would always be different, but with all of her limitations, she could still enjoy school. Mary did not mind helping because she still had her own identity, her own friends, her own time, and it seemed like her sister was not such a burden on everyone, after all.

The obvious differences between these stories highlight two possible scenarios regarding the special problems faced by siblings in school situations. These special situations were intensified not only by the structure of the school program, but also by the teachers and parents and the expectations of each. Positive school situations between siblings can be achieved by attending to potential problems and structuring the situation to respect the needs of each child. The school-age period for siblings may be the most intense in terms of their special needs. Itzkowitz (1989) found that during this period, siblings had the greatest needs for information and support services regarding their brothers' and sisters' disabilities. Since siblings spend much of their time in the school setting, it is the logical source for the provision of support services. The school, therefore, has a special responsibility for addressing those needs.

SPECIAL PROBLEMS
RELATED TO SCHOOL

Current special education laws and regulations, like PL 101-476 (Individuals with Disabilities Education Act), mandate that children with disabilities be educated in the "most inclusive environment." For most children, this implies the local public school. Even for students with the most severe disabilities, the local school is the least restrictive setting (Brinker, 1984; Lipsky & Gartner, 1992; Stainback & Stainback, 1992). This trend in service delivery means that a child with a disability will most likely attend the same school as siblings without disabilities.

When a child with a disability enters school for the first time, it poses a potential crisis for the entire family. This is typically the first time the child has been forced to interact with others without the constant protection of parents and siblings. Parents are naturally worried about whether the child will benefit from these opportunities for interaction and from the school experience in general. Will the child be accepted by teachers and other children? Will he or she be able to participate in class activities? Parents are often concerned about their role in preparing the child for school and may worry about other adults judging their parenting skills.

Likewise, siblings also have a number of special concerns about their brother or sister attending school. How will the brother's or sister's attendance at school affect the sibling? Will the child be accepted by others? Will there be teasing? These special concerns need to be addressed by professionals in order to ensure that the school experience is positive for all of the children. A number of specific sibling concerns are examined in more detail below.

Competition

It is natural for all siblings to compete with one another at school. Who earned the highest grade, who made the basketball team, or who was chosen for the school play may be the focus of attention among siblings. Competition is healthy in most cases, especially when both children have an opportunity to excel in different areas. However, competition becomes unhealthy when only *one* child is recognized, when one sibling is continually dominant, or when one receives all of the attention.

When there is a disability, competition will most likely favor the sibling without the disability. This may be especially evident in traditional academic situations. Unfair competition may result in the child with the disability experiencing extraordinary feelings of jealousy and anger toward a brother or sister. Competition should, of course, be limited. Grades and other school achievements should not be compared. Each child should be recognized for his or her unique accomplishments.

The "Brother's Keeper"

Many siblings worry that they will be expected to help care for their brother or sister at school as they do at home (Michaelis, 1980). Indeed, some siblings are asked to serve as caregivers for the child at school. They are asked to travel with the child, carry messages, keep assignments, interpret the child's communication, and even help instruct the child. This "brother's keeper" role may impinge unfairly upon siblings' freedom. It may keep a sibling from informal, yet im-

portant, social interactions with friends. School may provide the one opportunity for a sibling to have some needed respite from the necessary caregiving that must be performed at home. Expecting the sibling to perform similar caregiving activities at school will unduly burden the sibling with additional responsibilities.

Friends

Siblings often worry about the reactions of their school friends and peers to their brother or sister with a disability. In some cases, siblings may not have told their friends about their brother or sister. There may be some concern that they will be rejected by their friends if they are too closely associated with the child. Occasionally, some siblings may claim that the child is either adopted or a cousin. Some siblings also worry about the child's relationship with other children. Many siblings are concerned about how other children will treat their brother or sister with a disability.

Teasing

Even in the best school situations, children with disabilities will experience teasing by other children. The nature and intensity of such teasing will vary, depending on the school climate and attitude of the teachers and administrators. Siblings are concerned about this teasing and how they should handle it. Naturally, it is difficult for a sibling to hear jokes and rude remarks about a brother or sister. How should the sibling handle such teasing? Is it best to ignore it, respond with anger, join in, or report it to teachers and parents? How can the sibling defend the child and, at the same time, not risk rejection by peers?

The "Mysterious" Special Education Program

Siblings' knowledge of the special education program at the school may be limited. Depending on the school and the structure of the special education services, the classroom for students with disabilities may have a positive or negative reputation. In some situations, the special education program may consist of a resource room, and in others, a highly specialized self-contained classroom. Siblings may wonder what the child will experience in the room and how his or her education will differ from their own. The special education program typically contains special equipment and materials that may puzzle siblings and, at first appearance, may be frightening. Finally, special education programs are frequented by a full cadre of professionals, such as physical therapists, recreational specialists, psychologists, counselors, and social workers. Siblings, like other children who are not directly involved in special education, may be curious as to what these professionals do in school, especially with their brothers or sisters.

Other Special Situations

In addition to these five major concerns, some special situations may cause added worries:

Segregation versus Integration Segregated educational programs are rapidly becoming a service delivery model of the past as more and more children are being welcomed to integrated public schools. For some children, help with this transition from segregation to integration is necessary. Siblings, especially, may have adjustment problems and special concerns when their brother or sister suddenly begins to attend their school. The student with the disability, who may be accustomed to the social demands of an isolated school, may initially have difficulty adjusting to an integrated public school. Naturally, siblings' concerns may be intensified during this period. Special measures to help prepare siblings for these changes may be needed.

Younger Siblings in Class with Older Siblings Special concerns arise when an older brother or sister with a disability is placed in the same classroom with younger siblings. In some cases, the student with a disability is retained a year or attends remedial subjects in a lower grade, which is also attended by a younger brother or sister. Increased competition in terms of grades, friends, and teacher recognition between the siblings may be one result of this arrangement. Both siblings may also find it more difficult to establish independent identities since they are together for a major part of the day.

SCHOOL-BASED STRATEGIES

To address the special problems siblings may experience in the school situation, intervention strategies have been developed that focus on the roles of teachers, counselors, principals, and parents; sibling involvement in the IEP process; and the school structure.

Teachers

Both regular and special education teachers play a vital role in helping siblings deal with special problems. The teacher's assistance is enhanced by attention to a number of strategies.

Recognizing the Sibling as an Individual Teachers should respect the individuality of each family member, recognizing individual contributions and strengths. Because some siblings may be preoccupied with the notion that they, too, are considered disabled by others, the teacher must be particularly sensitive to the sibling's need to have his or her own achievements and individual differences recognized. This recognition can be conveyed through conversations with the sibling that revolve around the sibling's activities, not the activities of the child with a disability. Calling attention to accomplishments, asking questions, and providing words of encouragement and praise communicate a respect for the sibling as an individual.

Demystifying Special Education Special education teachers are in the best position to help siblings understand what the brother or sister will experience at school. Michaelis (1980) has suggested two strategies that might help demystify special education. The first strategy is informal in nature and readily implemented; in fact, it calls for the special education teacher to simply *be available* for the sibling. A brief, guided walk through the classroom and straightforward explanations of materials and content can be very helpful. Friends of the sibling should also be invited to visit. Michaelis's second strategy involves the establishment of a "sibling school." A sibling school is a more structured gathering where siblings have an opportunity to meet one another and learn about the special education program and the staff who work with their brothers and sisters. The "sibling school" program could be based upon the concepts presented in Chapter 5.

Another way to demystify special services is to explain all related services in an easy-to-understand manner. Meyer et al. (1985) provide an excellent example of explaining special services in a straightfor-

ward manner. Teachers may want to develop brief descriptions of these services. For example, a brief description of physical therapy will help clarify treatment goals and procedures. (Such a description may also be helpful to other professionals and adults in the school.)

Involving Siblings in Meetings Turnbull and Turnbull, (1990) suggest that it may be advantageous to ask older siblings to participate in the development of the individualized education program (IEP). Naturally, this should only be done with permission of the parents and, as appropriate, with the permission of the student with the disability. Siblings should be prepared prior to the meeting. The reasons, process, and outcomes of these meetings should be explained to them. These types of educational meetings, which involve positive future planning, will benefit from the active involvement of brothers and sisters.

Being Available To Talk Sometimes siblings need someone to talk to who will understand their special needs and respond in a nonjudgmental manner. Milstead (1988) notes that upon learning that her younger sister had a disability, she would have welcomed the comfort of a teacher. "Perhaps a teacher could have taken time to chat with me and to assure me that our family would eventually adjust and that our home would return to normalcy" (p. 537). As Michaelis (1980) has also noted, a sibling may have difficulty talking about feelings and problems with parents, therefore, the teacher is a likely and available adult alternative. Someone who will truly listen to problems and concerns and offer practical advice may help a sibling deal with problems more effectively. The keys to offering support are an understanding manner and a willingness to listen.

Providing "Space" It is also important to sense when the sibling would rather not be involved with teachers, especially special education teachers. Some siblings prefer not to be reminded of their sister or brother and actively avoid any association with the teacher. Sensitive teachers will recognize this and not presume that all siblings need or want to be involved with the special classroom.

Talking with Parents When arranging meetings with parents, teachers should remember to schedule separate conferences for each child, or to at least discuss each sibling separately within the same meeting. Conferring about one child at a time helps to reinforce the idea that children, even brothers and sisters, are unique individuals. Parents need to hear about the accomplishments of each child. For instance, by noting the accomplishments of a sibling in an informal meeting with parents, special education teachers can help parents feel recognized for some of their parenting skills. These positive aspects have been overlooked in the midst of concentrated efforts to help the child with a disability.

Providing Educational Experiences Jones (1983) has described an experience in which one of her children, Aaron, was actively encouraged to discuss his brother's Down syndrome as part of a science lesson on genes and chromosomes. This project grew into a formal report and the sharing of a photo album that depicted Aaron's brother, Jay, at several stages of development, as well as interacting with others in a natural way. According to Jones, "the children at school not only enjoyed the album but learned by looking at the pictures that Jay was pretty much a regular little guy . . ." (p. 121). Another wonderful and touching example of this involvement is reported by Turnbull and Bronicki (1986). The senior author (11 years old), who has a brother with mental retardation, reports on teaching her class about his disability. After the teaching session, a subsequent study was conducted to judge the students' attitudes about mental retardation. Similar presentations could be practiced by regular classroom teachers, provided the sibling is willing to share his or her experiences and knowledge. To ensure success, the sibling's teacher may wish to consult with the special education teacher when planning the project.

School Counselors

Many schools now employ professional counselors or social workers to serve the diverse needs of children and adolescents. One role for the school counselor is to establish sibling support groups in schools (Post-Kramer & Nickolai, 1985; Slade, 1988). As reviewed in Chapters 5 and 6, these support groups can serve to teach siblings new information as well as help them deal with their feelings in a proactive manner.

The school counselor, more than any other school professional, is in the best position to establish sibling groups. The counselor is likely to know which children with disabilities have brothers and sisters who can devote the time and energy to these special efforts. The counselor is also in a position to be a support for all children and, it is hoped, viewed as a nonthreatening, friendly adult.

In establishing a special-based group the counselor should attend to the suggestions in Chapters 5 and 6. In particular, the school counselor should:

1. Determine the goals of the support group (informational or affective).
2. Contact parents to explain the rationale for the group and how it will operate. It may be helpful to host an informational session for parents to answer their questions and seek their assistance and expertise.
3. Announce the establishment of the group. Children and adolescents should volunteer for these groups. Forcing them to participate will most likely lead to a negative outcome.
4. Explain the goals of the group to the teachers and other instructional personnel. The school counselor should not assume that the teachers or other professionals have knowledge or appreciation of sibling concerns. Teachers with strategies to support siblings will be helpful.

Principals

The principal, as the educational leader, defines the nature and tone of the school. Principals play a key role in helping all children learn and develop their skills. To support siblings, principals can affirm that brothers and sisters with disabilities are full members of the school community. This affirmation will benefit all children, especially the sibling who may have questions about the child's acceptance. Caring and concerned principals can offer real support and guidance to children who are presented with challenges. Not only can principals make themselves available to talk with siblings, but a simple suggestion, encouragement, or pat on the back from a principal can do much to support siblings. Finally, principals can take the leadership role in meeting special needs of siblings by encouraging and supporting teachers, counselors, and parents in the establishment of special sibling programs.

Parents

Parents also play a critical role in ensuring that school-related problems between siblings are minimal.

Arranging Separate Conferences Like teachers, parents should limit discussions about their children to one child at a time. Most children know when parents go to school to talk with teachers. Each sibling's needs, problems, and achievements should be discussed separately. After parent–teacher conferences, parents should sit down with the individual child and explain the meeting, stressing the positive aspects and noting problem areas discussed.

Being Careful Not To Overburden the Sibling Teachers need to give the sibling "space" at school, and parents need to limit caregiving demands placed on the sibling. Although it may be easier to ask the sibling to deliver messages, carry books and lunches, escort, or interpret, whenever possible parents should avoid expecting the sibling to perform such chores. These chores may interfere with the sibling's activities and/or restrict participation in extracurricular events. In families where the only possible alternative for providing these needed services is the sibling, the parents should discuss these needs with the sibling and reward the sibling for assuming these extra duties. In large families, responsibilities associated with school should be shared among the siblings.

Participating in School-Related Activities Parents should attempt to provide a balance in terms of attention and resources given to each child. With a child with a disability, the demands for parental time and energy are intense. Meetings with teachers and related medical professionals, medical evaluations, parent groups, and classroom observations may all demand so much parental time that parents cannot attend to the school-related activities of the other sibling. Parental participation in each child's school activities should be kept as equal as possible, even if it means forgoing a classroom observation or volunteer tutoring.

Taking Time To Discuss Schoolwork Some parents have found it helpful to set aside time each week to talk with the sibling about schoolwork and school activities. Setting aside a particular time in the afternoon or evening for this discussion communicates a recognition of the sibling's needs as well as his or her uniqueness.

Educational Involvement

Some siblings, especially those who have brothers and sisters with severe disabilities, may wish to take an active role in the school program. The two activities suggested below may allow the sibling to be involved with the school-based educational program, known as the individualized education program, or IEP.

Setting Educational Goals Many siblings have specific suggestions for what skills their brothers or sisters should learn. Parents and teachers should involve the sibling in the establishment of learning goals. The sibling can be asked to name skills the child should learn or to list possible skills by priority. Closely related to the setting of goals is participation in educational assessment activities. Professionals conducting assessments might find it valuable to talk with siblings about the current skills exhibited by the sister or brother as well as behavioral and learning characteristics. Siblings can be a rich source of information, but they are often overlooked in the assessment process. Finally, as noted above, some siblings may wish to attend educational meetings in which the child's school program is discussed. When parents agree that siblings should participate, they should be welcomed as active members of the child's educational team.

Using Sibling Tutors As discussed in Chapter 8, siblings often make effective instructors who are capable of teaching many skills. If the sibling wishes to be involved in actual teaching, time and resources should be given to ensure that the sibling is well prepared to tutor the brother or sister. The guidelines proposed in Chapter 8 should be followed for such school-based instruction.

School Structure

The physical and administrative structure of the school program can have an important impact on the sibling relationship. Schools should be set up to minimize problems that siblings experience when one child has a disability.

Making a Commitment to Integration The school must be structured so that all students interact on a regular basis. The days of segregating children or housing special education classes in "the basement" helped to perpetuate myths and mysteries about students with disabilities. These outmoded service delivery systems bred rumors, jokes, and prejudice toward children with disabilities. A strong commitment toward integration and full school inclusion implies that all students can, and are even expected to, participate in the school community. Integration implies attending the same classes, going to the cafeteria and playground with other students, attending assemblies, using the library, computer room, and gymnasium, as well as interacting with many teachers and a variety of students. Having a brother or sister in "the basement" or "special wing" can have a negative effect on a sibling. Seeing a brother or sister participate in an accepting school community and being involved in all aspects of school life can have a profound, positive effect on siblings.

Not Labeling the Classroom Special education classrooms should not be labeled. Classrooms with signs that say "Severe and Profound," "Learning Disabilities," "Blind," "Hearing Impaired," or "Noncategorized" stigmatize those within and outside of the classroom, especially family members. These signs have little purpose and can be the root of problems for siblings, not to mention the students who are forced to look at such signs day after day. Classrooms used for special instructional purposes should be identified using the same system applied to the other classrooms in the school—numbers or teachers' names.

Fostering School-Wide Awareness School systems can minimize sibling problems in the school setting by teaching students and teachers about disabilities. The school community can increase its awareness of the needs and problems experienced by students with disabilities as well as their achievements and contributions. Such training can foster positive attitudes toward students with special needs. (Anderson & Milliren, 1983). As positive attitudes toward these students increase, it will most assuredly have a positive impact on their siblings.

As a part of this awareness, school leaders should make it clear that teasing students with disabilities or joking about them will not be tolerated. Established policies and procedures regarding teasing and joking will make it easier for siblings to deal with these behaviors. Naturally, no policy will control all teasing or joking, but a policy may help prevent some of it and can be a source of support for siblings.

SUMMARY

Children with disabilities will, at some point, attend the same school as their siblings. This situation carries the potential either to increase problems for siblings or to help siblings see their brother or sister as a valued and contributing member of a total school community. To achieve the latter situation, teachers must play a critical role. Teachers need to recognize and reinforce each sibling's individuality and be available to talk with siblings and explain the special education program. They must also be sensitive to the sibling's need for anonymity and "space," if desired. Likewise, parents must be careful not to overburden the sibling with extra caregiving demands related to school. Both teachers and parents should provide an opportunity for the sibling to become involved in the child's educational program if both siblings are interested. Finally, school systems must make concerted efforts to fully integrate all children so that they can participate in all the aspects of school life. Making a commitment to integration and full inclusion will clearly communicate to siblings that their brothers and sisters are valued members of the school community.

10

Siblings
as Adults

It is inevitable that one day I will lose my parents. I will inherit whatever constitutes their estates, be it money or debts . . . but, their most important legacy will be in the form of my autistic brother. As his future guardian, I will acquire and accept the full responsibility of Douglas. As his only sister, I feel that I have already absorbed too much of this burden. I am hoping that long before my parents' demise, Doug's future will be guaranteed. The only alternative to my becoming his perpetual "other mother" is for him to be settled in a group home offering suitable living conditions
(p. 2).
Gerri Zatlow, 1982

The death of Walter, Bob, and Mary's mother was not a surprise. After their father died, their mother had become melancholy and was prone to colds and flu. These siblings had dealt with the loss of their parents as best they could. Now they were troubled by the evolution of their new sibling relationship; a relationship no longer bound by parents but by each other. Their passage into this new and inevitable sibling relationship was similar to the experience of most siblings in all but one way; Bob has a severe disability.

At an early age, Bob was institutionalized. His parents followed the predominant belief that this action would be more advantageous for his siblings, while allowing Bob to receive specialized education and therapy. When Bob turned 16, he returned home because state and local resources had changed. He was now able to receive the services he needed close to his natural home. For the past 10 years, Bob had lived with his mother and frequently visited his siblings, nieces, and nephews. Bob's speech was limited and barely understandable. During family gatherings, he would say, "Good, good, good!" over and over again. After so many years of institutional life, he relished the participation in a thriving family. With his mother's death, Bob and his siblings were faced with a serious dilemma.

Initially, Walter and Mary were confused about their role with Bob. They loved him dearly, but their personal responsibilities to their spouses and children precluded incorporating Bob into their day-to-day life. Immediately after their mother's death, Bob went to live with Mary until a permanent solution could be found.

The next few months were consumed with issues and problems associated with Bob's long-term care and treatment. Issues regarding guardianship, finances, SSI (Supplemental Security Income), community-based services, group homes, and institutional care occupied every spare moment. As Walter and Mary began their search for services for Bob, they were overwhelmed with conflicting advice from friends and professionals. Their attorney was unsure about guardianship. Bob's social worker from the county could not guarantee a group-home placement and suggested a state-run facility. Bob's instructors at the sheltered workshop argued against institutional placement and suggested a lawsuit to force the county to provide a group home. The Social Security division needed a "representative payee" if benefits were to continue. A representative of Social Security suggested that Bob's benefits would be terminated once his mother's estate was settled. Needless to say, Walter and Mary were quite confused and often felt helpless and afraid of what the future would hold.

Certainly, Walter and Mary thought about Bob's future before the death of their mother, but not in their wildest dreams did they anticipate that providing for his future would be so problematic. They assumed that some social service organization would come to the rescue and provide residential placement within the community. In the intervening months, Walter and Mary hired an attorney to pursue limited guardianship, which they received. They used their guardianship responsibility to ensure Bob's community placement in supported living and supported employment programs. In consultation with their attorney and an accountant, a financial plan was developed to enable Bob to enjoy the benefits of his mother's estate while still receiving state and federal entitlements.

Bob still visits Walter and Mary often. He usually spends holidays with them and, occasionally, goes on vacation with them. Sitting around with his siblings, their spouses, and his growing nephews and nieces, Bob still says, "Good, good, good!"

Adult siblings who have brothers or sisters with disabilities can face complex issues and problems, as Walter and Mary's story indicates. These problems are uniquely related to the family's situation, past relationships, and services that are available to the adult with the disability. Not all adult siblings have the same experience as Walter and Mary. Consider Patty and Jack:

Jack was born with severe cerebral palsy and was expected to die shortly after birth. Now, 38 years later, he was still living with his mother, who spent most of her waking hours attending to his needs. His younger sister Patty, an accountant, lived in the same town and visited her brother and mother frequently. Patty has become increasingly concerned about her mother's ability to care for Jack. She knew that her mother's age and fading health put her brother and mother in an unsafe situation. She also knew that the bond between them was great and that neither of them would agree to separation. She was concerned, not only with her mother's recent need for increased support, but also with her older brother's lifelong needs. How could she arrange to help them without sacrificing her personal life and career?

Luckily, Patty located several community services that provided home-health care to assist in dressing and bathing Jack; homemaker services, which provided assistance with household chores; and a nutrition program, which provided periodic meals to Jack and his mother. Because they lived in an area that supported community living for persons with disabilities, Patty was able to help her mother and brother by locating and arranging services rather than by directly providing them herself.

We know from the literature review that many adult siblings report that their experiences with brothers and sisters who have disabilities have had a profound influence on their adult life. Burton and Parks (1991) conducted a study with adult siblings that considered their self-esteem, locus of control, and career aspirations. *Locus of control* was defined as the extent to which these adult siblings viewed their control over personal choices and decision-making, which they exert to influence life events. Burton and Parks found that the adult siblings who had brothers and sisters with disabilities had a greater locus of control than siblings who did not have a brother or sister with a disability. They suggest that this may be because their unique experience enables them to more readily perceive and accept responsibility for their actions. While they did not find any statistically significant differences between siblings in regard to career aspirations, they noted that twice as many siblings with brothers and sisters who have disabilities were enrolled in helping profession majors in college (e.g., special education, counseling, social work).

Zeitlin (1986) conducted a participant observation study, involving 35 adults with mental retardation, to assess the nature and intensity of their relationships with their brothers and sisters. Her findings indicate that the vast majority of the adults maintained contact with their siblings. The relationships ranged from very warm with frequent contact and extensive involvement to hostile feelings with neither contact nor involvement. She notes that most of the contact appeared to be hierarchical, with siblings providing assistance to their brothers and sisters. Sisters tended to assume a caregiving role, and in families with multiple siblings, one adult sibling tended to assume most of the responsibility for the brother or sister with the disability. Not unexpectedly, Zeitlin found that the adult siblings' concern for their brothers and sisters followed the expressed wishes of their parents. To the adults with mental retardation, the notion of reciprocity in their relationship with a sibling appeared to be important. These adults expressed a desire to return favors and contribute to the relationship.

The concerns of adults who have brothers and sisters with disabilities are somewhat different from the concerns experienced by younger siblings. The main issue here is how the adults can attend to their own needs as they mature. Their natural concerns for their spouse, children, aging parents, and careers are often tempered with the added responsibility of being the sibling of a person who has special needs. These adult concerns fall into three broad areas:

1. Genetics
2. Long-term care of the brother or sister
3. Helping the sibling enjoy a quality life

These major concerns, outlined in Table 10.1 by a number of critical questions often posed by adult siblings, are examined below.

GENETICS

A major concern of most adult siblings who have brothers and sisters with disabilities is the possibility that they, themselves, will give birth to a child with a disability (Tingey, 1988). This concern increases substantially when the brother or sister has had a disability since birth and/or has an identified genetic disorder. Helping siblings with this

Table 10.1. Critical questions often posed by adult siblings

Concern	Questions
Genetic	What are my chances of parenting a child with a disability? Will I pass a disorder along to my children? How can I get specific advice about my genetic concerns? How will my spouse/fiancé feel about possible genetic problems?
Long-term care	What will happen when my parents die? Who will take care of my sibling? Will I be financially responsible for my sibling? Should I serve as a guardian? What responsibilities will a guardian have? Can my parents plan their estate to safeguard my sibling's financial future? Will a conservator be needed? How can we establish a guardianship or conservatorship?
Helping the sibling	How can I help improve my sibling's life? Can I get involved in services for my sibling? How can I advocate for my sibling?

concern requires a basic knowledge of genetics and the various genetic services available to siblings.

Many siblings have been helped by the scientific field of genetics, which involves the study of the structure and function of genes and the transmission of genes among generations. While this science has helped families understand more about heredity and particular genetic disorders, human genetics is a complex subject and knowledge is limited. Scientific technology has not advanced to the stage where all the genetically caused disabilities are known. Yet, a number of specific disorders have been identified as being genetically related. Naturally, this genetic uncertainty can be a major source of anxiety for many adult siblings.

Through advances in genetics, many siblings can receive advice and information concerning the risk of having a child with a disability or the risk of passing defective genes to their offspring. Fortunately, genetic screening and prenatal diagnosis have advanced to a stage where predictability is replacing chance and the prospects for the prevention of many inherited disabilities have dramatically improved (Connor, 1989).

The United States Department of Health and Human Services (1980) has published a brief checklist to alert individuals who may be in need of specific genetic counseling. The list includes the following questions:

Has anyone in your family had a child with a genetic disorder?
Is there a family history of birth defects or mental retardation?
Have the parents had a history of miscarriages, still births, or
    early infant death?
Do more than three relatives on one side of the family have the
    same disorder?
Do either of the parents have a history of excessive exposure to
    drugs, chemicals, or radiation?
Is the mother over age 35?

If either spouse answers "yes" to one or more of these questions, genetic counseling is recommended.

Genetic counseling includes a complete review of family history, with emphasis on the medical histories of both immediate and distant relatives. Parents who keep a complete family history and specific medical records will be able to assist children who may later seek genetic counseling. Comprehensive family records are invaluable to genetic counselors. Genetic counseling is discussed in more detail below, but first a brief review of how disorders can be inherited may be helpful.

A Brief Review of Heredity's Role

The two chief structures responsible for passing along hereditary information are the chromosomes and the genes.

Chromosomes are microscopic parts of living cells that direct the cell's activity. Within the chromosomes, 50,000–100,000 genes exist. These chromosomes also contain DNA (deoxyribonucleic acid), the hereditary material of life, which is of critical importance. In humans, the normal number of chromosomes in each cell is 46. This includes two sex chromosomes, which determine gender, and 44 autosomes, which determine other features of the individual. If the total number or arrangement of chromosomes varies for any reason, the individual may have certain identifiable disabilities.

Genes are located on the chromosomes. Humans are estimated to have 10,000–100,000 structural genes plus an unknown number of regulatory genes. The *gene* is defined chemically as a unit of inheritance encoded in a sequence of DNA. These specialized sub-units of chromosomes hold a code for the specific characteristics that parents pass to their children. Genes are responsible for the production of specific products, such as hormones and enzymes, needed for growth and development. Genes also control individual features, such as hair, eye, and skin color, as well as height. When a gene has an abnormal change or mutation, the production of specific proteins can be affected. The defective gene can be responsible for the occurrence of certain disabilities or a tendency toward them. Mutations in genes occur by chance or as the result of environmental factors such as radiation, viruses, drugs, or advanced maternal age. Typically, the defective gene affects all cells in the body, becomes part of the person's genetic code, and is then passed from one generation to another.

The genes passed to the new generation may be dominant or recessive. A dominant gene is one that, whether inherited from one or both parents, is evident in the child and the transmitting parent; that is, its characteristics are always visible. A dominant condition can also appear following a de nova mutation in the germ cells in one of the unaffected parents. In this case, neither of the parents will show any manifestations of the condition, although the infant will be affected. A recessive gene is one that has visible characteristics only if the gene is inherited from both unaffected parents.

In their review of genetics, Kolodny, Abuelo, Barsel-Bowers, and Pueschel (1990) note that genetic disabilities can be viewed as one of three types of disorders:

1. Chromosomal disorders
2. Mendelian disorders
3. Multifactorial disorders

Chromosomal Disorders   These disorders are the result of the loss or addition of an entire chromosome or changes in the structure of a chromosome, which may involve either autosomes or sex (X or Y) chromosomes. Abnormalities in the number of chromosomes include extra or missing chromosomes, while structural abnormalities include deletions, duplications, or inversions of chromosome material or translocation of material from one chromosome to another (Kolodny et al., 1990).

Autosomal chromosomal aberrations typically lead to mental retardation. These syndromes happen randomly and are very unlikely. In the general population, the incidence of autosomal chromosomal disorders is only approximately 0.7% (Maxson & Daugherty, 1992).

Sex chromosomal abnormalities do not cause as severe physical and intellectual problems as autosomal chromosomal malformations. Typical chromosomal malformations include:

Down syndrome (Trisomy 21)
Patau syndrome (Trisomy 13)
Edwards syndrome (Trisomy 18)
Klinefelter syndrome (XXY syndrome)
Turner syndrome (XO syndrome)
cri du chat syndrome

Mendelian Disorders These disorders refer to a mutation of a gene or its allele. An allele is a specific form of a gene that occupies a specific location on a chromosome. This gene is also one of many possible molecular sequences that directs a particular characteristic. As with chromosome disorders, Mendelian disorders occur randomly (Maxson & Daugherty, 1992). McKusick (1990) notes that over 2,000 diseases are known to be caused by Mendelian disorders.

Mendelian disorders are classified as either autosomal recessive disorders, autosomal dominant disorders, or X-linked disorders (Kolodny et al., 1990).

Autosomal Recessive Disorders These disorders become apparent when an individual has a pair of defective genes. The disorder results from parents who are not affected, but who carry the defective gene and pass it to the child. Maxson and Daugherty (1992) note that at least 626 traits in humans have been identified as the result of mutated recessive genes. Another 851 traits are strongly suspected to be the result of recessive disorders. Figure 10.1 shows the inheritance pattern of autosomal recessive disorders. If two carriers mate (as shown in Figure 10.1A), according to the laws of probability, 75% of the children would be clinically normal; however, 50% would carry the recessive gene and 25% would have the disorder. If a carrier mates with a noncarrier (Figure 10.1B), statistically speaking, 50% of the children would not be affected and 50% would be carriers, but would not show signs of the disorder. As Batshaw and Perret (1992) note, this is simply a *statistical* risk as inheritance occurs by chance. As each pregnancy is an independent event, the laws of probability apply in an independent fashion for each pregnancy.

As can be seen from the diagram, it is the carriers who pass the gene from one generation to the next. Siblings of persons with the recessive disorder are statistically likely to be carriers of the defective gene. Recessive disorders only occur if two carriers mate and because this is a rare occurrence, these disorders are rather uncommon. When relatives marry, the chances of a recessive disorder occurring are substantially higher since there is a higher probability that two relatives carry a recessive gene. Unlike X-linked disorders (discussed below), males and females have an equal chance of being affected by an autosomal recessive disorder, because the responsible gene is carried on an autosome rather than on a sex chromosome.

Autosomal recessive disorders usually result in an enzyme deficiency, which may lead to biochemical abnormalities and subsequent mental retardation or early death (Batshaw & Perret, 1992). Since a specific biochemical abnormality is typically present with an autosomal recessive disorder, detection of carriers as well as prenatal

Autosomal Recessive Disorders

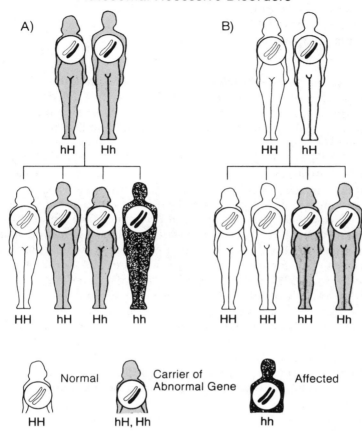

Figure 10.1. The inheritance of autosomal recessive disorders. A) Inheritance pattern, according to the laws of probability, when two carriers mate. B) Inheritance pattern when a carrier and a normal person mate. (From Batshaw, M. L., & Perret, Y. M. [1992]. *Children with disabilities: A medical primer,* 3rd ed., p. 14. Baltimore: Paul H. Brookes Publishing Co.; reprinted by permission.)

diagnosis is often possible (Kolodny et al., 1990). Autosomal recessive disorders include:

  Congenital hypothyroidism
  Cystic fibrosis
  Galactosemia
  Homocystinuria
  Hurler syndrome
  Maple syrup urine disease

Metachromatic leukodystrophy
Methylmalonic aciduria
Phenylketonuria (PKU)
Retinitis pigmentosa
Tay-Sachs disease

Autosomal Dominant Disorders With autosomal dominant disorders, the inheritance of an abnormal gene from just one parent leads to the manifestation of the disease (Singer, 1978). A single dominant gene is abnormal with these disorders. Maxson and Daugherty (1992) note that some 1,443 traits have been identified as autosomal dominant traits, while another 1,141 traits are suspected as being dominant. Figure 10.2 illustrates the inheritance pattern of autosomal dominant disorders. If an affected person mates with an unaffected person, there is a 1 in 2 chance of having an affected infant and a 1 in 2 chance of having an unaffected infant with each pregnancy (see Figure 10.2A). The unaffected children will not have the abnormal gene and, therefore, cannot pass the disorder to their children. If two affected individuals mate (see Figure 10.2B), on the average, 25% of the offspring will be normal; 50% will receive one abnormal gene and, thus, be affected; and 25% of the children will receive two of the abnormal dominant genes, a rare and often fatal combination.

Dominant disorders usually involve physical or structural abnormalities, and mental retardation is less common. Males and females are equally affected (Batshaw & Perret, 1992). With autosomal dominant disorders, a family history of the disorder is typical, although in some cases no family history is evident. Autosomal dominant disorders include:

Achondroplasia
Apert syndrome
Huntington's chorea
Marfan syndrome
Neurofibromatosis
Noonan syndrome
Osteogenesis imperfecta
Stickler syndrome
Treacher Collins syndrome
Tuberous sclerosis

X-Linked Disorders This form of Mendelian disorder specifically involves the genes located on the X, or female, sex chromosome. Maxson and Daugherty (1992) note that at least 140 genes have been identified with the X chromosome and 171 other genes are suspected of being X-linked. Sometimes the terms *X-linked disorder* and *sex-linked*

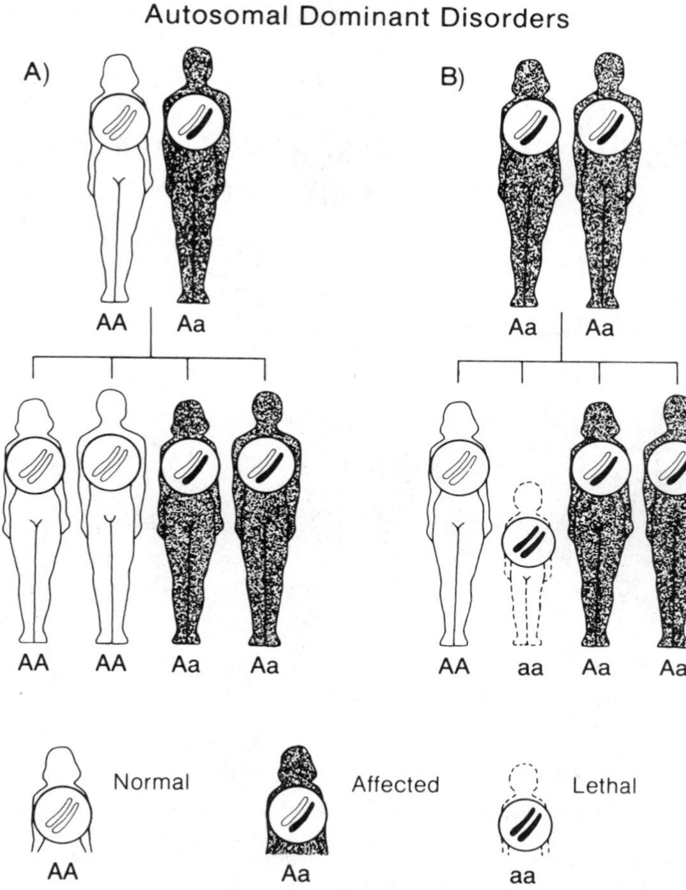

Autosomal Dominant Disorders

Figure 10.2. The inheritance of autosomal dominant disorders. A) Inheritance pattern, according to the laws of probability, when an affected person and a normal person mate. B) Inheritance pattern when two affected persons mate. (From Batshaw, M. L., & Perret, Y. M. [1992]. *Children with disabilities: A medical primer*, 3rd ed., p. 16. Baltimore: Paul H. Brookes Publishing Co.; reprinted by permission).

disorder are used synonymously. These disorders are passed from one generation to the next by carrier females and the genes can be either dominant or recessive. It should be noted that dominant X-linked disorders are extremely rare (Kolodny et al., 1990). Figure 10.3 illustrates how the disorder is passed along. A carrier woman will have one affected X chromosome (Xa) and one normal X chromosome. She, herself, will not be affected if the gene is recessive, but she can pass the disorder to her children, typically her sons. If a carrier female mates with an unaffected male (who will contribute either a normal X chromosome, producing a girl, or a normal Y chromosome, produc-

Sex-Linked Disorders

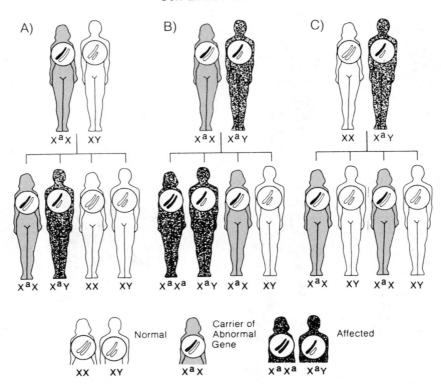

Figure 10.3. The inheritance of X-linked disorders. A) Inheritance pattern, according to the laws of probability, when a carrier female and normal male mate. B) Inheritance pattern when a carrier female and an affected male mate. C) Inheritance pattern when an affected male mates with a noncarrier female. (Adapted from Batshaw, M. L., & Perret, Y. M. [1992]. *Children with disabilities: A medical primer*, 3rd ed., p. 19. Baltimore: Paul H. Brookes Publishing Co.; reprinted by permission.)

ing a boy), statistically, 50% of the male children will be normal and 50% of the male children will be affected. Since males only have one X chromosome, they express the X-linked recessive disorder. Of the female children, 50% will be normal and 50% will carry the disorder (see Figure 10.3A). In the rare case when a carrier female mates with an affected male, on the average, 50% of the male children will be affected and 50% will be normal, whereas 50% of the female children will be affected and 50% will be carriers (see Figure 10.3B). In cases where an affected male mates with an unaffected, noncarrier female, the female offspring will be carriers of the disorder and the male offspring will neither have the disorder nor carry the defective gene (see Figure 10.3C).

X-linked disorders may involve biochemical abnormalities and may be the cause of mental impairments. In males, 25% of intellectual defects are related to X-linked syndromes as are 10% of the learning impairments in females. The most common of these types of X-linked disorders is referred to as Fragile X syndrome (Batshaw & Perret, 1992). Family histories of persons with Fragile X syndrome usually reveal X-linked disorders. These persons usually have a brother, maternal uncle, or maternal male cousin with the disease. X-linked disorders include:

Hemophilia
Hunter syndrome
Lesch-Nyhan syndrome
Muscular dystrophy
Fragile X syndrome

Multifactorial Disorders   Some disabilities are the result of the interaction of multiple predisposing genes and unknown environmental factors. These traits are referred to as multifactorial disorders and include disorders such as:

Anencephaly
Cardiac defects
Cleft lip/palate
Clubfoot
Spina bifida
Thalidomide toxicity

As noted by Kolodny et al. (1990), multifactorial disorders differ from Mendelian disorders in the following ways:

1. Risk of recurrence is typically 2%–5% provided there is only one affected relative. If there is an affected parent or several offspring the recurrence rate is greater.
2. The occurrence rate seems to depend on the severity of the disability; that is, the more severe the disability the more likely it is to recur.
3. When the disorder typically appears in one sex and the parents have a child of the opposite sex with a disorder, the chances of recurrence increase.

Genetic Counseling, Screening, & Prenatal Diagnosis

Any woman who is planning to become pregnant should undergo a physical examination that screens for high risk conditions and have certain diagnostic tests performed (Evrard & Scola, 1990). This is even more important for siblings who have brothers or sisters with disabilities. Many siblings want to take advantage of available genetic counseling, screening services, and prenatal diagnosis. These services cannot guarantee 100% predictive accuracy (just as no one can guarantee ultimately how many male and female children a couple will have—it's a 50/50 chance each time), or can they identify the presence of all disabilities. However, they can help increase the sibling's knowledge of present and potential risks. In other words, genetic counseling and screening can provide the opportunity for the sibling to make informed decisions about pregnancy.

Genetic Counseling Given the increasing knowledge of genetics as well as the improvements in techniques for diagnosis and treatment of genetic disorders, most adult siblings interested in having a family will benefit from genetic counseling. Since genetic disabilities are many and complex, siblings (independent of the nature of the disability of their brother or sister) are wise to seek the advice of genetic counselors.

Genetic counseling is conducted by professionals who aim to provide the latest information on medical genetics to persons seeking such advice. The genetics counselor, working with a physician, helps the sibling understand the basis of specific genetic disorders, the risk of having a child with the disorder, and the treatment that is available.

When seeking genetic counseling, it is usually most helpful for the counselor and physician to examine the person with the disability to establish the exact nature of the disorder. When this is not an option, the sibling should provide the professionals with as much information as possible on the brother or sister and the nature of the disability.

After determination of the exact nature of the disability, genetic counseling proceeds with a pedigree analysis. This analysis is a diagram of genealogy, constructed with reference to a particular genetic trait. The pedigree analysis helps the siblings and professionals understand how and when the disability was passed along or whether it just appeared as a random occurrence, and it reveals the mode of inheritance of a particular trait.

Once the nature of the disability is determined, the genetic counselor can provide education to help the sibling understand the genetics involved in passing along the disability. The goal of genetic counseling is to help siblings make informed decisions concerning their potential children. The genetic counseling process is usually non-directive, providing information and enabling individuals to make their own decisions about parenting (Kolodny et al., 1990).

It is important to note that genetic counseling can do much to alleviate fear and anxiety experienced by siblings. Cohen (1985) shared an experience in which genetic counseling helped her understand her brother's disability and dissipated her concerns about having a child with a disability. While she recognized that genetic counseling does not offer a guarantee, a confirmation of her averageness served as significant reassurance.

Genetic counseling services are available in all states. A directory of each state's genetic counseling centers is available from:

National Clearinghouse for Human Genetic Diseases
805 15th Street, N.W., Suite 500
Washington, DC 20005
(800)336-2590
(703)522-2590

National Genetics Federation, Inc.
184 Fifth Avenue
New York, NY 10010
(212)371-1030

Genetic Screening This refers to the identification of known genetic disorders via the evaluation of susceptible individuals in order to identify either those who are affected or who are carriers of the disorder. Genetic screening can be helpful either prenatally or postnatally. A good example of genetic screening is the test for phenylketonuria (PKU). Within a day after birth, a blood sample is taken from the child and a test is conducted to determine the presence of the disorder. A special diet is prescribed for affected children preventing the serious, disabling effects of PKU. Other screening is available for Tay Sachs disease, sickle cell anemia, cystic fibrosis, and congenital hypothyroidism.

Prenatal Diagnosis This type of diagnosis for genetic disorders focuses on a biochemical and/or DNA analysis of the chromosomes of the developing fetus or mother. Over 400 disorders can be diagnosed prenatally (Maxson & Daugherty, 1992). With the advancement of genetics and diagnostic techniques, it is likely that many more disorders will be able to be identified prenatally during the 1990s.

One widely used prenatal diagnostic test is *alpha-fetoprotein* (AFP) *screening*. In this screening, amniotic fluid and/or blood are analyzed for the amount of AFP present. Elevated levels of AFP can indicate the risk of neural tube closure disorders (e.g., spina bifida, anencephaly), while lower levels of AFP can indicate the risk of Down syndrome. When abnormal AFP levels are detected, other tests to confirm the findings are conducted.

The most common prenatal diagnostic technique is *amniocentesis*. In this procedure, amniotic fluid is withdrawn from the pregnant mother's womb for chemical and chromosomal analysis. Over 100 disorders can be detected via amniocentesis. The most common disabilities detected by this prenatal detection method are Down syndrome and neural tube closure disorders.

Another prenatal diagnostic technique is *chorionic villus sampling* (CVS) in which cells of the chorionic membrane of the fetus are removed and analyzed. This procedure can be performed in the very early stages of pregnancy (from the fifth to the eighth week). Additional techniques, *fetoscopy* and *ultrasonography*, provide for the detection of physical disorders. In some cases, prenatal surgery or intravenously administered therapies can be implemented to prevent or minimize disabilities (Pueschel & Mulick, 1990). *Percutaneous umbilical blood sampling (PUBS)* is yet another prenatal diagnostic procedure in which fetal blood is removed and analyzed. Since the blood is from the fetus, more precise tests can be conducted.

Choices & Decisions for Adult Siblings

The new screening and diagnostic techniques help to provide adult siblings with information that they can use to make decisions about parenting. As with many life decisions, some siblings and their spouses will be faced with difficult and complex choices. Decisions made by siblings should be based upon a thorough information base and balanced with values and experience.

PROVIDING FOR LONG-TERM CARE

Eventually, most people face the inevitable fact that their parents will not live forever. Sudden illness or an accident may precipitate an acute realization of parental mortality. When a family has a member with a disability, the ramifications of parental mortality can increase substantially. When parents are no longer around, or are unable to care for the individual with a disability, who will provide for that person's future? In many cases, responsibility is awarded to the siblings. Seltzer (1991) describes the results of a survey of 126 siblings who had a brother or sister with developmental disabilities. Only about a third of these siblings had a thorough discussion with their parents about who will assume future responsibility for their brothers or sisters. The remaining siblings had only talked a little or some (51%) about the issue, while 14% of the siblings had not talked at all with their parents about future responsibilities. Seltzer expresses concern over the lack of information regarding siblings' perceptions of their present and future roles and responsibilities. Siblings faced with this responsibility will need to be familiar with guardianship, conservatorship, wills, and trusts.

Guardianship

Guardianship is a legal relationship between two persons, one serving as a guardian and the other as a ward. This legal relationship provides the guardian with the duty and right to act on behalf of the ward in making important decisions. Guardianship is intended for persons who have disabilities that render them unable to make decisions that would be in their best interest. Guardianship attempts to protect the person in situations regarding services, finances, residences, and property, while still maintaining the person's individuality. A court may grant a guardian responsibility for personal affairs (called guardianship of the person) or for financial affairs (called guardianship of the property), or for both. A "limited guardianship" may also be established in which the guardian only has responsibility for certain areas of decision in the ward's life.

While guardianship may be necessary for some individuals, for others, the legal situation may be too restrictive. In determining the need for guardianship, siblings should attempt to answer the following questions:

1. Is my brother or sister, due to a lack of social, vocational, academic, and personal skills, vulnerable to extraordinary exploitation and/or abuse?
2. Does he or she wish to have a guardian?
3. Does he or she have property or resources that need management beyond his or her ability?
4. Is it likely that the individual will require additional services, will change residence, or will interact with many service agencies?

Answering "yes" to these questions may indicate that the person would benefit from a legal guardian, even though he or she is an adult.

Who Should Be a Guardian? Selecting the proper guardian for an individual is a serious matter that requires consideration from several perspectives. Often, the guardian is a sibling or other close relative, but this is not necessary. An interested friend may, in some cases, be a better guardian than family members. Other alternatives include public guardianship or corporate (group) guardianship; in the latter, a private agency or organization serves as guardian. This arrangement can offer numerous advantages over individual guardianship, because the full resources of a professional group are available to the individual with a disability. Corporate guardianship programs in both the United States and Canada have been reviewed in detail by Apolloni and Cooke (1984).

According to the American Association on Mental Deficiency (1975), guardians should be able to demonstrate such prerequisite criteria as:

1. A willingness to serve as guardian
2. The ability to focus on the best interest of the person in all decisions made on their behalf
3. Freedom from any conflict of interest that may interfere with decision-making
4. Availability to serve as a guardian over a reasonable number of years
5. Accessibility to the person and the services in which the person is involved

How Is Guardianship Established? Guardianship is always a legal arrangement and, thus, requires sanction by a court or appointed panel. Specific procedures for establishing guardianship vary according to state statutes. Guardianship should be pursued by parents, siblings, or interested friends who *first* seek the counsel of an attorney. Attorneys who specialize in family matters have specific expertise on state guardianship laws. Attempting to establish guardianship without the advice of an attorney is not wise.

In many cases, the parents of children with disabilities may wish to appoint a guardian in their will. This is sometimes referred to as a testamentary nomination of a guardian. In most states, such nominations are respected, provided that the nominated person agrees to serve in this capacity, does not present any conflict of interest, and is of good character. Nomination of a specific guardian should be thoroughly discussed among the attorney, parents, and the nominated person.

In cases where a will does not declare a specific guardian or in cases where the parent is unable to serve as guardian (because of sickness, etc.) one may be appointed via a court petition. In these situations, an interested individual or the person requests that a court appoint a guardian for the person. Typically, the individual who wishes to be appointed as guardian employs an attorney to pursue this legal procedure.

As mentioned, guardianship laws vary according to state law. Usually, the procedure to establish guardianship will entail:

1. Appointment of an attorney to protect the interests of the person
2. Evaluation of the individual by a physician and a psychologist
3. Interviews of all parties by a court-appointed "visitor," usually a social worker or counselor, who will make an independent recommendation to the court
4. A court hearing to review the petition and make a judgment

What Does a Guardian Do? The powers given to the guardian by the court vary according to the needs of the person. In some cases, the guardian's power is all-inclusive; in others, it is restricted to specific decision-making areas. This latter form, as mentioned earlier, is called "limited guardianship." Guardianship powers may include:

1. Giving or withholding consent for treatment and admission to a program
2. Applying for community-based services on behalf of the person
3. Using the person's funds to provide for needs
4. Applying for government assistance for the person
5. Monitoring the person's progress in various treatment programs

Once guardianship is established, the guardian should:

1. Allow the individual to participate as fully as possible in all decisions affecting his or her future.
2. Interact with the person on a regular basis.
3. Solicit professional expertise when necessary to ensure that decisions made for the individual are in the person's best interest.
4. Serve as an intermediary for the person with social services and other community representatives or agencies.

A guardian does *not* assume financial responsibility for the individual; however, the guardian will typically manage the person's finances, if the individual does not have a conservator. If a conservator has been appointed for the person, the guardian may be asked to report to the conservator all expenses incurred during the guardianship period.

Conservatorship

Unlike guardianship, conservatorship has a single focus. A conservator is a person appointed by the court to manage the estate of a person. In some situations, it may be more advantageous for the sibling to become a conservator rather than a guardian. When several siblings are willing to be involved in long-term protection, one sibling can serve as a conservator, managing financial affairs, while another may serve as a guardian. Conservatorship is established in a manner similar to guardianship. An attorney should be retained to legally establish a conservatorship.

Estate Planning

A common concern among adult siblings is their financial responsibility in regard to long-term care and treatment for their brother or sister. Proper estate planning by parents may help alleviate unnecessary worries, and enables all of the siblings, including the person with a disability, to realize the benefits from parental property. Given the rapid changes in social services policy, benefits, and community services, future estate and financial planning are strategic steps to help ensure the family member's future.

Estate and financial planning are typically done by attorneys via wills and trusts. However, Fee (1990) notes that simple wills and special needs trusts are typically insufficient in ensuring a secure future for the person with a disability. Fee advocates for a life planning approach, which utilizes a letter of intent (Russell, 1990) that allows the family to specify what they want for the family member in terms of residential, vocational, recreational, religious, medical, and social services. Naturally, the first option is to allow the individual with the disability to be actively involved in specification of future life styles and services; however, when the individual has difficulty expressing desires, the family's letter of intent can inform care providers of the preferred future.

Another future planning option for families is the self-sufficiency trust set up in several states to help supplement the individual's government benefits. These trusts are managed in a manner that allows families to set aside resources in a way that does not interfere with the individual's benefits. They are used to provide services and materials to enhance the family member's quality of life.

Apolloni (1989) described a service model called the National Continuity Program, which is aimed at supporting long-term financial, advocacy, and guardianship services for persons with disabilities. This program serves to assist local advocacy programs in ensuring provision of quality services. The National Continuity Program provides seven key services to participants and their families, as follows:

1. A file is established for each participant and updated to ensure proper services.
2. When a parent dies or becomes permanently disabled, the program monitors the participant's receipt of government benefits.
3. The participant is provided representation at individual habilitation planning sessions with state agencies.
4. The participant is visited twice a month to monitor quality of life standards and advocate on the individual's behalf.
5. The delivery of all services is monitored and an advocate acts to correct problems.
6. A guardian is ensured when necessary.
7. Legal, dental, and medical services that supplement government services are made available.

In addition to the obvious long-term support such a program can provide to families, it may offer more immediate support in alleviating some stress about future care for the brother or sister who has a disability.

ENSURING A QUALITY LIFE

Not every sibling can be, or is willing to serve as, a guardian or conservator for a brother or sister with a disability. However, an adult sibling can have a significant, positive impact on his or her brother's or sister's life by serving as an advocate. An advocate is a person who promotes the interests of another and helps him or her enjoy a quality life.

Broadly defined, advocacy is a set of beliefs that results in action aimed at defending, maintaining, or promoting the best interests of another or a group of persons (Neufeld, 1975). An advocate may be another sibling who seeks to protect the human and legal rights of his or her brother or sister. Sibling advocates may be actively engaged in representing the interest of the individual or an entire group of persons with disabilities.

Unlike guardians or conservators, advocates typically do not have legal status. Anyone can serve as an advocate, although family members may be best suited for the role. Minimal prerequisites for advocates include the following:

1. An interest in the needs of the person with a disability
2. A specific knowledge of the needs and resources available to meet those needs
3. A willingness to secure needed services
4. An ability to be assertive
5. A desire to promote the human rights of people
6. The courage to help systems change to meet the needs of persons with disabilities

Advocacy can occur at many levels, be pursued with varying intensity, and achieve a multitude of ends. First and foremost, advocacy focuses on the family member and attempts to ensure that he or she will experience a quality life. A dramatic example of vigorous advocacy is the legislation and policies spearheaded by President John F. Kennedy, who had a sister with mental retardation. During his administration, services for people with disabilities were given a definite direction and their resources expanded; thus, they experienced rapid growth. No doubt, President Kennedy's sense of sibling responsibility helped to motivate his advocacy effort. Luckily, siblings do not need to be presidents or even elected officials to be effective advocates.

Over the past years we have met a number of adult siblings who have become quite active in advocacy roles. Consider these examples:

Nancy's youngest sister, Melinda, still attends a public school for students with cerebral palsy. Although their mother and father are both alive, Nancy attends educational team meetings about Melinda and is an active team member. Nancy is a cashier at a grocery store and has arranged a flexible work schedule with her employer so that she can be involved in Melinda's education. She often observes Melinda at school and visits with her teachers. Recently, she suggested that the team investigate another developmental placement, an integrated public school program for Melinda. Nancy enhances her educational advocacy by reading books and articles on special education.

Patrick is an attorney with a private law firm that specializes in corporate law. He recently donated his services to help a group of professionals start a corporation to serve families who have children with disabilities. He was eager to help since his family could have used such services when he was growing up. His advocacy effort, dedicated to his sister, will have a substantial impact on many people with disabilities.

Cathy's busy schedule as a sales representative to large department stores keeps her on the road most weeks. Her advocacy efforts for her brother, Tim, involve her membership in The Association for Persons with Severe Handicaps (TASH). She often donates money on behalf of her brother.

Alex is a personnel manager at a large manufacturing company. Each year, the employees select a charitable organization and donate money raised at various company functions. For the last 3 years, thanks to Alex's efforts, the proceeds went to the Foundation for Exceptional Children. No one at his company knows that Alex has a sister with spina bifida.

Marsha and her husband, Bill, stop by Jim's group home every Sunday and take him to church and dinner. Jim is Marsha's older brother who has Down syndrome. Marsha and Bill take the opportunity to visit with Jim and monitor his progress and living situation. They often visit with the group home staff to inquire about Jim and the other residents in the home.

Tracy finds it difficult to get along with her older sister, Alice, who has visual disabilities. Even though they do not visit on a regular basis, Tracy keeps track of developments in regard to services to people with disabilities. She often writes her elected officials, especially her senator, expressing her support for services for people with disabilities.

Henry's brother, Joe, has a learning disability. As a school board member, Henry actively advocates special education services at board meetings. Although Henry is known as an advocate, few people know that his brother has a learning disability.

Jan wanted to do something for her brother, Jeff, who is in an institution. She decided her best advocacy effort would be to join the Association for Retarded Citizens. Now, Jan regularly attends local chapter meetings, volunteers to serve on committees, and assists with chapter events.

Kent loved to play soccer as an adolescent. His brother Chris, who died of muscular dystrophy, never played soccer. Kent is now an adult volunteer for a community recreation program that has made a commitment to including children with disabilities. Every year, he attends the local competition and helps serve refreshments.

In a major lawsuit aimed at improving educational services, Sarah was asked to testify as to her family's needs. Sarah willingly testified, noting the special needs of her brother, Jerome, who has mental retardation, as well as the needs of her family.

Susan is a physician at a large metropolitan hospital. Her brother, Tony, has multiple disabilities. She recently formed and chaired a task force to consider medical ethics involving involuntary euthanasia and newborns with severe disabilities.

Linda serves as a representative payee for her brother's Social Security benefits. She meets Robert weekly to go over his finances and to do his banking. Linda always escorts him to the Social Security office for periodic reviews and to complete new applications. Recently, she helped Robert apply for food stamps.

Sally, a professor of Special Education and a sister to a person with disabilities, organizes special sibling groups at the university to help siblings who have brothers and sisters with disabilities. She organizes positive, upbeat sessions to help other siblings celebrate their unique relationship.

Russ, a professor of Educational Psychology, is the brother of Linda who has Down syndrome. In his classes to teachers-in-training he stresses human similarities, rather than human differences. He teaches his students about concepts like full school inclusion and speaks out against the problems of "tracking" in schools. He makes a commitment to his sister by preparing caring teachers who will respect everyone's right to be a part of school communities.

Advocacy can take on many forms. These examples are just a small sample of the work being done and the various avenues advocates can choose. What unifies these different activities is the desire to help improve the quality of life experienced by siblings with disabilities or by other people with similar problems.

SUMMARY

Adults who are siblings of persons with disabilities face a number of unique concerns and challenges. On the one hand, they have lives of their own, often with responsibilities toward their spouses and their own children; on the other hand, they have a bond with their sibling, which has its own set of responsibilities. As parents age and pass away, the responsibilities toward siblings with disabilities usually increase. The main issue for adult siblings seems to be the delicate balancing act of meeting all of their responsibilities to themselves, their spouse, their children, and to their sibling.

Meeting those special responsibilities leads to a number of concerns, unique to adult siblings. A genetic concern has obvious implications for married couples and future children. Concerns about the long-term care for the brother or sister after parents pass away focus on the responsibilities the sibling may need to assume. Guard-

ianship, conservatorship, and estate planning are all aimed at enabling the person to live as independently and safely as possible while
not placing undue burden or hardship on siblings. Advocacy activities
also help adults contribute to the quality of life of their brothers and
sisters. Adult siblings who are concerned about the welfare of their
sister or brother can help influence services by actively serving as
advocates.

Finally, it is necessary to reassert a sibling bond at various stages
of our lives. Adulthood is a period of uncertainty between siblings.
Most adult siblings establish their own families and friends. During
this period, the sibling bond may be strained, yet it remains ever
present. When one sibling does not or cannot establish a new family
or friends, dependency on other siblings and their families may increase rather than decrease. A clear role for adult siblings is to open
some space in their lives for their brother or sister. In doing so, adult
siblings reassert their sibling bond and provide testimony to the
power of the family.

11

Capstone—
Strategies for
Parents & Siblings

*Siblings can experience an impact in many different ways. To plan
effective interventions for them, you should recognize their variety
of feelings and needs. Addressing siblings' needs is one important
way of enabling the entire family to help the child with
exceptionality grow and develop (p. 58).*
Ann and Rud Turnbull, 1986

Seven adult siblings sat at the table as the audience,
mostly parents and professionals, awaited their guidance. Each sibling came with a different experience. Lori's older sister has Down
syndrome and lives in an institution; Bill's brother had Hunter syndrome and died when Bill was 18; Marion's brother has cystic fibrosis
and is often hospitalized; Jackie's sister has cerebral palsy and is severely retarded; Debbie's brother has a severe learning disability; Nor-
een's brother is deaf due to meningitis; and Dan's brother has autism.
The panel assembled in an effort to share their experiences and their
advice with parents who have children and with the professionals
who work with them.

After panel members introduced themselves and described their
siblings, the moderator posed similar questions to each panelist.

What do you remember most about growing up with a brother or
sister who has a disability?
What were some of the problems you faced while growing up?
When did you learn about your sibling's disability?

Did you experience any fears associated with the disability?
Were there any positive aspects for you or your family?

Although each sibling grew up with a different set of experiences, had
a sibling with a different type of disability, and came from families of a
different size and economic status, the commonality of the responses
was astounding. The siblings' stories about their problems focused on
play and social interactions, their friends, extra family duties and
caregiving responsibilities, and some loss of freedom because, as
most of the siblings noted, their family stayed close to services for the
child with a disability. Not surprisingly, the siblings all presented a
common litany of benefits they feel they received as a result of their
experiences. They stated that they are more understanding of human
problems; that they accept people better; and that they are less judg-
mental and more easygoing. Several said they learned to teach; others
said they developed patience; still others claimed to have learned to
deal effectively with embarrassment. Two of the siblings were human
services professionals, which they said was a result of their sibling
experience. Most of the siblings stated that their family communicates
more effectively. All of the siblings said their family members are
closer, more open, and more honest with each other as a result of
their experiences.

Listening to each sibling elaborate on the positive aspects of life with a brother or sister who has a disability, one could call into question the "scientific" value of this exercise. Were these seven a representative group of all siblings? They were outspoken and willing to talk to strangers. What about those who are not? Indeed, it would be nearly impossible to clearly discern if the benefits these siblings discussed were a direct result of their special sibling experience, but the issue of cause was not the point here. What did matter was that these siblings, when given a chance to talk, spoke primarily about the benefits they received. Their negative experiences, although important, seemed to be outweighed by the positive.

The moderator shifted gears a bit and posed another question: "Why, when we know that some siblings have problems, were your experiences so positive? What made the difference?" Almost in unison and without hesitation, the siblings responded, "My parents." "Well, what did they do? What advice can you give the parents assembled here?" As the siblings responded, the difficult task of parenting children became increasingly apparent. The parents of these seven were hardly *superparents;* they were parents who had extraordinary responsibilities and were able to balance, indeed juggle, responsibility effectively. It was unfortunate that none of the parents of the siblings were in the audience to hear these personal testimonials.

The strategies below are broken into two parts that summarize the suggestions for parents and for siblings themselves as set forth by other experienced siblings. Each strategy has been discussed to some extent in the previous chapters of this volume; here, they are simply clarified and succinctly assembled for use by parents and siblings.

The strategies are not listed in any particular order. Each is as important as the next, although not every strategy will be appropriate for every family. Families should read and consider all of the suggestions, choosing those that best meet individual needs and abilities, and disregarding the rest. Not every parent or sibling can nor should adopt every strategy. Most importantly, we hope parents recognize that we understand some of the parameters of their unique and often difficult mission and have summarized these suggestions only to assist families in re-evaluating their situation. Balancing and juggling emotions and responsibilities can be done most successfully by utilizing strategies based on the parents' knowledge of themselves and their children.

THIRTY STRATEGIES FOR PARENTS

1. *Be open and honest.* Siblings need parents to be available for questions and to provide straight answers to these questions. If par-

ents don't know the answer, they should say so and work together with siblings to find answers to their questions. Welcome
questions from siblings and, if they aren't forthcoming, pose
some of your own questions.

2. *Value each child individually.* It is natural to compare children,
   especially their physical features, strengths, and weaknesses.
   When one child has a disability, the comparison will almost
   always benefit the other children and will lead to problems between and among the children. Talk about each child individually.

3. *Limit caregiving responsibilities.* When one child has a severe disability, the siblings may be recruited to perform a number of
   direct care activities. Older siblings usually help with child-
   rearing, although these activities may be greatly extended when
   one child needs extraordinary care. Sharing these responsibilities or utilizing nonfamily helpers when appropriate may
   help achieve a workable balance. Remember, siblings always
   appreciate recognition for these extra caregiving responsibilities.

4. *Use respite care and other supportive services.* Respite care services
   were designed to help families with the constant and intense
   caregiving needs of children with disabilities (see Salisbury &
   Intagliata, 1986). Respite care can be used to enable parents to
   spend more time with other siblings.

5. *Be fair.* Parents should always attempt to be fair in terms of
   discipline, attention, and resources. The child with a disability
   should be treated as normally as possible. Siblings are quick to
   recognize when parents are acting fairly or unfairly. An important time for parents to be fair is when settling sibling disputes.
   Always taking one child's side over the other is certain to cause
   problems between the children.

6. *Accept the disability.* If parents do not accept their child's disability, it is doubtful if other family members will. When parents
   accept the disability, the family can begin to make plans to deal
   with the problems associated with the disability in a fair and
   constructive manner. When a disability is denied, sibling adjustment will be problematic.

7. *Put together a library of children's books on disabilities.* One of the
   best ways in which parents can share information with their
   children is to provide children's literature for them to read. Local
   libraries typically carry many books on disabilities and sibling
   relationships for all ages of children (see Appendix A).

8. *Schedule special time with the sibling.* Everyone recognizes that
   children with disabilities require extra parental time. As siblings
   mature, they come to realize the necessity of this additional

parental attention. Parents can partially balance this inequity by scheduling special time for the sibling. For example, one father set aside Thursday evenings from 7:00–8:00 P.M. to build models with his sons. One couple took turns taking their daughter to the movies. Scheduling special times helps to reassert how important the siblings are to their parents.

9. *Let siblings settle their own differences.* Fighting between siblings is natural and, in many cases, healthy. It helps the siblings get to know each other and helps them work out the rules of cooperative relationships. Always interrupting fights will deny siblings the opportunity to solve their own problems. (Of course, parents should never let siblings hurt one another.)

10. *Welcome other children and friends into the home.* The siblings' relationships with others outside of the family are a universal concern. Parents can minimize potential problems by providing a home that welcomes other children and friends. This sharing provides a powerful model of accepting a child's disability and reasserts the family's willingness to fully participate in community life.

11. *Praise siblings.* All children need parental praise. Siblings should receive acknowledgment and be encouraged when parents notice that they have sacrificed, been patient, or been particularly helpful. Parents should be liberal with their praise; it is a commodity that cannot be exhausted and is always valued. Parental praise will help the siblings develop a positive self-image.

12. *Recognize that you are the most important, most powerful teacher of your children.* Siblings typically follow the lead set forth by their parents. They model parental behavior. Parents need to recognize the power of their informal lessons and provide an example in terms of their interactions with the child. Likewise, they should provide an example in terms of their acceptance and involvement with people.

13. *Recognize the uniqueness of your family.* Feeling good about your family and your children implies that comparisons to other families and other children are made infrequently. Other families and other children usually have a full range of problems that stay hidden from public scrutiny. If parents continually compare their family to the public image of other families, the children are being taught to set up unrealistic goals.

14. *Listen to siblings.* Siblings will know the child with a disability in a way different from their parents. Theirs is a unique relationship. As siblings mature, they will have observations, comments, and suggestions about the child. Their statements and concerns should fall on attentive ears. Active listening also im-

plies that parents attend to unspoken messages and behaviors.

Asking the sibling to talk, or in other ways prompting communication between parents and siblings, will let the siblings know that their thoughts and suggestions are valued.

15. *Involve the siblings.* As siblings mature, they may wish to become actively involved in decisions regarding their brother or sister with a disability. Parents can involve siblings by:

   a. Inviting them to attend school meetings (e.g., IEP meetings)
   b. Discussing future plans with them
   c. Soliciting their ideas on treatment and service needs
   d. Having them visit with professionals working with the child
   e. Helping them develop competencies to teach the child new skills
   f. Providing opportunities to advocate for the child

16. *Require the child with a disability to do as much for himself or herself as possible.* When the child performs life skills independently, it limits dependency on siblings. Setting the stage for ultimate independence starts with parental expectations that children do as many activities for themselves as is feasible. These expectations clearly communicate that parents recognize the limits of the siblings' responsibilities and provide a foundation for the characteristics of the future relationship between the siblings.

17. *Recognize each child's unique qualities and family contribution.* As often as possible, remind each child of his or her positive qualities and contributions to other family members. Siblings, like the rest of us, cannot hear this too much.

18. *Help establish special sibling programs.* Through their contact with other parents and professionals, parents are best able to facilitate the establishment of sibling support groups. These support groups, organized by age levels, can help siblings share their feelings and concerns with others in similar situations. Parents should recognize the advantages of siblings talking with one another and lend their support to efforts that provide such opportunities. Encouraging a parent organization or school to start a "sibling day" or "sibling workshop" will help siblings receive some of the information they need.

19. *Recognize special stress times for siblings and plan to minimize negative effects.* Like parents, siblings experience greater levels of stress at different times. From what we know, it seems that sibling stress may be greatest when:

   a. Another child is born
   b. The child goes to school
   c. The sibling starts to date
   d. Friends reject the child

    e.   Friends ask questions about the child

    f.   The child becomes critically ill

    g.   Problems related to the child are handled in secrecy

    h.   Parents die

    i.   Siblings marry

       These tend to be more stressful times, often because of a lack of information and/or communication between the parents and siblings. The stress can be minimized through recognition of potential problems and frank, open discussion about the problems and possible solutions. Siblings may not always recognize why they feel more angry, resentful, frightened, sad, or lonely. Parents can help by opening the door for discussions and mutual problem solving.

20.   *Use professionals to help siblings.*   Sometimes, siblings need some special attention from teachers, social workers, counselors, and psychologists. If the parent feels that such service is needed, it should be provided in as vigorous a manner as services for the child who has a disability. Luckily, these times are rare because most siblings never need professional help; however, when problems arise, service for the sibling should be sought promptly.

21.   *Teach the siblings to interact.*   Many siblings need help in learning how to socially interact with their brother or sister who has a disability. Parents should provide recreational activities and materials that their children can enjoy and use together. Parents can teach social interaction by modeling appropriate behavior through their own interactions, as well as by more formal teaching activities (see Chapter 8). Always reward the siblings when they interact with each other. Siblings typically exert much energy and patience when interacting with a brother or sister, and their efforts should not go unnoticed. Occasionally, parents note that siblings are more capable than they are in eliciting positive behaviors from the child who has a disability.

22.   *Provide opportunities for a normal family life and normal family activities.*   Problems with siblings tend to develop when all of the family's energy and resources are focused on providing care to the child with the disability. In these situations, siblings are denied normal opportunities for personal growth and experience. No outsider can ever determine what comprises "normal" family activities. Each family values a different set of experiences. However, if the family wants to participate in some activities but cannot due to the demands of a child with a disability, extra effort should be taken to ensure that the family does not have to forgo such activities. This extra effort may mean

buying a larger car, adding a special room to the house, modifying traditional activities, or seeking respite services.

Siblings should participate in community activities, like scouting, 4-H, sports, clubs, and hobby groups, with their parents' encouragement and as much parental participation as possible. Families should have fun together. They should take vacations, pursue special projects, and spend time together. When a child's disability precludes these activities, respite care, and other supportive social services are in order. Respite care may, in fact, benefit the siblings more directly than the parents. Allowing normal family activities to occur, in spite of a disability, will help to strengthen the family unit.

23. *Don't expect siblings to be saints.*   Sometimes parents expect too much from their children who do not have disabilities. Sometimes parents expect these children to excel and to grow up before their time. Like all people, siblings will occasionally lose their patience, understanding, and compassion. They will become angry at their brother or sister and may even reject him or her. Healthy relationships imply a full range of emotions. Siblings who are always patient and kind are rather rare. Not expecting siblings to be saints allows them to be real, honest people. This means they will fight, argue, compete, laugh, share secrets, and play together as they grow together. The boundaries of typical sibling feelings are rather broad. We cannot expect siblings to behave in extraordinary ways within a narrow definition of acceptable sibling behavior.

24. *Provide understandable answers and repeat them as often as requested.* Siblings, like all people, understand information differently at different times. Parents need to explain disabilities and the ramifications using language and terms understood by the sibling. Most likely the information will need to be shared many times before it is fully understood. Patience!

25. *Ask.*   So many siblings have told us that if only their parents had asked, "Would it be OK if your brother came along?" or "Would it be OK if you stayed with your sister while I make a run to the store?" or "Would it be OK if John sat next to you at the movies?" More often than not, the answer will be yes, but the act of asking reasserts the parents' understanding of the siblings' concerns and needs. Naturally if they say, "no," then other plans will need to be made. Ask first and respect the answer.

26. *Let them know that they come first sometimes.*   Occasionally, it is important to let your other children know that they come first. It

is advisable to let your child with the disability know that they will have to wait while you attend to their brother or sister.

27. *Let siblings teach you what it is like.* Let your children know that they are having experiences that you did not. Let them know that you want to understand what it is like to have a brother or sister with a disability.

28. *Give siblings a set of strategies.* Some siblings have found it helpful to have a list of actions that they can use to help them with their unique situation. (We have included a list of 20 strategies, generated by siblings which follows this list. Use the list to create your own set of strategies to share.)

29. *Talk about the future with them.* The future plans for the individual with a disability should not be a mystery. Siblings and, most importantly, the person with the disability should be actively engaged in discussing future plans including knowledge of wills, trusts, and guardianship.

30. *Don't forget to laugh.* We know several families who have a family laughter book where they write down the funny moments of their life together. These laughter memories come out, especially during stressful times or when the family is just feeling low. Soon one hears, "Remember when . . . .?" or "I was never so embarrassed as when . . . now I can really laugh about it!" These laughter memories help to keep the balance for all family members and communicate a powerful message.

So what can siblings do to contribute more fully to their family and in turn help themselves? Over the past 15 years we have asked that question of hundreds of siblings young and old. We have been fortunate that they have taught us so much. Here are some ideas that siblings may find helpful.

TWENTY STRATEGIES FOR SIBLINGS

1. Talk to others, especially parents, teachers, and other siblings, about your feelings and concerns.

2. Read about your brother's or sister's disability. The knowledge you receive will empower you.

3. Learn from other siblings who have had similar experiences. Sometimes it is easier to follow the lead of others with more experience.

4. Join sibling groups and attend special sessions for siblings.

5. Be willing to teach your parents what it is like to grow up with a brother or sister who has a disability. Remember that most parents have never experienced what you are experiencing.

6. Recognize that your brothers or sisters with disabilities are more like other siblings than they are different. All brothers and sisters embarrass us and make us angry or sad at times.

7. Know that it is okay to have mixed feelings toward your brother or sister. Having these feelings makes you human.

8. Be proud that your special family experience provides you with many opportunities for growth and maturity.

9. Don't be afraid to ask for help when you need it.

10. Teach your friends and others. Remember that many people naturally have questions about people with disabilities and want to learn how they can help. By watching you and your interactions with your brother or sister, they will learn.

11. Be an advocate for people with disabilities. Let others know that your brother or a sister is first and foremost, a *person*, who just happens to have a disability.

12. If your friends tease a person with a disability or say something thoughtless, don't join in; it will only make you feel guilty later.

13. Be kind to your parents. Even though they may make mistakes, know that they love you and that they want the best for you and all their children.

14. Remember that you are not alone.

15. Keep your sense of humor. Look at the bright side. As in all families, funny things happen. Take time to laugh, smile often, and be happy.

16. Keep a positive outlook. While it may be easier to make a list of someone's shortcomings, everyone has strengths. Keep a balanced perspective by reminding yourself and your friends about your brother's or sister's good points.

17. When you get older, seek genetic counseling. It cannot hurt and it will usually help you feel more at ease.

18. Remember that your brother or sister, like you, needs to make his or her own way in the world. And, just like you, it is comforting to have a brother or sister whom you can count on when you need them.

19. Your brother or sister needs you to be the best sibling you can be. That means getting to know yourself, getting in touch with your feelings, and developing your abilities.

20. Get involved in some way. Your involvement does not need to be extensive or exciting; small acts will make the world a better place for people with disabilities and their families.

Good luck!

References

Abramovitch, R., Corter, C., & Lando, B. (1979). Sibling interaction in the home. *Child Development, 50,* 997–1003.

Abramovitch, R., Corter, C., & Pepler, D. J. (1980). Observations of mixed sex sibling dyads. *Child Development, 51,* 1268–1271.

Abramovitch, R., Corter, C., Pepler, D. J., & Stanhope, L. (1986). Sibling and peer interaction: A final follow-up and comparison. *Child Development, 57,* 217–229.

Abramovitch, R., Pepler, D. J., & Corter, C. (1982). Patterns of sibling interaction among preschool-age children. In M. E. Lamb & B. Sutton-Smith (Eds.), *Sibling relationships* (pp. 61–68). Hillsdale, NJ: Lawrence Erlbaum Associates.

Abramovitch, R., Stanhope, L., Pepler, D. J., & Corter, C. (1987). The influence of Down's syndrome on sibling interaction. *Journal of Child Psychology and Psychiatry, 28,* 865–879.

Aldous, J., Klaus, E., & Klein, D. M. (1985). The understanding heart: Aging parents and their favorite children. *Child Development, 56,* 303–316.

Allen, K. E., Hart, B. M., Buell, J. S., Harris, F. R., & Wolf, M. M. (1964). Effects of social reinforcement on isolate behavior of a nursery school child. *Child Development, 35,* 511–518.

American Association on Mental Deficiency. (1975). *Guardianship for mentally retarded persons.* Washington, DC: Author.

Anderson, K., & Milliren, A. (1983). *Structured experiences for integration of handicapped children.* Rockville, MD: Aspen Publications.

Apolloni, T. (1989). Guardianship, trusts and protective services. In G. Singer & L. Irvin (Eds.), *Support for caregiving families: Enabling positive adaptation to disability* (pp. 283–296). Baltimore: Paul H. Brookes Publishing Co.

Apolloni, T., & Cooke, T. P. (1975). Peer behavior conceptualized as a variable influencing infant and toddler development. *American Journal of Orthopsychiatry, 45,* 4–17.

Apolloni, T., & Cooke, T. P. (Eds.). (1984). *A new look at guardianship: Protective services that support personalized living.* Baltimore: Paul H. Brookes Publishing Co.

Ausubel, D. P. (1958). *Theory and problems of child development.* New York: Grune & Stratton.

Baer, D. M. (1981). *How to plan for generalization.* Lawrence, KS: H & H Enterprises.

Baker, B., & Brightman, A. (1989). *Steps to independence: A skills training guide for parents and teachers of children with special needs* (2nd ed.). Baltimore: Paul H. Brookes Publishing Co.

Bank, S., & Kahn, M. D. (1982a). *The sibling bond.* New York: Basic Books.

Bank, S., & Kahn, M. D. (1982b). Intense sibling loyalties. In M. E. Lamb & B. Sutton-Smith (Eds.), *Sibling relationships* (pp. 251–266). Hillsdale, NJ: Lawrence Erlbaum Associates.

Barton, M. E., & Tomasello, M. (1991). Joint attention and conversation in mother–infant–sibling triads. *Child Development, 62,* 517–529.

Batshaw, M. L., & Perret, Y. M. (1992). *Children with disabilities: A medical primer* (3rd ed.). Baltimore: Paul H. Brookes Publishing Co.

Battle, C. U. (1974). Disruptions in the socialization of a young severely handicapped child. *Rehabilitation Literature, 35,* 130–140.

Becker, W. (1971) *Parents are teachers.* Champaign, IL: Research Press.

Beckman, P. J. (1983). The influence of selected child characteristics on stress in families of handicapped infants. *American Journal of Mental Deficiency, 88,* 150–156.

Beckman, P. J., & Bristol, M. M. (1991). Issues in developing the IFSP: A framework for establishing family outcomes. *Topics in Early Childhood Special Education, 11*(3), 19–31.

Beckman-Bell, P. (1980). *Characteristics of handicapped infants: A study of the relationship between child characteristics and stress as reported by mothers.* Unpublished doctoral dissertation, University of North Carolina–Chapel Hill.

Begun, A. (1989). Sibling relationships involving disabled people. *American Journal on Mental Deficiency, 93,* 566–574.

Bell, R. (1968). A reinterpretation of the direction of effects in studies of socialization. *Psychological Review, 75,* 81–95.

Belmont, L., & Marolla, F. A. (1973). Birth order, family size and intelligence. *Science, 182,* 1096–1101.

Belmont, L., Stein, Z. A., & Zybert, P. (1978). Child spacing and birth order: Effect on intellectual ability in two child families. *Science, 202,* 995–996.

Bennett, C. W. (1973). A four-and-a-half year old as a teacher of her hearing impaired sister: A case study. *Journal of Communication Disorders, 6,* 67–75.

Benson, G. (1982, November). *Siblings: Research and implications for family programming.* Paper presented at the 9th annual meeting of The Association for the Severely Handicapped, Denver.

Bigner, J. A. (1974). A Wernerian developmental analysis of children's descriptions of siblings. *Child Development, 45,* 317–323.

Binger, C. (1973). Childhood leukemia: Emotional impact on siblings. In J. Anthony & C. Koupernik (Eds.), *The child in his family.* New York: Wiley.

Bodenheimer, C. (1979). For the sake of others. *Journal of Autism and Developmental Disorders, 9*(3), 291–293.

Borders, K., Borders, S., Borders, L., Watts, D., & Watts, D. (1982). Our sibling group. *Sibling Information Network Newsletter, 1*(4), 2.

Bossard, J., & Boll, E. S. (1960). *The sociology of child development.* New York: Harper & Brothers.

Boyd, R. (1980). Systematic parent training through a home based model. *Exceptional Children, 45,* 647–650.

Brammer, L. M. (1973). *The helping relationship: Process and skills.* Englewood Cliffs, NJ: Prentice Hall.

Brammer, L. (1977). Who can be a helper? *Personnel and Guidance Journal, 55,* 303–308.

Brammer, L., & Shostrom, E. (1982). *Therapeutic psychology: Fundamentals of counseling and psychotherapy.* Englewood Cliffs, NJ: Prentice Hall.

Breslau, N. (1982). Siblings of disabled children: Birth order and age spacing effects. *Journal of Abnormal Child Psychology, 10,* 85–96.

Breslau, N., Weitzman, M., & Messenger, K. (1981). Psychological functioning of siblings of disabled children. *Pedatrics, 67,* 344–353.

Brim, O. J. (1958). Family structure and sex role learning by children: A further analysis of Helen Koch's data. *Sociometry, 21,* 1–16.

Brinker, R. P. (1984). *Executive summary.* Division of Education Policy Research and Services. Educational Testing Service, Princeton, NJ.

Bristol, M. M. (1979). *Maternal coping with autistic children: Adequacy of interpersonal support and effect of child's characteristics.* Unpublished doctoral dissertation, University of North Carolina–Chapel Hill.

Bristol, M. M., Reichle, N. C., & Thomas, D. D. (1987). Changing demographics of the American family: Implications for single parent families of young handicapped children. *Journal of the Division for Early Childhood, 12*(1), 56–69.

Brody, G. H., & Stoneman, Z. (1986). Contextual issues in the study of sibling socialization. In J. J. Gallagher & P. M. Vietze (Eds.), *Families of handicapped persons: Research, programs, and policy issues* (pp. 197–217). Baltimore: Paul H. Brookes Publishing Co.

Brody, G. H., Stoneman, Z., & Burke, M. (1987). Child temperaments, maternal differential behavior and sibling relationships. *Developmental Psychology, 23,* 354–362.

Brody, G. H., Stoneman, Z., & Burke, M. (1988). Child temperament and parental perceptions of individual child adjustment: An intrafamilial analysis. *American Journal of Orthopsychiatry, 58*(4), 532–542.

Brody, G. H., Stoneman, Z., & MacKinnon, C. E. (1982). Role asymmetries in interactions between school aged children, their younger siblings and their friends. *Child Development, 53,* 1364–1370.

Brody, G. H., Stoneman, Z., & MacKinnon, C. E. (1986). Contributions of maternal child-rearing practices and play contexts to sibling interactions. *Journal of Applied Developmental Psychology, 7,* 225–236.

Brody, G. H., Stoneman, Z., MacKinnon, C. E., & MacKinnon, R. (1985). Role relationships and behavior between preschool-aged and school-aged sibling pairs. *Developmental Psychology, 21*(1), 124–129.

Bronfenbrenner, U. (1977). Toward an experimental ecology of human development. *American Psychologist, 32,* 513–531.

Bryant, B. K. (1982). Sibling relationships in middle childhood. In M. E. Lamb & B. Sutton-Smith (Eds.), *Sibling relationships* (pp. 87–122). Hillsdale, NJ: Lawrence Erlbaum Associates.

Bryant, B., & Crockenberg, S. (1980). Correlations and dimensions of prosocial behavior: A study of female siblings and their mothers. *Child Development, 51,* 354–362.

Buell, J., Stoddard, P., Harris, F. R., & Baer, D. M. (1968). Collateral social development accompanying reinforcement of outdoor play in a preschool child. *Journal of Applied Behavior Analysis, 1,* 167–174.

Buhrmester, D., & Furman, W. (1990). Perceptions of sibling relationships during middle childhood and adolescence. *Child Development, 61,* 1387–1398.

Burbach, D. J., & Peterson, L. (1986). Children's concepts of physical illness: A review and critique of the cognitive-developmental literature. *Health Psychology, 5,* 307–325.

Burton, L. (1975). *The family of sick children*. London, England: Routledge, Kehan Paul.

Burton, S. (1991). *Kidpower*. Moscow: University of Idaho, Idaho Center on Developmental Disabilities.

Burton, S. L., & Parks, A. L. (1991). *The self-esteem, locus of control, and career aspirations of college-aged siblings of individuals with disability*. Moscow: Idaho Center on Developmental Disabilities, The University of Idaho.

Byrnes, C., & Love, M. (1983). Sibling day workshops: A holistic approach. *Sibling Information Network Newsletter, 2*(1), 4.

Caldwell, B. M., & Guze, S. B. (1960). A study of the adjustment of parents and siblings of institutionalized and noninstitutionalized retarded children. *American Journal of Mental Deficiency, 64*, 845–861.

Cash, W. M., & Evans, I. N. (1975). Training preschool children to modify their retarded siblings' behavior. *Journal of Behavior Therapy and Experimental Psychiatry, 6*, 13–16.

Cerreto, M., & Miller, N. B. (1981). *Siblings of handicapped children: A review of the literature*. Unpublished paper, University of California–Los Angeles.

Chintz, S. P. (1981). A sibling group for brothers and sisters of handicapped children. *Children Today*, 21–23.

Cicirelli, V. G. (1972). The effect of sibling relationships on concept learning of young children taught by child teachers. *Child Development, 43*, 282–287.

Cicirelli, V. G. (1976a). Mother–child and sibling–sibling interactions on a problem solving task. *Child Development, 47*, 588–596.

Cicirelli, V. G. (1976b). Siblings teaching siblings. In V. L. Allen (Ed.), *Children as teachers*. New York: Academic Press.

Cicirelli, V. G. (1982). Sibling influence throughout the lifespan. In M.E. Lamb & B. Sutton-Smith (Eds.), *Sibling relationships* (pp. 267–284). Hillsdale, NJ: Lawrence Erlbaum Associates.

Clark, H. B., Greene, B. F., Macrae, J. N., McNees, N. P., Davis, J. L., & Risley, T. R. (1977). A parent advice package for family shopping trips: Development and evaluation. *Journal of Applied Behavior Analysis, 10*, 605–624.

Clements, J. E., & Alexander, R. N. (1975). Parent training: Bringing it all back home. *Focus on Exceptional Children, 7*(5), 1–12.

Cleveland, D., & Miller, N. (1977). Attitudes and life commitments of older siblings of mentally retarded adults: An exploratory study. *Mental Retardation, 15*, 38–41.

Cohen, B. (1985). Good news genetic counseling. *Sibling Information Network Newsletter, 4*(1), 1.

Colletti, G., & Harris, S. L. (1977). Behavior modification in the home: Siblings as behavior modifiers, parents as observers. *Journal of Abnormal Child Psychology, 5*(1), 21–30.

Connor, J. M. (1989). Genetic aspects of prenatal diagnosis. *Journal of Inherited Metabolic Disease, 12*, 89–96.

Conway, A. (1986). A sibling living with schizophrenia: Some personal reflections. *Sibling Information Network Newsletter, 4*(4), 4–5.

Correa, V. I., Silberman, R. K., & Trusty, S. (1986). Siblings of disabled children: A literature review. *Education of the Visually Handicapped, 18*(1), 5–13.

Corter, C., Abramovitch, R., & Pepler, D. J. (1983). The role of the mother in sibling interaction. *Child Development, 54*, 1599–1605.

Cowan, E. L., Pederson, A., Babigan, H., Izzo, L. D., & Trost, M. A. (1973). Long term follow-up of early detected vulnerable children. *Journal of Consulting and Clinical Psychology, 41*, 438–446.

Crnic, K. A., & LeConte, J. (1986). Understanding sibling needs and influences. In R. Fewell & P. Vadasy (Eds.), *Families of handicapped children: Needs and supports across the life span* (pp. 75–98). Austin, Texas: PRO-ED.

Crocker, A. C. (1983). Sisters and brothers. In J. A. Mulick & S. M. Pueschel (Eds.), *Parent-professional partnerships in developmental disability services.* Cambridge, MA: Ware Press.

Daniels, D., Dunn, J., Furstenberg, F. F., Jr., & Plomin, R. (1985). Environmental differences within the family and adjustment differences within pairs of adolescent siblings. *Child Development, 56,* 764–774.

Daniels, D., & Plomin, R. (1985). Differential experience of siblings in the same family. *Developmental Psychology, 21,* 747–760.

Davis, D., Cahan, S., & Bashi, J. (1977). Birth order and intellectual development: The confluence model in the light of cross-cultural evidence. *Science, 196,* 1470–1472.

Day, R., Lindeman, D., Powell, T., Fox, J. J., Stowitscheck, J., & Shores, R. (1984). The investigation of an empirically derived teaching package for socially withdrawn handicapped children and non-handicapped children. *Teacher Education and Special Education, 7*(1), 46–55.

Day, R., Powell, T., & Stowitschek, J. (1981). *Social competence intervention package for preschool youngsters* (SCIPPY). Logan: Exceptional Child Center, Utah State University.

DeMyer, M. K. (1979). Comments on siblings of autistic children. *Journal of Autism and Developmental Disorders, 9*(3), 296–298.

DeRisi, W. J., & Butz, G. (1975). *Writing behavioral contracts.* Champaign, IL: Research Press.

Dunn, J. (1983). Sibling relationships in early childhood. *Child Development, 54,* 787–811.

Dunn, J. (1985). *Sisters and brothers.* Cambridge, MA: Harvard University Press.

Dunn, J., & Kendrick, C. (1979). Interaction between young siblings in the context of family relationships. In M. Lewis & L. Rosenblum (Eds.), *The child and its family.* New York: Plenum.

Dunn, J., & Kendrick, C. (1980). The arrival of a sibling: Changes in patterns of interaction between mother and first born child. *Journal of Child Psychology and Psychiatry and Allied Disciplines, 21*(2), 119–132.

Dunn, J., & Kendrick, C. (1982). *Siblings.* Cambridge: Harvard University Press.

Dunn, J., & Plomin, R. (1990). *Separate lives: Why siblings are so different.* New York: Basic Books.

Dunn, J. F., Plomin, R., & Daniels, D. (1986). Consistency and change in mothers' behavior toward younger siblings. *Child Development, 57,* 348–356.

Dunn, J., & Shatz, M. (1989). Becoming a conversationalist despite (or because of) having an older sibling. *Child Development, 60,* 399–410.

Dunn, J., & Stocker, C. (1989). The significance of differences in siblings' experiences within the family. In K. Kreppner & R. Lerner (Eds.), *Family systems and life span development* (pp. 289–301). Hillsdale, NJ: Lawrence Erlbaum Associates.

Dunn, J., Stocker, C., & Plomin, R. (1990). Nonshared experiences within the family: Correlates of behavioral problems in middle childhood. *Development and Psychopathology, 2,* 113–126.

Dyson, L. L. (1989). Adjustment of siblings of handicapped children: A comparison. *Journal of Pediatric Psychology, 14,* 215–229.

Dyson, L., Edgar, E., & Crnic, K. (1989). Psychological predictors of adjustment by siblings of developmentally disabled children. *American Journal on Mental Retardation, 94*(3), 292–302.

Dyson, L., & Fewell, R. R. (1989). The self-concept of siblings of handicapped children: A comparison. *Journal of Early Intervention, 13,*(3), 230–238.

Egan, G. (1975). *The skilled helper.* Monterey, CA: Brooks/Cole.

Ellifritt, J. (1984). Life with my sister. *Exceptional Parent, 8*(14), 16–21.

Evrard, J. R., & Scola, P. S. (1990). Preparation for parenthood. In S. M. Pueschel & J. A. Mulick (Eds.), *Prevention of developmental disabilities* (pp. 27–36). Baltimore: Paul H. Brookes Publishing Co.

Faber, A., & Mazlish, E. (1988). *Siblings without rivalry.* New York: Avon.

Fairfield, B. (1983). Workshops for siblings and parents. *Sibling Information Network Newsletter, 2*(2), 5.

Falbo, T. (1982). Only children in America. In M. E. Lamb & B. Sutton-Smith (Eds.), *Sibling relationships* (pp. 285–304). Hillsdale, NJ: Lawrence Erlbaum Associates.

Farber, B. (1959). Effects of a severely mentally retarded child on family integration. *Monographs of the Society for Research in Child Development, 24,* (2, Serial No. 71).

Farber, B. (1960). Effects of a severely mentally retarded child on family integration. *Monographs of the Society for Research in Child Development, 21*(1, Serial No. 75).

Farber, B. (1964). *Family: Organization and interaction.* San Francisco: Chandler.

Farber, B. (1968). *Mental retardation: Its social context and social consequences.* Boston: Houghton Mifflin.

Farber, B., & Jenné, W. C. (1963). Interaction with retarded siblings and life goals of children. *Marriage and Family Living, 25,* 96–98.

Farber, B., & Rychman, D. (1965). Effects of severely mentally retarded children on family relationships. *Mental Retardation Abstracts, 2,* 1–17.

Featherstone, H. (1980). *A difference in the family: Living with a disabled child.* New York: Basic Books.

Fee, R. W. (1990, Fall). The life planning approach. *New Ways,* 18–19.

Feigon, J. (1981). A sibling group program. *Sibling Information Network Newsletter, 1*(2), 2.

Ferrari, M. (1984). Chronic illness: Psychosocial effects on siblings—I. Chronically ill boys. *Journal of Child Psychology and Psychiatry, 25,* 459–476.

Fewell, R. R. (1986). A handicapped child in the family. In R. R. Fewell & P. F. Vadasy (Eds.), *Families of handicapped children: Needs and supports across the life span* (pp. 3–34). Austin, TX: PRO-ED.

Fewell, R. R., & Vadasy, P. F. (1986). *Families of handicapped children: Needs and supports across the lifespan.* Austin, TX: PRO-ED.

Fischer, J., & Roberts, S. (1983). The effect of the mentally retarded child on his siblings. *Education, 103,* 399–401.

Fotheringham, J., & Creal, D. (1974). Handicapped children and handicapped families. *International Review of Education, 20,* 355–373.

Fowle, C. M. (1968). The effect of the severely mentally retarded child on his family. *American Journal of Mental Deficiency, 73,* 468–473.

Frank, R. A. (1988). Building self-esteem in persons with Down syndrome. In S. M. Pueschel (Ed.), *The young person with Down syndrome* (pp. 205–213). Baltimore: Paul H. Brookes Publishing Co.

Freeman, K. (1984). Twinning it: How to survive. *Sibling Information Network Newsletter, 2*(4), 3.

Furman, W., & Buhrmester, D. (1985). Children's perceptions of the qualities of sibling relationships. *Child Development, 56,* 448–461.

Gallagher, P. A., & Powell, T. H. (1989). Brothers and sisters: Meeting special needs. *Topics in Early Childhood Special Education, 8*(4), 24–37.

Gamble, W. G., & McHale, S. M. (1989). Coping with stress in sibling relationships: A comparison of children with disabled and nondisabled siblings. *Journal of Applied Developmental Psychology, 10*, 353–373.

Gath, A. (1974). Sibling reactions to mental handicap: A comparison of the brothers and sisters of mongol children. *Journal of Child Psychology and Psychiatry, 15*, 187–198.

Gath, A., & Gumley, D. (1987). Retarded children and their siblings. *Journal of Child Psychology and Psychiatry, 28*, 715–730.

Gazda, G. (1978). *Group counseling: A developmental approach.* Boston: Allyn & Bacon.

George, R. L., & Christiani, T. S. (1981). *Theory, methods and processes of counseling and psychotherapy.* Englewood Cliffs, NJ: Prentice Hall, Inc.

Graliker, B. V., Fishler, K., & Koch, R. (1962). Teenage reaction to a mentally retarded sibling. *American Journal of Mental Deficiency, 66*, 838–843.

Green, D., Budd, K., Johnson, M., Lang, S., Pinkston, E., & Rudd, S. (1976). Training parents to modify problem behaviors. In E. J. Marsh & L. C. Hammerlynck (Eds.), *Behavior modification approaches to parenting.* New York: Brunner/Mazel.

Grossman, F. K. (1972). *Brothers and sisters of retarded children: An exploratory study.* Syracuse, NY: Syracuse University Press.

Guralnick, M. J. (1976). The value of integrating handicapped and nonhandicapped preschool children. *American Journal of Orthopsychiatry, 46*, 236–245.

Guralnick, M. J. (Ed.). (1978). *Early intervention and the integration of handicapped and nonhandicapped children.* Baltimore: University Park Press.

Hannah, M. E., & Midlarsky, E. (1985). Siblings of the handicapped: A literature review for school psychologists. *School Psychology Review, 14*, 510–520.

Harris, I. D. (1964). *The promised seed: A comparative study of eminent first and later sons.* Glencoe, IL: Free Press.

Harris, V., & McHale, S. M. (1989). Family life problems, daily caregiving activities, and the psychological well-being of mothers of mentally retarded children. *American Journal on Mental Retardation, 94*, 231–239.

Hartup, W. W. (1978). Peer interaction and the process of socialization. In M. J. Guralnick (Ed.), *Early intervention and the integration of handicapped and nonhandicapped children.* Baltimore: University Park Press.

Hartup, W. W. (1979, March 15). *Current issues in social development.* Paper presented at the biennial meeting of the Society for Research in Child Development, San Francisco. (ERIC Reproduction Service No. ED 168 709).

Hayden, V. (1974). The other children. *The Exceptional Parent, 4*, 26–29.

Heifetz, L. J. (1977). Behavioral training for parents of retarded children: Alternative formats based on instructional manuals. *American Journal of Mental Deficiency, 82*, 194–203.

Helsels, E. (1985). The Helsels' story of Robin. In A. P. Turnbull & H. R. Turnbull (Eds.), *Parents speak out: Then and now* (pp. 94–115). Columbus, OH: Charles E. Merrill.

Hendrickson, J. M., Strain, P., Tremblay, A., & Shores, R. E. (1981). Relationship between toy and material use and the occurrence of social interactive behaviors by normally developing children. *Psychology in the Schools, 18*, 500–504.

Hoffman, M. (1970). Moral development. In P. Mussen (Ed.), *Carmichael's manual of child psychology* (Vol. 2). New York: John Wiley & Sons.

Holt, K. (1958). The home care of severely retarded children. *Pediatrics, 22*(4), 744–755.

Homme, L. (1970). *How to use contingency contracting in the classroom.* Champaign, IL: Research Press.

Itzkowitz, J. S. (1989). *The needs and concerns of brothers and sisters of individuals with disabilities.* Unpublished doctoral dissertation, The University of Connecticut.

Jacobs, B. S., & Moss, H. A. (1976). Birth order and sex of sibling as determinants of mother–infant interaction. *Child Development, 47,* 315–322.

James, S. D., & Egle, A. L. (1986). A direct prompting strategy for increasing reciprocal interactions between handicapped and non-handicapped siblings. *Journal of Applied Behavior Analysis, 19,* 173–186.

Jiao, S., Ji, G., & Jing, C. C. (1986). Comparative study of behavioral qualities of only children and sibling children. *Child Development, 57,* 357–361.

Johnson, C. A., & Katz, R. G. (1973). Using parents as change agents for their children: A review. *Journal of Child Psychology and Psychiatry and Allied Disciplines, 14,* 181–200.

Jones, C. P., & Adamson, L. B. (1987). Language use in mother–child and mother–child–sibling interactions. *Child Development, 58,* 356–366.

Jones, L. T. (1983). A suggestion for siblings. *Down's Syndrome News, 7*(9), 121.

Kaiser, A. P., & Fox, J. J. (1986). Behavioral parent training research: Contributions to an ecological analysis of families of handicapped children. In J. J. Gallagher & P. M. Vietze (Eds.), *Families of handicapped persons: Research, programs, and policy issues* (pp. 219–235). Baltimore: Paul H. Brookes Publishing Co.

Kaplan, B. J., & McHale, F. J. (1980). Communication and play behaviors of a deaf preschooler and his younger brother. *Volta Review, 82,* 476–482.

Kaplan, F. (1969). Siblings of the retarded. In S. B. Savason & J. Doris, *Psychological problems in mental deficiency* (4th ed.). New York: Harper & Row.

Kaplan, F., & Colombatto, J. (1966). Headstart program for siblings of mentally retarded children. *Mental Retardation, 4*(6), 30–32.

Kelly, A. (1982). Always been one of us. *Sibling Information Network Newsletter, 1*(5), 3.

Kirk, S. A., & Bateman, B. D. (1964). *Ten years of research at the Institute for Research on Exceptional Children,* Urbana: University of Illinois.

Kirkman, M. (1986, September). *Sibling relationships with and without a disabled child in the family.* Keynote address to NY Conference on Siblings of Mentally Retarded and Developmentally Disabled Persons, New York City.

Klein, S. D. (1972). Brother to sister/Sister to brother. *The Exceptional Parent, 2*(1), 10–16; 2(2), 24–27; 2(3), 24–28.

Knapczyk, D. R. (1989). Peer-mediated training of cooperative play between special and regular class students in integrated play settings. *Education and Training in Mental Retardation, 24,*(3), 255–264.

Koch, H. L. (1955). Some personality correlates of sex of sibling position and sex of sibling among five- and six-year-old children. *Genetic Psychology Monographs, 52,* 3–50.

Koch, H. L. (1960). The relation of certain formal attributes of siblings to attitudes held toward each other and toward their parents. *Monographs of the Society for Research in Child Development, 25* (4, Serial No. 78).

Kohl, F., & Beckman, P. (1990). The effects of directed play on the frequency and length of reciprocal interactions with preschoolers having moderate handicaps. *Education and Training in Mental Retardation, 25*(3), 258–266.

Kohn, M., & Rosman, B. L. (1972). Relationship of preschool social–emotional functioning to later intellectual achievement. *Developmental Psychology, 6,* 445–452.

Kolin, K., Scherzer, A., New, B., & Garfield, M. (1971). Studies of the school-age child with myelomeningocele: Social and emotional adaptation. *Pediatrics, 78,* 1013–1019.

Kolodny, E. H., Abuelo, D. N., Barsel-Bowers, G., & Pueschel, S. M. (1990). Preconceptual genetic screening and counseling. In S. M. Pueschel & J. A. Mulick (Eds.), *Prevention of developmental disabilities* (37–51). Baltimore: Paul H. Brookes Publishing Co.

Konig, T. J. (1986). A special brother. *Sibling Information Network Newsletter, 5*(1), 4.

Korner, A. F. (1971). Individual differences at birth: Implications for early experience and later development. *American Journal of Orthopsychiatry, 41,* 608–619.

Kowalski, J. L. (1980). The attitude and self concept of adolescent siblings of handicapped children (Doctoral dissertation, University of Cincinnati). *Dissertation Abstracts International, 41/03A,* 1020.

Lamb, M. (1978a). Interactions between 18-month-olds and their preschool-aged siblings. *Child Development, 49,* 51–59.

Lamb, M. (1978b). The development of sibling relationships in infancy: A short term longitudinal study. *Child Development, 49,* 1189–1196.

Lamb, M. (1982). Sibling relationship across the lifespan: An overview and introduction. In M. E. Lamb & B. Sutton-Smith (Eds.), *Sibling relationships* (pp. 1–11). Hillsdale, NJ: Lawrence Erlbaum Associates.

Lamb, M., & Sutton-Smith, B. (Eds.). (1982). *Sibling relationships.* Hillsdale, NJ: Lawrence Erlbaum Associates.

Laureys, K. (1982, November). Speech given at the National Society for Children and Adults with Autism, Washington, DC. Reprinted in the *Sibling Information Network Newsletter* (1984), *3*(1), 5.

Lefrancois, G. R. (1973). *Of children: Introduction to child development.* Belmont, CA: Wadsworth Publishing.

Lent, J. R., & McLean, B. M. (1976). The trainable retarded: the technology of teaching. In N. G. Haring & R. L. Schiefelbusch (Eds.), *Teaching special children.* New York: McGraw-Hill.

Lettick, S. (1979). Ben. *Journal of Autism and Developmental Disorders, 9*(3), 293–294.

Levy, D. M. (1934). Rivalry between children of the same family. *Child Study, 11,* 233–261.

Lindsey, J. O., & Stewart, D. (1989). The guardian minority: Siblings of children with mental retardation. *Education and Training in Mental Retardation, 24*(4), 291–296.

Lipsky, D. K., & Gartner, A. (1992). Achieving full inclusion: Placing the student at the center of educational reform. In W. Stainback & S. Stainback (Eds.), *Controversial issues confronting special education* (pp. 3–12). Boston: Allyn and Bacon.

Lloyd-Bostock, S. (1976). Parents' experiences of official help and guidance in caring for a mentally handicapped child. *Child: Care, Health, and Development, 2,* 325–338.

Lobato, D. J. (1981). *Multiple assessment of a workshop program for siblings of handicapped children.* Unpublished doctoral dissertation, University of Massachusetts.

Lobato, D. J. (1983). Siblings of handicapped children: A review. *Journal of Autism and Developmental Disorders, 13*(4), 347–364.

Lobato, D. J. (1985). Preschool siblings of handicapped children—Impact of peer support and training. *Journal of Autism and Developmental Disorders, 15*(3), 345–350.

Lobato, D. J. (1990). *Brothers, sisters and special needs: Information and activities for helping young siblings of children with chronic illnesses and developmental disabilities.* Baltimore: Paul H. Brookes Publishing Co.

Lobato, D., Barbour, L., Hall, L. J., & Miller, C. T. (1987). Psychosocial characteristics of preschool siblings of handicapped and nonhandicapped children. *Journal of Abnormal Child Psychology, 15,* 329–338.

Lobato, D., & Tlaker, A. (1985). Sibling intervention with a retarded child. *Education and Treatment of Children, 8,* 221–228.

Mackeith, R. (1973). The feelings and behavior of parents of handicapped children. *Developmental Medicine and Child Neurology, 15,* 524–527.

Mager, R. (1975). *Preparing instructional objectives.* Palo Alto, CA: Fearon Publishers.

Mannle, S., & Tomasello, M. (1987). Fathers, sibling, and the bridge hypothesis. In K. E. Nelson & A. VanKleeck (Eds.), *Children's language* (Vol. 6, pp. 23–42). Hillsdale, NJ: Lawrence Erlbaum Associates.

Mash, E. J., & Mercer, B. J. (1979). A comparison of the behavior of deviant and non-deviant boys while playing alone and interacting with a sibling. *Journal of Child Psychology and Psychiatry and Allied Disciplines, 20*(3), 197–207.

Mates, T. E. (1982, July). *Which siblings of autistic children are at greater risk for the development of school and/or personality difficulties?* Paper presented at the National Society for Autistic Children, Omaha, NE.

Maxson, L. R., & Daugherty, C. R. (1992). *Genetics: A human perspective.* Dubuque, IA: Wm. C. Brown Publishers.

McCallum, N. (1981, November). My brother Jon. *Sibling Information Network Newsletter, 1*(3), 2.

McDermott, J. (1980). *The complete book on sibling rivalry.* New York: Wideview Books.

McEvoy, M., Shores, R., Wehby, J., Johnson, S., & Fox, J. (1990). Special education teachers' implementation of procedures to promote social interaction among children in integrated settings. *Education and Training in Mental Retardation, 25*(3), 267–275.

McEvoy, M. A., Nordquist, V. M., Twardosz, S., Heckaman, K., Wehby, J. H., & Denny, R. K. (1988). Promoting autistic children peer interaction in mainstreamed settings using affection activities. *Journal of Applied Behavior Analysis, 21,* 193–200.

McHale, S. M., & Gamble, W. C. (1987). Sibling relationships and adjustment of children with disabled brothers and sisters. *Journal of Children in Contemporary Society, 19,* 131–158.

McHale, S. M., & Gamble, W. C. (1989). Sibling relationships of children with disabled and nondisabled brothers and sisters. *Developmental Psychology, 25*(3), 421–429.

McHale, S. M., & Harris, V. S. (1992). Children's experiences with disabled and nondisabled siblings: Links with personal adjustment and relationship evaluation. In F. Boer and J. Dunn (Eds.), *Children's relationships with their siblings: Developmental and clinical implications.* (pp. 83–100). Hillsdale, NJ: Lawrence Erlbaum Associates.

McHale, S. M., & Pawletko, T. M. (1992). Differential treatment of siblings in two family contexts. *Child Development, 63,* 68–81.

McHale, S. M., Simeonsson, R. J., & Sloan, J. L. (1984). Children with handicapped brothers and sisters. In E. Schopler & G. Mesibov (Eds.), *The effects of autism on the family* (pp. 327–342). New York: Plenum.

McHale, S. M., Sloan, J., & Simeonsson, R. J. (1986). Sibling relationships of children with autistic, mentally retarded, and nonhandicapped brothers and sisters. *Journal of Autism and Developmental Disorders, 16,* 399–413.

McKeever, P. (1983). Siblings of chronically ill children: A literature review with implications for research and practice. *American Journal of Orthopsychiatry, 53*(2), 209–218.

McLinden-Mott, S. E., & Braeger, T. (1988). The impact on family scale: An adaptation for families of children with handicaps. *Journal of the Division for Early Childhood, 12,* 217–223.

Meyer, D. J. (1983). A sibshop for siblings. *Sibling Information Network Newsletter, 2*(1), 1.

Meyer, D. J., Vadasy, P. F., & Fewell, R. R. (1985). *Living with a brother or sister with special needs: A book for sibs.* Seattle: University of Washington Press.

Michaelis, C. T. (1980). *Home and school partnerships in exceptional education.* Rockville, MD: Aspen Publications.

Miller, L. G. (1969). The seven stages in the life cycle of a family with a mentally retarded child. *Washington Institution Department Proceedings of the 9th Annual Research Meeting, 2,* 78–81.

Miller, N. B., & Maruyama, G. (1976). Ordinal position and peer popularity. *Journal of Personality and Social Psychology, 33,* 123–131.

Miller, N. B., & Miller, W. H. (1976). Siblings as behavior change agents. In J. D. Kromboltz & C. E. Thoresen (Eds.), *Counseling methods.* New York: Holt, Rinehart, & Winston.

Miller, S. (1985). Siblings. *Sibling Information Network Newsletter, 4*(3), 4.

Miller, S. G. (1974). An exploratory study of sibling relationships in families with retarded children (Doctoral dissertation, Columbia University). *Dissertation Abstracts International, 35,* 2994B–2995B.

Milstead, S. (1988). Siblings are people too. *Academic Therapy, 23*(5), 537–540.

Minnett, A. M., Vandell, D. L., & Santrock, J. W. (1983). The effects of sibling status on sibling interaction: Influence of birth order, age spacing, sex of child, and sex of sibling. *Child Development, 54,* 1064–1072.

Minuchin, S. (1974). *Families and family therapy.* Cambridge, MA: Harvard University Press.

Mischel, W. (1970). Sex typing and socialization. In P. Mussen (Ed.), *Carmichael's manual of child psychology.* New York: John Wiley & Sons.

Munson, H. L. (1971). *Foundations of developmental guidance.* Boston: Allyn & Bacon.

Murphy, A., Pueschel, S., Duffy, T., & Brady, E. (1976, March/April). Meeting with brothers and sisters of children with Down's syndrome. *Children Today, 5,*(2), 20–23.

Murphy, L., & Corte, S. D. (1989). Siblings. *Special Parent, Special Child, 5*(1), 1–6). (ERIC Document Reproduction Service No. ED 309 605).

Myers, R. (1978). *Like normal people.* New York: McGraw-Hill.

Neufeld, G. R. (1975). Council as advocate. In J. Paul, R. Wiegerink, & G. R. Neufeld (Eds.), *Advocacy: A role for DD councils.* Chapel Hill, NC: The University of North Carolina.

O'Dell, S. (1974). Training parents in behavior modification: A review. *Psychological Bulletin, 31,* 418–433.

Ogle, P. A. (1982). *The sibling relationship: Maternal perceptions of the nonhandicapped and handicapped/nonhandicapped sibling dyads.* Unpublished doctoral dissertation, University of North Carolina–Chapel Hill.

Parten, M. (1932). Social participation among preschool children. *Journal of Abnormal Social Psychology, 27,* 243–269.

Patterson, G. R. (1976). The aggressive child: Victim and architect of a coercive system. In E. J. Mash, L. A. Hamerlynck, & L. C. Hardy (Eds.), *Behavior modification and families* (pp. 267–316). New York: Brunner/Mazel.

Patterson, L. E., & Eisenberg, S. (1983). *The counseling process* (3rd ed.). Boston: Houghton Mifflin.

Peck, C. A., Donaldson, J., & Pezzoli, M. (1990). Some benefits nonhandicapped adolescents perceive for themselves from their social relationships with peers who have severe handicaps. *Journal of The Association for Persons with Severe Handicaps, 15*(4), 241–249.

Peltz, L. G. (1977). An exploratory study of the interactional behavior of psychotic children with psychotic peers and with normal siblings (Doctoral dissertation, Columbia University, 1977). *Dissertation Abstracts International, 38*, 2380B.

Pepler, D. J., Abramovitch, R., & Corter, C. (1981). Sibling interaction in the home: A longitudinal study. *Child Development, 52*, 1344–1347.

Perske, R. (1981). *Hope for families: New directions for parents of persons with retardation or other disabilities.* Nashville, TN: Abingdon Press.

Perske, R. (1990). *Circle of friends.* Nashville, TN: Abingdon Press.

Pietrofesa, J. J., Hoffman, A., & Splete, H. H. (1984). *Counseling: An introduction.* Boston: Houghton Mifflin.

Plomin, R., & Daniels, D. (1987). Why are children in the same family so different from one another? *Behavioral and Brain Sciences, 10*, 1–16.

Post-Kramer, P., & Nickolai, S. (1985). Counseling services for siblings of the handicapped. *Elementary School Guidance and Counseling, 20*(2), 115–120.

Potter, P. C., & Roberts, M. C. (1984). Children's perceptions of chronic illness: The roles of disease symptoms, cognitive development, and information. *Journal of Pediatric Psychology, 9*, 13–27.

Powell, T. H. (1982). *Parents, siblings, and handicapped children: A social interaction program.* Storrs: The University of Connecticut.

Powell, T. H., Salzberg, C., Rule, S., Levy, S., & Itzkowitz, J. (1983). Teaching mentally retarded children to play with their siblings using parents as trainers. *Education and Treatment of Children, 6*, 343–362.

Pueschel, S. M., & Mulick, J. A. (Eds.). (1990). *Prevention of developmental disabilities.* Baltimore: Paul H. Brookes Publishing Co.

Robson, K. S., & Moss, H. A. (1970). Patterns and determinants of maternal attachment. *Journal of Pediatrics, 77*, 976–985.

Roff, M., Sells, B., & Golden, M. (1972). *Social adjustment and personality development in children.* Minneapolis: University of Minnesota Press.

Ross, H. G., & Milgram, J. I. (1982). Important variables in adult sibling relationships: A qualitative study. In M. E. Lamb & B. Sutton-Smith (Eds.), *Sibling relationships* (pp. 225–250). Hillsdale, NJ: Lawrence Erlbaum Associates.

Rowe, D. C., & Plomin, R. (1981). The importance of nonshared environmental influences in behavioral developments. *Developmental Psychology, 17*, 517–531.

Russell, M. (1990, Fall). Writing the letter of intent. *New Ways, 20*–25.

Salisbury, C. L., & Intagliata, J. (Eds.). (1986). *Respite care: Support for persons with developmental disabilities and their families.* Baltimore: Paul H. Brookes Publishing Co.

Sameroff, A. J., & Chandler, M. J. (1975). Perinatal risk and the continuum of caretaking casualty. In M. F. D. Horowitz et al. (Eds.), *Review of child development research* (Vol. IV). Chicago: University of Chicago Press.

Samuels, H. (1980). The effect of an older sibling on infant locomotor exploration in a new environment. *Child Development, 51*, 607–609.

San Martino, M., & Newman, M. B. (1974). Siblings of retarded children: A population at risk. *Child Psychiatry and Human Development, 4*(3), 168–177.

Schachter, F. F. (1982). Sibling deidentification and split-parent identification. In M. E. Lamb & B. Sutton-Smith (Eds.), *Sibling relationships: Their nature and significance across the lifespan*. Hillsdale, NJ: Lawrence Erlbaum Associates.

Schachter, F. F., & Stone, R. K. (1985). Difficult sibling, easy sibling: Temperament and the within-family environment. *Child Development, 56,* 1335–1344.

Schaefer, E., & Edgerton, M. (1979, November). *Sibling Inventory of Behavior.* Caroline Institute for Research on Early Education of the Handicapped, University of North Carolina–Chapel Hill.

Schaefer, E., & Edgerton, M. (1981). *Short description of the Sibling Inventory of Behavior.* Unpublished manuscript, University of North Carolina–Chapel Hill.

Schaffer, H. R., & Emerson, P. E. (1964). Patterns of response to physical contact in early human development. *Journal of Child Psychology and Psychiatry, 5,* 1–13.

Schild, S. (1976). The family of the retarded child. In R. Koch & J. Dobson (Eds.), *The mentally retarded child and his family*. New York: Brunner/Mazel.

Schipper, M. T. (1959). The child with Mongolism in the home. *Pediatrics, 24,* 132–144.

Schneider-Corey, M., & Corey, G. (1987). *Groups: Process and practice* (3rd ed.). Pacific Grove, CA: Brooks/Cole.

Schreiber, M. (1984). Normal siblings of retarded persons. *Social Casework: The Journal of Contemporary Social Work, 67*(7), 420–427.

Schreiber, M., & Feeley, M. (1965). Siblings of the retarded: A guided group experience. *Children, 12*(6), 221–225.

Schreibman, L., O'Neill, R. E., & Koegel, R. L. (1983). Behavioral training for siblings of autistic children. *Journal of Applied Behavior Analysis, 16*(2), 129–138.

Schvaneveldt, J. D., & Ihinger, M. (1979). Sibling relationships in the family. In W. R. Burr, R. Hill, F. I. Nye, & I. L. Reiss (Eds.), *Contemporary theories about the family* (Vol. 1, pp. 453–467). New York: The Free Press.

Seligman, M. (1983). Siblings of handicapped persons. In M. Seligman (Ed.), *The family with a handicapped child: Understanding and treatment* (pp. 147–174). New York: Grune & Stratton.

Seltzer, G. B. (1985). Informal supports for aging mentally retarded persons. *American Journal of Mental Deficiency, 90,* 259–265.

Seltzer, G. B. (1991). *Stress, health, and social support among families and caregivers of older adults with developmental disabilities.* Cincinnati, OH: Research and Training Center Consortium on Aging and Developmental Disabilities.

Seltzer, G. B., Begun, A., Seltzer, M. M., & Krauss, M. W. (1991). Adults with mental retardation and their aging mothers: Impacts of Siblings. *Family Relations, 40,* 310–317.

Senapti, R., & Hayes, A. (1988). Sibling relationships of handicapped children: A review of conceptual and methodological issues. *International Journal of Behavioral Development, 11*(1), 89–115.

Shapiro, B. (1983). Informational interviews. *Sibling Information Network Newsletter, 2*(1), 5.

Shertzer, B., & Stone, S. C. (1980). *Fundamentals of counseling* (3rd ed.). Boston: Houghton Mifflin.

Shores, R. E. (1981). *Social competence intervention project: Final report.* Nashville, TN: Vanderbilt University. (U.S. Office of Education Grant No. G007802088).

Shores, R. E. (1987). Overview of research on social interaction: A historical and personal perspective. *Behavior Disorders, 12*(4), 233–241.

Simeonsson, R. J., & Bailey, D. B. (1983, September). *Siblings of handicapped children.* Paper presented at NICHD Conference on Research on Families with Retarded Children.

Simeonsson, R. J., & Bailey, D. B. (1986). Siblings of handicapped children. In J. J. Gallagher & P. M. Vietze (Eds.), *Families of handicapped persons: Research, programs, and policy issues* (pp. 67–77). Baltimore: Paul H. Brookes Publishing Co.

Simeonsson, R. J., & McHale, S. M. (1981). Review: Research on handicapped children: Sibling relationships. *Child: Care, Health, and Development, 7,* 153–171.

Simeonsson, R. J., & Simeonsson, N. E. (1981). Parenting handicapped children: Psychological aspects. In J. L. Paul (Ed.), *Understanding and working with parents of children with special needs* (pp. 51–88). New York: Holt, Rinehart, & Winston.

Skrtic, T. M., Summers, J. A., Brotherson, M. J., & Turnbull, A. P. (1984). Severely handicapped children and their brothers and sisters. In J. Blacher (Ed.), *Severely handicapped young children and their families: Research in review* (pp. 215–246). New York: Academic Press.

Slade, J. C. (1988). Why siblings of handicapped children need the attention and help of the counselor. *The School Counselor, 36,* 107–111.

Snell, M. E. (1987). *Systematic instruction of persons with severe handicaps.* Columbus, OH: Charles E. Merrill.

Snell, M. E., & Gast, D. L. (1981). Applying time delay procedure to the instruction of the severely handicapped. *Journal of The Association for the Severely Handicapped, 6*(3), 3–14.

Snell, M. E., & Zirpoli, T. J. (1987). Intervention strategies. In M. Snell (Ed.), *Systematic instruction of persons with severe handicaps* (pp. 110–149). Columbus, OH: Charles E. Merrill.

Sobol, H. L. (1977). *My brother Steven is retarded.* New York: Macmillan Publishing Co.

Stainback, S., & Stainback, W. (1992). Schools as inclusive communities. In W. Stainback & S. Stainback (Eds.), *Controversial issues confronting special education* (pp. 29–43). Boston: Allyn and Bacon.

Stainback, W., & Stainback, S. (1987). Facilitating friendships. *Education and Training in Mental Retardation, 22*(1), 18–25.

Starr, L. A. (1984). The siblings' survival: Forget me not. *Sibling Information Network Newsletter, 2*(4), 2.

Stewart, J. C. (1986). *Counseling parents of exceptional children* (2nd ed.). Columbus, OH: Charles E. Merrill.

Stewart, R. B., Mobley, L. A., VanTuyl, S. S., & Salvador, M. A. (1987). The firstborn's adjustment to the birth of a sibling: A longitudinal assessment. *Child Development, 58,* 341–355.

Stocker, C., Dunn, J., & Plomin, R. (1989). Sibling relationships: Links with child temperament, maternal behavior, and family structure. *Child Development, 60,* 715–727.

Stoneman, Z., & Brody, G. H. (1982). Strengths inherent in sibling interactions involving a retarded child: A functional role theory approach. In N. Stinnett, B. Chesser, J. DeFrain, & P. Knaub (Eds.), *Family strengths: Positive models for family life* (pp. 113–129). Lincoln: University of Nebraska Press.

Stoneman, Z., & Brody, G. H. (1984). Research with families of severely handicapped children: Theoretical and methodological considerations. In J.

Blacher (Ed.), *Severely handicapped young children and their families* (pp. 179–214). Orlando, FL: Academic Press.

Stoneman, Z., Brody, G. H., Davis, C. H., & Crapps, J. M. (1987). Mentally retarded children and their older same-sex siblings: Naturalistic in-home observations. *American Journal of Mental Retardation, 92,* 290–298.

Stoneman, Z., Brody, G. H., Davis, C. H., & Crapps, J. M. (1988). Childcare responsibilities, peer relations, and sibling conflict: Older siblings of mentally retarded children. *American Journal of Mental Retardation, 93,* 174–183.

Stoneman, Z., Brody, G. H., Davis, C. H., & Crapps, J. M. (1989). Role relations between children who are mentally retarded and their older siblings: Observations in three in-home contexts. *Research in Developmental Disabilities, 10,* 61–76.

Stoneman, Z., Brody, G. H., & MacKinnon, C. (1984). Naturalistic observations of children's activities and roles while playing with their siblings and friends. *Child Development, 55,* 617–627.

Stoneman, Z., Brody, G. H., & MacKinnon, C. E. (1986). Same-sex and cross-sex siblings: Activity choices, roles, behavior, and gender stereotypes. *Sex Roles, 15*(9/10), 495–511.

Stoneman, Z., & Crapps, J. M. (1990). Mentally retarded individuals in family care homes: Relationships with the family-of-origin. *American Journal on Mental Retardation, 94,* 420–430.

Strain, P. S., Cooke, R. P., & Apolloni, T. (1976). *Teaching exceptional children: Assessing and modifying social behavior.* New York: Academic Press.

Strain, P. S., & Fox, J. J. (1981). Peers as behavior change agents for withdrawn classmates. In B. B. Lahey & A. E. Kazdin (Eds.), *Advances in clinical child psychology* (Vol. 4). New York: Plenum Press.

Strain, P. S., Shores, R. E., & Timm, M. A. (1977). Effects of peer social initiations on the behavior of withdrawn preschool children. *Journal of Applied Behavior Analysis, 10,* 289–298.

Strain, P. S., & Timm, M. A. (1974). An experimental analysis of social interaction between a behaviorally disordered child and her classroom peers. *Journal of Applied Behavior Analysis, 7,* 583–590.

Strully, J. L., & Bartholomew-Lorimer, K. (1988). Social integration and friendship. In S. M. Pueschel, (Ed.), *The young person with Down syndrome* (pp. 65–76). Baltimore: Paul H. Brooks Publishing Co.

Stubblefield, H. W. (1965). Religion, parents, and mental retardation. *Mental Retardation, 3,* 4, 8–11.

Sullivan, R. C. (1979). Siblings of autistic children. *Journal of Autism and Developmental Disorders, 9*(3), 287–298.

Sulzer-Azaroff, B., & Mayer, G. R. (1977). *Applying behavior analysis procedures with children and youth.* New York: Holt, Rinehart, & Winston.

Summers, J. A., Behr, S. K., & Turnbull, A. P. (1989). Positive adaptations and coping strengths of families who have children with disabilities. In G. H. S. Singer & L. K. Irvin (Eds.), *Support for caregiving families: Enabling positive adaptation to disability* (pp. 27–40). Baltimore: Paul H. Brookes Publishing Co.

Summers, M., Bridge, J., & Summers, C. R. (1991, Summer). Sibling support groups. *Teaching Exceptional Children,* 20–25.

Sutton-Smith, B., & Rosenberg, B. G. (1968). Sibling consensus on power tactics. *Journal of Genetic Psychology, 112*(1), 63–72.

Sutton-Smith, B., & Rosenberg, B. G. (1970). *The sibling.* New York: Holt, Rinehart, & Winston.

Swenson-Pierce, A., Kohl, F., & Egle, A. (1987). Siblings as home trainers: A strategy for teaching domestic skills to children. *Journal of The Association for Persons with Severe Handicaps*, 12(1), 53–60.

Taylor, L. S. (1974). *Communication between mothers and normal siblings of retarded children: Nature and modification.* Unpublished doctoral dissertation, University of North Carolina–Chapel Hill.

Teti, D. M., & Ablard, K. E. (1989). Security of attachment and infant–sibling relationships: A laboratory study. *Child Development*, 60, 1519–1528.

Tew, B., & Laurence, K. M. (1973). Mothers, brothers, and sisters of patients with spina bifida. *Developmental Medicine and Child Neurology*, 15, 69–76.

Tingey, C. (1988). Cutting the umbilical cord: Parental perspectives. In S. M. Pueschel (Ed.), *The young person with Down syndrome: Transition from adolescence to adulthood* (pp. 5–22). Baltimore: Paul H. Brookes Publishing Co.

Tomasello, M., & Mannle, S. (1985). Pragmatics of sibling speech to one-year-olds. *Child Development*, 56, 911–917.

Torisky, J. A. (1979). My brother Eddie. *Journal of Autism and Developmental Disorders*, 9(3), 288–290.

Travis, G. (1976). *Chronic illness: Its impact on child and family.* Stanford: Stanford University Press.

Tremblay, A., Strain, P. S., Hendrickson, J. M., & Shores, R. E. (1981). Social interactions of normal preschool children: Using normative data for subject and target behavior selection. *Behavior Modification*, 5(2), 237–253.

Trevino, F. (1979). Siblings of handicapped children: Identifying those at risk. *Social Casework*, 60, 488–493.

Turnbull, A. P., & Bronicki, G. J. (1986). Changing second graders' attitudes toward people with mental retardation: Using kid power. *Mental Retardation*, 24, 44–45.

Turnbull, A. P., & Turnbull, H. R. (1986). *Families, professionals and exceptionality: A special partnership.* Columbus, Ohio: Merrill.

Turnbull, A. P., & Turnbull, H. R. (1990). *Families, professionals, and exceptionality: A special partnership* (2nd ed.). Columbus, OH: Merrill.

United States Department of Health and Human Services. (1980). *Learning together: A guide for families with genetic disorders.* Washington, DC: U.S. Government Printing Office (DHHS Publication No. HSA 80-5131).

Unruh, S. G., Grosse, M. E., & Zigler, E. (1971). Birth order, number of siblings, and social reinforcer effectiveness in children. *Child Development*, 42, 1,153–1,163.

Vandell, D. L., Minnett, A. M., & Santrock, J. W. (1987). Age differences in sibling relationships during middle childhood. *Journal of Applied Developmental Psychology*, 8, 247–257.

Vandell, D. L., & Wilson, K. S. (1987). Infants' interactions with mother, sibling, and peer: Contrasts and relations between interaction systems. *Child Development*, 58, 176–186.

Van Hasselt, V. B., Hersen, M., Whitehill, M. B., & Bellack, A. A. (1979). Social skills assessment and training for children: An evaluation review. *Behavioral Research and Therapy*, 17, 413–437.

Wagner, M. E., Schubert, H. J. P., & Schubert, D. S. P. (1985). Effects of sibling spacing on intelligence, interfamilial relations, psychosocial characteristics, and mental and physical health. In H. W. Reese (Ed.), *Advances in child development and behavior* (Vol. 19, pp. 149–206). New York: Academic Press.

Wasserman, R. (1983). Identifying the counseling needs of siblings of mentally retarded children. *Personnel and Guidance Journal*, 61, 622–627.

Weinrott, M. R. (1974). A training program in behavior modification for siblings of the retarded. *American Journal of Orthopsychiatry, 44,* 362–375.

Weiss, J. H. (1970). Birth order and physiological stress response. *Child Development, 41,* 461–470.

Whitman, T. L., Sciback, J. W., & Reid, D. H. (1983). *Behavior modification with the severely and profoundly retarded.* New York: Academic Press.

Wikler, L. (1983). Chronic stresses of families of mentally retarded children. *Family Relations, 30,* 281–288.

Wikler, L., Wasow, M., & Hatfield, E. (1981). Chronic sorrow revisited: Attitude of parents and professionals about adjustment to mental retardation. *American Journal of Orthopsychiatry, 51,* 63–70.

Willenz-Issacs, I. (1983). Brothers and sisters are special: A sibling program at the Kendall Demonstration School. *Sibling Information Network Newsletter, 2*(1), 2.

Wilson, J., Blacher, J., & Baker, B. L. (1989). Siblings of children with severe handicaps. *Mental Retardation, 27*(3), 167–173.

Wing, L. (1972). *Autistic children.* Secaucus, NJ: Citadel Press.

Wishart, J. G. (1986). Siblings as models in early infant learning. *Child Development, 57,* 1232–1240.

Wood, M. J., Vaughn, B. E., & Robb, M. D. (1988). Social–emotional adaptation and infant–mother attachment in siblings: Role of the mother in cross-sibling consistency. *Child Development, 59,* 643–651.

Woolett, A. (1986). The influence of older siblings on the language environment of young children. *British Journal of Developmental Psychology, 4,* 235–245.

Young, C. C. (1981). Children as instructional agents for handicapped peers: A review and analysis. In P. S. Strain (Ed.), *The utilization of classroom peers as behavior change agents.* New York: Plenum Press.

Young, C., Hecimovic, A., & Salzberg, C. L. (1983). Tutor–tutee behavior of disadvantaged kindergarten children during peer teaching. *Education and Treatment of Children, 6*(2), 123–135.

Zajonc, R. B., & Bargh, J. (1980). Birth order, family size and decline in SAT scores. *American Psychologist, 35,* 662–668.

Zatlow, G. (1982). A sister's lament. *Sibling Information Network Newsletter, 1*(5), 2; reprinted from 1981 *Citizens Future.*

Zeitlin, A. G. (1986). Mentally retarded adults and their siblings. *American Journal of Mental Deficiency, 91*(3), 217–225.

Zuk, G. H., Miller, R. L., Bartram, J. B., & Kling, F. (1961). Maternal acceptance of retarded children: A questionnaire study of attitudes and religious background. *Child Development, 32,* 525–540.

Appendices

Resources

A

Literature for Brothers & Sisters

Bibliographies

Attitude toward disability, A bibliography of children's books. Santa Monica, CA: Pediatric Projects, Inc. (P.O. Box 2175, Santa Monica, CA 90406).

Baskin, H., & Harris, H. (1977). *Notes from a different drummer: A guide to juvenile fiction portraying the handicapped.* New York: R. R.Bowker and Co.

Communication and communication disability, A bibliography of children's books. Santa Monica, CA: Pediatric Projects, Inc. (P.O. Box 2175, Santa Monica, CA 90406).

Moore, B., & Morton, A. (1977). *A reader's guide for parents of children with mental, physical or emotional disabilities.* Rockville, MD: U.S. Department of Health and Human Services. (Available from Bureau of Community Health Services, Publication No. HSA-77-5290x.)

Retardation, A bibliography of children's books. Santa Monica, CA: Pediatric Projects, Inc. (P.O. Box 2175, Santa Monica, CA 90406).

Rost, S. *A selected annotated bibliography for parents and siblings of mentally retarded individuals.* Arlington, TX: National Association for Retarded Citizens. (P.O. Box 2175, Santa Monica, CA 90406).

Siblings, A bibliography of children's books. Santa Monica, CA: Pediatric Projects, Inc. (P.O. Box 2175, Santa Monica, CA 90406).

General Disabilities

Adams, B. (1979). *Like it is: Facts and feelings about handicaps from kids who know.* New York: Walker & Co.

This book neatly summarizes the nature of various disabilities, including mental retardation, learning disabilities, orthopedic impairments, speech and hearing disorders, visual impairment, and behavioral disorders.

Nonfiction   Middle school level

Barnes, E., & Berrigan, C. (1978). *What's the difference? Teaching positive attitudes toward people with disabilities.* New York: Human Policy Press.

This is a book of activities containing ideas that are meant to be acted upon, not just read. The activities suggest ways to become involved in

experiences that foster contact, empathy, and responsive behavior toward people with disabilities. It also offers background information on a range of disabilities and a list of resources for further research. This book will encourage the reader to reexamine expectations and stereotypes, questions and answers, and feelings and behaviors toward people who have disabilities.
Nonfiction   High school level

Brown, T. (1984). *Someone special, just like you.* New York: Holt, Rinehart, & Winston.

This book contains photographs of young children who are enjoying themselves in a variety of activities. Many of the children pictured do not appear to have a disability, while others do. The text and the photographs emphasize the similarities between the children, despite their apparent differences.
Nonfiction   Primary school level

Edrington, M. J., Moss, S. A., & Young, J. (1978). *Friends.* Monmouth, OR: Instructional Development Corp.

This book offers simulation activities for children to help them better understand the daily life of their friends who have disabilities, and to better recognize their problems and accomplishments. This book will be helpful for both siblings and friends of children with disabilities.
Nonfiction   Primary-middle school level

Haskins, J., with Stifle, J. M. (1979). *The quiet revolution: The struggle for the rights of disabled Americans.* New York: Thomas Y. Crowell.

Civil rights are not just a matter of race. This book thoroughly discusses the disabled rights movement and the philosophy and history behind it. Topics include the right to treatment, education, employment and compensation, and the right to a barrier-free environment.
Nonfiction   High school level

Kamien, J. (1979). *What if you couldn't . . . ? A book about special needs.* New York: Charles Scribner's Sons.

This resource book for children examines the effects of various disabilities and treatments. Mental retardation, visual and hearing impairments, physical and learning disabilities, and emotional disturbances are each covered in a separate chapter. Facts are presented and situations are described to stimulate critical thinking. Activities that simulate various aspects of a particular disability are suggested, and controversial issues are covered in an unbiased manner.
Nonfiction   Middle-junior high school level

McConnell, N. P., & Duell, N. (1982). *Different and alike.* Colorado Springs, CO: Current, Inc.

This colorfully illustrated book provides a brief and easy-to-understand overview of disabilities, including deafness, blindness, physical disabilities, speech disorders, learning disabilities, mental retardation, and multiple disabilities. The book concludes with practical suggestions for helping people with disabilities. These suggestions would be meaningful to siblings and their friends.
Nonfiction   Middle-junior high school level

Sullivan, M. B., Brightman, A. J., & Blatt, J. (1979). *Feeling free*. Reading, MA: Addison-Wesley.

This activity book was spawned by an acclaimed children's television series of the same title. Included are short stories and nonfictional accounts about the lives of children with learning disabilities or physical disabilities. These stories are so effective because they are written by the children themselves. Games and activities are provided as well.

Nonfiction   Middle-junior high school level

Asthma and Allergies

Silverstein, A., & Silverstein, V. B. (1978). *Itch, sniffle, and sneeze. All about asthma, hay fever and other allergies*. New York: Four Winds Press.

In a comical light, this book discusses what allergies, hay fever, and asthma are and how to cope with them.

Nonfiction   Primary school level

Autism

Bodenheimer, C. (1979). *Everybody is a person: A book for brothers and sisters of autistic kids*. Syracuse, NY: Jowonio: The Learning Place. (Jowonio: The Learning Place, 215 Bassett Street, Syracuse, NY 13210).

This booklet covers some of the basic concerns and questions siblings might have about a brother or sister with autism. Chapter titles include: What is autism? What to tell your friends? You can't catch it. It's okay to get mad. Smiling is important for everyone.

Nonfiction   Middle school level

Gold, P. (1975). *Please don't say hello*. New York: Human Services.

This story depicts a family with two boys, one of whom has autism, moving into a new neighborhood. Although the story is told from the brother's perspective, autism is explained through the mother's conversations with the neighborhood children and is vividly described throughout the story. The issue of how to tell newfound friends about a sibling with a disability and cope with their reactions is fully addressed in the story.

Fiction   Primary-middle school level

Parker, R. (1974). *He is your brother*. Nashville, TN: Thomas Nelson, Inc.

"Orry," a 6-year-old with autism, spends much of his time in a closet under the stairs. Mike, his older brother, becomes instrumental in helping to draw Orry out of his shell by sharing his interest in trains. As the story unfolds, Orry has begun to teach himself classical melodies by using a tape recorder. This book illustrates the important influence that a sibling can have on a brother or sister who has a disability.

Fiction   Middle-junior high school level

Spence, E. (1977). *The devil hole*. New York: Lothrop, Lee, and Shepard Books, Division of William Morrow & Co.

The story begins before Carl, a boy with autism, is born and covers a 4-year period in the life of his Australian family. As Carl grows, his bewildering behavior and the subsequent reactions of his parents, siblings, and others are explored.

Fiction   Middle-junior high school level

Cancer

Jampolsky, G. G., & Taylor, P. (Eds.). (1978). *There is a rainbow behind every dark cloud*. Tiburon, CA: Center for Attitudinal Healing.

This is a collection of artwork—drawings and words—of children who have had cancer.

Nonfiction   Primary-middle school level

Jampolsky, G. G., & Taylor, P. (Eds.). (1982). *Another look at the rainbow. Straight from the siblings*. Tiburon, CA: Center for Attitudinal Healing.

Similar to their first volume, this collection focuses on the experiences of children whose brothers and sisters have had cancer.

Nonfiction   Primary-middle school level

Cardiac Problems

Lenski, L. (1952). *We live in the South*. Philadelphia: J. B. Lippincott.

Seven-year-old Evelina has an enlarged heart. Her frequent chest pains are met with insensitivity from her peers, and communication between her mother and siblings regarding her problem is poor. Hurt feelings and general lack of awareness by others toward Evelina's special needs result.

Fiction   Primary school level

Cerebral Palsy

Fassler, J. (1975). *Howie helps himself*. Chicago: Albert Whitman & Co.

Howie is accustomed to accepting assistance from others, however, his dream is to learn how to independently work his own wheelchair. Howie succeeds with the help of his father—they celebrate this long-awaited milestone together.

Nonfiction   Middle school level

Perske, R. (1986). *Don't stop the music*. Nashville: Abingdon Press.

This book generates an action-packed adventure as it shows how persons with disabilities contribute positively to the community. Joe and Jessica, two teens with cerebral palsy, become key elements in cracking an auto-theft ring. The reader will be amazed as Joe and Jessica use their wits and their motorized wheelchairs to capture the thieves, while making some very special friends along the way.

Fiction   Middle-high school level

Emotional Disturbance

Green, P. (1978). *Walkie-talkie*. Reading, MA: Addison-Wesley.

In this story, two young teenage boys befriend each other when no one else will. Richie is behind in school, hyperactive, and engages in impulsively cruel acts. Norman's cerebral palsy severely limits his speech and movement abilities.

Fiction   Middle-junior high school level

Hamilton-Paterson, J. (1970). *The house in the waves*. Chatham, NY: S. G. Phillips.

Hospital life and therapy are realistically portrayed in this story of a withdrawn 14-year-old boy. Having suffered abuse at the hands of his father, he is now trying to cope with reality.
Fiction   Junior high school level

Epilepsy

Girion, B. (1981). *A handful of stars*. New York: Charles Scribner's Sons.

Information about epilepsy and its diagnosis, prognosis, and treatment are relayed to the reader in this story of a young high school girl. Her memory lapses have recently been attributed to epilepsy. This is a realistic presentation of an adolescent coming to grips with her own worries, and the ignorance and bias she encounters.
Fiction   Junior high school level

Hermes, P. (1980). *What if they knew?* San Diego: Harcourt, Brace, Jovanovich.

This story depicts a 10-year-old girl, Jeremy, who wants to keep her epilepsy a secret from her classmates. When she has a seizure at school, Jeremy gains some insight into friendship.
Fiction   Middle school level

Silverstein, A., & Silverstein, V. B. (1975). *Epilepsy.* Philadelphia: J. B. Lippincott Junior Books.

This clear and informative book discusses epilepsy as a misunderstood disease and describes the condition, manifestations, probable causes, treatment, and societal attitudes of epilepsy. Well-known people with epilepsy are featured in this book, such as Julius Caesar, Roman emperor, and John Considine, a famous hockey player.
Nonfiction   Primary-middle school level

Hearing Impaired

Glazzard, M. H. (1978). *Meet Camille and Danielle, they're special persons.* Lawrence, KS: H & H Enterprises.

Camille and Danielle are sisters; in fact, they are twins who are both hearing impaired. In this book, they are shown attending class with hearing children in an integrated atmosphere. The story and photographs explain speech training, lipreading, and hearing aids.
Biography   Primary school level

Hanlon, E. (1981). *The swing.* New York: Dell.

Beth is a young teenage girl whose overprotective mother discourages her from participating in most activities. Finally allowed to walk alone to the nearby mountains, Beth discovers a bear and her cub but tells no one. In the woods at the same time, Danny, a 13-year-old neighbor, accidentally discharges his father's gun causing the mother bear to charge. Much to his embarrassment, Beth courageously saves Danny from harm, and so he lies, claiming that he rescued her from the bear. After a very hostile relationship, Beth and Danny are tragically brought together to overcome their bitterness for each other and they become friends.
Fiction   High school level

Hlibok, B. (1981). *Silent dancer.* New York: Messner, Division of Simon & Schuster.

Written by her brother, this book depicts the life of his deaf sister, Nancy. She and her family live in suburban New York City. Despite her hearing impairment, Nancy attends ballet class at the Joffrey School of Ballet in Greenwich Village. This story recounts the events that occur in ballet class, such as the performance of routines, the use of hearing aids, and the feeling of musical vibrations.

Nonfiction Primary-middle school level

Hyman, J. (1980). *Deafness.* New York: Franklin Watts.

This factual book contains information on the diagnosis and causes of hearing impairments. Treatment and educational issues are discussed along with various communication options. Limitations, special problems, and special devices are also delineated.

Nonfiction Middle school level

Levine, E. (1974). *Lisa and her soundless world.* New York: Human Sciences Press.

Lisa is an 8-year-old who is hearing impaired. She cannot speak and does not have any friends until she receives a hearing aid. Now she participates in lipreading, speech classes, and sign language. Lisa progresses in all areas, and diagnosis predicts that she will speak clearly when she is an adult.

Nonfiction Primary school level

Litchfield, A. (1976). *A button in her ear.* Chicago: Albert Whitman and Company.

Angela is hearing impaired and often doesn't understand conversation with family, friends, and teachers, which results in confusion and hard feelings. Angela is fitting with a hearing aid and given instructions for care. Her teacher asks her to demonstrate the use of her hearing aid to the class and, surprisingly, the class is impressed, possibly even envious. Angela is now happy that she knows what people are saying and even a little smug about her ability to tune them out when she doesn't want to hear them.

Fiction Primary-middle school level

Peter, D. (1976). *Claire and Emma.* Charles Black.

The author is the mother of 4-year-old Claire and 2-year-old Emma. Both girls have been hearing impaired since birth. The children's mother explains and illustrates the components of the hearing aid and describes daily activities with hearing friends and the girls' brother. Included are helpful suggestions and responses that are direct, clear, and informative.

Nonfiction Primary school level

Peterson, W. (1977). *I have a sister, my sister is deaf.* New York: Harper & Row.

In this warm story for young children, a girl describes the limitations and strengths of her younger sister, who is hearing impaired.

Nonfiction Primary school level

Riokind, M. (1982). *Apple is my sign.* Boston: Houghton Mifflin.

This story tells of Harry's adventures and solid friendships that develop when he is sent to boarding school to learn needed skills. Henry's skill in

drawing, designing, and football strategies is illustrated in detail throughout the story.
Fiction   High school level

Robinson, V. (1965). *David in silence.* Philadelphia: J. B. Lippincott Co.

In this novel, Michael befriends a new neighbor who is hearing impaired. The difficulties experienced by an individual who is deaf are initially explained to Michael and his family by David's older brother. Throughout the story, David's difficulties and experiences with language are carefully illustrated through his thoughts and his interactions with the neighborhood children.
Fiction   Junior high school level

Sullivan, M. B., & Bourke, L. (1980). *A show of hands.* Reading, MA: Addison-Wesley.

This informational book introduces sign language and finger spelling with an index of 150 signs. The author uses cartoon-like drawings in black and white, and also uses African-American and white people for illustrations. A variety of people with a range of opinions on hearing impairments are also presented. As an example, the author uses a girl who is hearing impaired, a boy who signs because he has a brother who is hearing impaired, and another boy who sees no point in learning to talk with his hands.
Nonfiction   Primary-middle school level

Wolf, B. (1977). *Anna's silent world.* Philadelphia: J. B. Lippincott Co.

In this photo essay, we meet Anna, who is a 6-year-old with a hearing impairment. She attends a regular first grade and enjoys ballet lessons. She is learning to communicate through speech and lipreading. The process and devices used to facilitate Anna's communication abilities are described in great detail.
Biography   Primary-middle school level

Language Problems

Kelley, S. (1976). *Trouble with explosives.* Scarsdale, NY: Bradbury.

Polly, who is 11 years old, leads an ordered, conventional life. She also has a language disability—she stutters. Her friend, Sis Hawkins, is colorful, casual, and unorthodox which leads to their envying each other's lifestyles. Needless to say, they become close friends and throughout the story they take risks for each other in a school setting.
Fiction   Primary-middle school level

Learning Disabilities

Albert, L. (1976). *But I'm ready to go.* Scarsdale, NY: Bradbury.

Judy Miller, 15 years old, is the oldest of four children but is jealous of her sister Emily, who is bright, pretty, and clever. Judy has difficulty in following discussions and concentrating on her lessons; however, she is very unhappy about being placed in a special school. Her fantasy is to have a successful audition as a singer, so she boldly sets out to pursue her career. Faced with barriers, Judy is ready to abandon her pursuit when Emily comes

through and helps her overcome the barriers. In conclusion, the rift between them is ready to be bridged.
Fiction   Middle-high school level

Fassler, J. (1969). *One little girl.* New York: Human Science.

Although it takes Laurie a long time to learn, she is involved in many activities. Laurie will soon discover that she is learning disabled after taking a psychological examination. However, she remains happy and well-adjusted due to the positive attitudes projected by those around her.
Nonfiction   Middle school level

Gillham, B. (1981). *My brother Barry.* Bergenfield, NJ: Andre Deutsch.

James Oakley, 9 years old, has much of the responsibility for his older brother Barry, who has a mental disability. The two brothers befriend two gypsies, who find Barry lost and confused. In return, James and Barry help their new friends fight unfair charges of arson.
Fiction   Primary-middle school level

Glazzard, M. H. (1978). *Meet Scott, he's a special person.* Lawrence, KS: H & H Enterprises.

This book introduces the reader to a variety of teaching methods. Even though Scott, who has a disability, enjoys art and plays outside with the other children, he requires some unusual teaching methods to help him learn. The special teacher introduces him to unique ways of learning, such as drawing words in sand and reading aloud to a tape recorder.
Nonfiction   Primary school level

Lasker, J. (1974). *He's my brother.* Niles, IL: Albert Whitman and Company.

Jamie's big brother describes Jamie's learning disabilities in this story for young children. Both the level of mental and the level of physical development are characteristic of a learning disability.
Fiction   Preschool-primary school level

Pevsner, S. (1977). *Keep stompin' till the music stops.* New York: Seabury Press.

A 12-year-old boy with perceptual disabilities comes to a new level of maturity while attending a family reunion. In this story, self-confidence is gained when others recognize his strengths.
Fiction   Middle school level

Smith, D. B. (1975). *Kelly's creek.* New York: Harper & Row.

Kelly's interest in nature eventually wins him the respect of others. Throughout the story, this 9-year-old's feelings about his motor and perceptual disabilities are empathetically depicted. Special education technology used to teach Kelly is also detailed.
Fiction   Middle school level

Mental Retardation

Anders, R. (1976). *A look at mental retardation.* Minneapolis: Lerner Publications.

This book is written for children in the primary grades as a means of increasing learner awareness. Attractive photos are used that show children with mental retardation and children without disabilities in a variety of ac-

tivities and school settings. The book also describes retardation and its causes, abilities to learn, and points out the need for love, encouragement, and acceptance.
Nonfiction   Primary school level

Baldwin, A. N. (1978). *A little time*. New York: Viking Press.

Matt, a 4-year-old, has Down syndrome. Matt's older sister, Sarah, feels she is the only one of his four siblings who understands him. At the same time, she is convinced that his presence in the family deprives her of the opportunity to make close friends. When Matt is placed in a foster home, life is easier but the whole family agrees that Matt belongs at home with them.
Fiction   Middle-high school level

Brightman, A. (1976). *Like me*. Boston: Little, Brown.

A young boy explores the differences that exist among people. The awareness of his own mental retardation facilitates a deeper understanding of the emotions and thoughts that individuals with disabilities experience. The strongest aspects of the book are the colorful photographs of children in a variety of social and recreational settings.
Nonfiction   Middle school level

Byars, B. (1970). *The summer of the swans*. New York: Viking Press.

In this story about growing up, a young girl's miseries are pushed aside as she searches for her brother, a boy with mental retardation who has gotten lost. Petty personal concerns are put into perspective in the light of her brother's predicament. The helping hand extended by Joe, a boy she "can't stand," proves to be a pleasant surprise.
Fiction   Middle-junior high school level

Cairo, S. (1985). *Our brother has Down's Syndrome*. Toronto: Annick Press Ltd.

Tara and Jasmine are sisters who enjoy playing with their little brother, Jai, who has Down syndrome. The book explains the causes of Down syndrome and what can be done to help. Tara and Jasmine describe their daily life of playing, walking on the beach, and reading stories with Jai. Being the typical little brother, Jai also gets into things and is generally very curious about the world. The sisters are understanding of the extra attention that Jai requires from their parents. They both proclaim that Jai gives "terrific kisses."
Nonfiction   Primary school level

Cleaver, V. (1973). *Me too*. Philadelphia: J. B. Lippincott Co.

This novel for children is about twin girls, one of whom has mental retardation. When their father deserts the family, Lydia becomes responsible for her sister, Lornie, who must now come home from boarding school. Lydia battles neighborhood ignorance and prejudice while attempting, in one summer, to do what no one else has done—to teach her sister. Lornie does not learn much from Lydia, but Lydia gains valuable insight into their relationship.
Fiction   Middle-junior high school level

Clifton, L. (1980). *My friend Jacob*. New York: E. P. Dutton.

Jacob and Sam are neighbors and best friends. Although Jacob is much older than Sam, they teach each other a lot. Jacob may be a great basketball player, but Sam has a better memory. The day Sam remembers to knock

before entering becomes a memorable day for both of them.
Fiction   Primary school level

Friis-Baastad, B. (1967). *Don't take Teddy* [Translated from the Norwegian version by L. S. McKinnon]. New York: Charles Scribner's Sons.

This novel tells the story of a Norwegian family with two sons. The younger son, Mikkel, is fiercely loyal to his 15-year-old brother, who has mental retardation. A lack of communication within the family prompts Mikkel to believe his parents have decided to institutionalize Teddy. The need for community-based services, the hardship encountered by families with a family member who has mental retardation, and the struggle to do what is best are underlying themes in the story.
Fiction   Junior high school level

Garrigue, S. (1978). *Between friends.* Scarsdale, NY: Bradbury.

This story illustrates a typical friendship triangle in which Jill befriends Dede, a girl who has mental retardation. Jill receives peer pressure about her new friendship with Dede from Marla, one of her self-centered friends. Jill is forced to make a choice that, in the end, proves to be rewarding. The book reflects common attitudes toward mental retardation including aversion, hostility, and irrational fears, but balances out with feelings of admiration and affection.
Fiction   Middle-high school level

Hanlon, E. (1978). *It's too late for sorry.* Scarsdale, NY: Bradbury.

Rachel befriends Harold, a boy with mental retardation, and includes him in many of her social activities which irritates her boyfriend Kenny. To make matters worse, Kenny's friend Phil makes jokes about Rachel and Harold that lead Kenny to react violently toward Harold. After Harold is forced into foster care, Kenny finally understands the importance of their contribution in providing Harold with sufficient skills and opportunities for social and personal growth.
Fiction   Middle-high school level

Hirsch, K. (1977). *My sister.* Minneapolis: Carol Rhoda Books.

In this story of a boy with an older sister who has mental retardation, the boy's own play activities and friendships are contrasted with his sister's social abilities. Through various scenarios, the brother's emotions (resentment, embarrassment, anger, pride, and love) are explored. His sister is depicted as gentle, kind, and capable of learning.
Fiction   Primary school level

Larson, H. (1978). *Don't forget Tom.* New York: Thomas Y. Crowell.

This books portrays what it would be like to have mental retardation. The author takes the reader through a day with Tom, a 6-year-old boy with mental retardation who lives at home with his family. Activities experienced with Tom include feeding and dressing, outdoor play, lessons with a teacher, a family dinner, and bathing with his brother.
Nonfiction   Primary school level

Lynch, M. (1979). *Mary Fran and me.* New York: St. Martin's Press.

This book describes the year the author spent living with her sister. Their goal was for Mary Fran to become, in her words, more "capable." This is not

only an account of their trials, tribulations, and personal successes, but also a firsthand glimpse into the life of a person with mental retardation and her needs. The author provides recollections of the siblings' childhood together and Mary Fran's growing need to acquire respect and independence.
Nonfiction   High school-adult level

Ominsky, E. (1977). *Jon O: A special boy.* Englewood Cliffs, NJ: Prentice-Hall.

In this small book for young children, complete with photographs, Jon O is a young boy with Down syndrome who is very much an active person in the mainstream of life. His activities at home with his brother and at school with his friends are described. His disabilities, and his own knowledge of them, are brought out along with the corresponding successes and pleasures of his life.
Biography   Primary school level

Perske, R. (1987). *Show me no mercy.* Nashville: Abingdon Press.

Andy and Maggie Banks and their teenage twins, Beth and Ben, were a family like any other—tempering their disagreements and occasional squabbles with mutual love and support. Beth, an academically gifted high school cheerleader, and her brother, who has Down syndrome, were close, in spite of her occasional feelings of frustration at some of Ben's efforts. Nevertheless, his enthusiasm and tenacity had earned him a special place in a sometimes hostile world—until an automobile accident changed his life forever.
Fiction   Middle-high school level

Shyer, M. F. (1978). *Welcome home, Jellybean.* New York: Charles Scribner's Sons.

A brother tells the story of his sister, who has mental retardation, and her return home after living for 13 years in an institution. The book realistically portrays a child with mental retardation who is accustomed to institutional life, and the stress placed on the family. The boy must struggle not only with the acceptance of his sister, but also with his anguish over his parent's ensuing marital difficulties.
Fiction   Middle-junior high school level

Slepian, J. (1980). *The Alfred summer.* New York: Macmillan Publishing Co.

Lester is a young man with cerebral palsy and impaired speech. Alfred Burt is Lester's newfound friend, a boy with mental retardation. Myron is a teenage neighbor who is spending his summer constructing a boat. Together, the three boys join forces to construct the boat in Myron's basement. They are discovered by Claire who also joins in the project. The quartet spends their whole summer building their boat for a long-awaited launch that is tragically postponed due to Alfred's sudden illness.
Fiction   Middle school level

Smith, L. B. (1977). *A special kind of sister.* New York: Holt, Rinehart, & Winston.

The word "special" in this title emphasizes qualities of a sister who does not have a disability. It is on her feelings that the story focuses. Her brother, who has mental retardation, is ill frequently, which prompts her to contemplate feigning illness to gain the parental attention her brother receives. Reactions of the girl's friends and of the general public are observed.
Fiction   Primary school level

Sobol, H. L. (1977). *My brother Steven is retarded*. New York: Macmillan Publishing Co.

In this book, illustrated with photographs, an 11-year-old girl speaks directly to the reader about her oscillating feelings toward her older brother, which range from anger and acute embarrassment to pleasure. Steven is portrayed as an integral member of the family, a person capable of accomplishment. His sister, Beth, worries about his future and the reactions of her friends, and reexamines her old fears that mental retardation might be "catching."
Biography   Primary school level

Wright, B. R. (1981). *My sister is different*. Milwaukee: Raintree Publishers, Inc.

What is it like to have a sibling with mental retardation? In this book, the reader can see what it is like for Carlo, whose older sister Terry has mental retardation. At first we learn of the responsibility Carlo must bear—responsibility that leads to resentment toward his sister. It is only after Carlo almost loses Terry that he, and the reader, begin to appreciate the special qualities Terry possesses and the gifts she gives to those around her. As a result, Carlo discovers the love that underlies his veneer of resentment.
Fiction   Primary school level

Physical Disabilities

Allen, A. (1981). *Sports for the handicapped*. New York: Walker & Co.

The author surveys six sports in which people with disabilities engage: skiing, basketball, swimming, track and field, football, and horseback riding. Sports, once considered beyond the reach of most people with disabilities, are shown here to be accessible in some measure to participants of all descriptions.
Nonfiction   Primary school level

Berger, G. (1979). *Physical disabilities*. New York: Franklin Watts.

This concise and comprehensive resource book offers information on a wide variety of physical disabilities. Nerve and muscle disorders, bone and joint disorders, chronic health problems, and sensory impairments are treated in detail. Family problems and the position that a person with physical disabilities holds in society are also discussed.
Nonfiction   Middle-junior high school level

Brightman, A., & Storey, K. (1978). *Ginny*. Scholastic's Feeling Free.

Ginny, a young girl in a family of seven children, is left paralyzed and visually impaired after being hit by a truck. The book focuses on the child's struggle to live and reenter the mainstream of life. This story should hold appeal for teenagers who like inspiring stories that involve close, loving families and good neighbors.
Nonfiction   Middle-high school level

Fanshawe, E. (1975). *Rachel*. Scarsdale, NY: Bradbury.

Rachel is a typical young girl. The most remarkable aspect about her is that she must use a wheelchair to get around and to engage in activities common to other children her age. The full, happy life she leads is inspirational for those who have an orthopedic impairment.
Nonfiction   Middle school level

Greenfield, E. (1981). *Alesia*. New York: Philomel, Division of Putnam Publishing Co.

A young lady with a disability chronicles her emotions and insights. Her disability is the result of an automobile accident. In this book for older children, she tells the reader about her family, friends, and school activities.
Biography   Junior high school level

Griese, A. (1969). *At the mouth of the luckiest river.* New York: Thomas Y. Crowell.

Set in Alaska, young Tatlek, an Athabascan Indian, despite having an orthopedic impairment, leads a happy life. He believes that the good spirits that his grandfather has told him about are watching over him. He recognizes his problems and also learns to compensate for them as he develops his skills at wrestling, learns to push a sled, and confronts the village's crooked medicine man.
Fiction   Primary-middle school level

Nadas, B. P. (1975). *Danny's song.* New York: Hubbard Scientific.

This book was developed by the producer of "Mister Roger's Neighborhood." It tells the story of Danny, who despite leg braces and crutches, is a boy capable of doing many activities well.
Biography   Preschool-primary school level

Rosenberg, M. R. (1983). *My friend Leslie.* New York: Lothrop, Lee, & Shepard Books.

Leslie and Karin attend kindergarten in the same school and have been friends for a long time. Despite Leslie's visual, hearing, and coordination impairments, the girls enjoy similar activities at school and find comfort in their friendship.
Nonfiction   Primary school level

Savitz, H. M. (1979). *Run, don't walk.* Denver, CO: Accent Special Publications.

A fateful dive left Samantha with no sensation in her lower limbs. The book describes Samantha's fight to participate in a 26-mile race and her friendship with the rebellious Johnny, who is part of an advocacy group for accessibility in their school. Eventually, Samantha gets involved with a planned walk-out at their school and gains the right to participate in the race of her dreams.
Fiction   Middle school level

Savitz, H. M. (1978). *Wheelchair champions.* New York: Harper and Row.

This book presents the history of wheelchair sports from 1940 to 1970, and includes personal stories of the people involved in these sports. A conclusion entitled "If You Were Suddenly Disabled," suggests provocative questions for the reader. Also provided are lists of organizations and publications related to disabilities and wheelchair sports.
Nonfiction   Primary-middle school level

Stein, S. B. (1974). *About handicaps: An open family book for parents and children together.* New York: Walker & Co.

This straightforward text for children describes Matthew and his friend with cerebral palsy, Joe. A man with a prosthetic arm is also featured. Matthew's exaggerated fears regarding his own physical disabilities and his deep

concerns about the disability he encounters are handled with sensitivity and thoroughness. A detailed text for parents, to promote discussion and greater understanding, accompanies the story.
Nonfiction   Preschool-primary school level

Turnbull, A. S. (1968). *The white lark.* Boston: Houghton Mifflin.

Following an accident, Suzy has had to depend upon leg braces for mobility. While visiting her aunt, she meets a man who was born with short legs. Together, Suzy and her friend share stories of their experiences.
Fiction   Middle school level

Wolf, B. (1974). *Don't feel sorry for Paul.* Philadelphia: J. B. Lippincott Co.

This book depicts the day-to-day life of a second-grader who must wear prosthetic devices on his hands and feet. The photographs and text take the mystery away from such equipment, while portraying Paul and his family in their varied activities, including preparations for Paul's birthday party.
Biography   Primary school level

Speech Impairment

Christopher, M. (1975). *Glue fingers.* Boston: Little, Brown.

Even though Billy Joe is an outstanding athlete, he fears joining the football team. He is afraid that he will be ostracized because he stutters, but his older brothers finally convince him that his speech problem does not have to affect his enjoyment of football. Upon making a key pass and scoring, rather than jeering at his stuttering, Billy Joe is delighted to find that the crowd is cheering at his impressive play.
Fiction   Middle school level

Jupo, F. (1967). *Atu, the silent one.* New York: Holiday House.

Set in a distant time, Atu is an African bushman who cannot speak. He is loved by the other members of his tribe and known for his ability to communicate artistically through his drawings. Atu not only develops into a great hunter, but also becomes the pictorial storyteller of the tribe's successes.
Fiction   Primary-middle school level

Spina Bifida

White, P. (1978). *Janet at school.* New York: Harper & Row.

Through 5-year-old Janet, this book explains the condition of an open spine. A tiny, pretty, and bespectacled girl, Janet has spina bifida. Each page contains pictures that show Janet in a wheelchair at school, on the playground participating in activities, learning to walk using leg braces and walking frame, with her family at home, and at a camping site.
Nonfiction   Primary school level

Visual Impairment

Bouchard, L. (1969). *The boy who wouldn't talk.* Garden City, NY: Doubleday.

Upon arriving in New York City from Puerto Rico, Carlos is lonely and frustrated with his inability to learn English and decides to communicate through drawing pictures and making gestures. Then he meets Ricky, a boy with visual impairments, who appears to be lost. Carlos finds that he must speak to his new friend in order to communicate with him. The two boys

share special moments such as Carlos's first exposure to braille books and an exploration of a park for the blind. Carlos returns home, finally able to speak with his family.
Fiction   Middle school level

Eyerly, J. (1981). *The seeing summer*. Philadelphia: J. B. Lippincott.

This story reveals several misconceptions that people have about the abilities of people with visual impairments. Jenny, who is visually impaired, is able to use other senses or various techniques to accomplish tasks that are completed by her sighted peers. Her friend, Corey, learns that many of her assumptions about persons with disabilities are incorrect when faced with finding her kidnapped friend.
Fiction   High school level

Goodsell, J. (1965). *Katie's magic glasses*. Boston: Houghton Mifflin.

For 5-year-old Katie, everything is often a blur. A visit to the doctor is followed up by an appointment with an ophthalmologist who informs her that she will be receiving a pair of magic glasses soon. In preparation, Katie tries on her father's glasses, which being the wrong prescription, make her feel sick. She decides that she is no longer looking forward to receiving her own glasses, but abruptly changes her mind when they arrive and her surroundings take on previously unknown sharpness.
Fiction   Primary school level

Heide, F. P. (1970). *Sound of sunshine, sound of rain*. New York: Parents' Magazine Press.

This book illustrates how hearing and touch become very important when they are a child's best tools for discovering the world. The life of a child who is visually impaired is presented with sensitivity.
Nonfiction   Primary school level

Keats, E. (1971). *Apt. 3*. New York: Macmillan Publishing Co.

Kept inside all day due to rain, two brothers decide to track down the source of music that they can hear in their apartment building. Their investigation brings them to the door of a man with a visual impairment playing his harmonica. Captivated by the man's ability to use hearing as a tool for learning about the world, they invite him on a walk, and the three become fast friends.
Fiction   Primary-middle school level

Kent, D. (1979). *Belonging*. New York: Ace Books.

Meg, who is visually impaired, yearns to be treated like other teenagers and fantasizes about her acceptance into the social crowd at school. Instead she finds pity, exaggerated concern, and appalling ignorance toward her disability. Fortunately, she also finds two genuine offers of friendship from Lindy, a loner, and Keith, an opera buff. The story continues as the trio bands together to fight the victimization of their teacher, Miss Kellogg.
Fiction   Middle school level

Little, J. (1972). *From Anna*. New York: Harper & Row.

When 9-year-old Anna's family moves to Canada to escape the political situation in Nazi Germany, a doctor discovers that she has visual impairment necessitating special education services. Her four older siblings' scorn and even her mother's reaction cause her to withdraw and build a defensive communicative barrier.

Fiction   Middle-junior high school level

Little, J. (1977). *Listen for the singing.* New York: E. P. Dutton.

This is a continuation of Anna's life depicted in *From Anna.* She is now nervous about entering high school, expecting difficult times. She finds a surprise resource in her oldest brother who often treated her unkindly in the past, but now seems quite changed. Anna's disabilities and her fears and doubts, as well as the experience of a sighted person becoming totally blind are thoughtfully detailed.

Fiction   Middle-junior high school level

Marcus, R. (1981). *Being blind.* Mamaroneck, NY: Hastings House.

This book simulates visual impairments to help the reader imagine and experience what it would be like to have such an impairment. The author also discusses society's treatment of people with disabilities and the various devices used in the past and present. There is no sentimentality or illusion, just pure day-to-day experiences.

Nonfiction   Primary-middle school level

McPhee, R. (1981). *Tom and Bear.* New York: Thomas Y. Crowell.

Tom, who is visually impaired and has diabetes, writes about the day-to-day training of a golden retriever in his journal. The 24-year-old's writings demonstrate the typical pattern of denial, isolation, anger, and depression, that people who are visibly impaired experience. While dealing with his denial, Tom is training his golden retriever, Bear, who fast becomes his trusted friend.

Nonfiction   Middle school level

Navior, P. (1967). *Jennifer Jean, the cross-eyed queen.* Minneapolis: Lerner.

Due to an inward-turned eye, 4-year-old Jennifer Jean squints and tilts her head in order to see. Even though other children tease her, Jennifer Jean maintains her spirit. Jennifer begins wearing a patch, then eye glasses, and finally does regular eye exercises to improve her sight.

Fiction   Primary school level

Newith, P. (1981). *Roly goes exploring.* New York: Philomel, Division of Putnam Publishing Co.

This is a unique book designed for children with visual impairments, as well as for the sighted. It is "in Braille and standard type, with pictures to feel as well as see." The subject matter is geometric shapes.

Nonfiction   Preschool-primary school level

Vance, M. (1956). *Windows for Rosemary.* New York: E. P. Dutton.

This book explores the adjustments that are necessary for dealing with visual impairments. Rosemary depends upon the location of furniture to make her way around the house. Her warm, up-beat family is a source of strength as she finds that even her friends have misconceptions about her impairment.

Nonfiction   Middle school level

Weiss, M. E. (1980). *Blindness*. New York: Franklin Watts.

This is a short outline containing personal accounts by individuals with visual impairments. Sight, itself, and the structures of the eye are explained. Mechanical aids and learning technology are also discussed.
Nonfiction   Middle school level

Wolf, B. (1976). *Connie's new eyes*. Philadelphia: J. B. Lippincott Co.

In this photo essay, the reader first becomes acquainted with a puppy being raised for Seeing Eye, Inc. The training process for both the dog and her new owner, Connie, is described. Connie is followed through her daily activities at home and at her new job as a preschool teacher for youngsters who are visually impaired.
Biography   Middle school level

Information & Service Sources for Siblings & Parents

Adaptive Environments Center
374 Congress Street
Suite 301
Boston, MA 02210
(617)695-1225

The Adaptive Environments Center offers consultation, workshops, courses, conferences, and resource materials on adaptive design. The Center's library contains a comprehensive collection of materials on adaptive design.

Administration on Developmental Disabilities (ADD)
200 Independence Avenue, S.W.
329D Humphrey Building
Washington, DC 20201
(202)245-2890

ADD is responsible for administering the provisions of the Developmental Disabilities Act of 1984 (PL 98-527). The administration oversees the following: state protection and advocacy agencies to assure that persons with developmental disabilities in each state obtain their rights and quality services; formula grants to states for the purpose of planning and administering programs, and delivering services to people with developmental disabilities; special project grants to improve the quality of services and programs, and for technical assistance and training of specialized personnel; and grants to university affiliated facilities that operate demonstration facilities for services to individuals with developmental disabilities and interdisciplinary training of specialized personnel.

Alexander Graham Bell Association for the Deaf, Inc.
3417 Volta Place, N.W.
Washington, DC 20007
(202)337-5220 (Voice/TDD)

The Alexander Graham Bell Association for the Deaf is committed to the idea that children with hearing impairments should be afforded the opportunity to develop verbal communication through the effective use of amplified residual hearing and speechreading skills.

American Association on Mental Retardation (AAMR)
1719 Kalorama Road, NW
Washington, DC 20009-2683
(202)387-1968

AAMR promotes cooperation among those involved in services, training, and research in mental retardation. The association also disseminates information about mental retardation and measures to reduce its incidence.

American Cleft Palate-Craniofacial Association
1218 Grandview Avenue
Pittsburgh, PA 15211
(412)481-1376
1-800-24-CLEFT

Individuals and their families affected by cleft lip, cleft palate, or other craniofacial disorders can receive information and referrals to health care teams and parent support groups. Brochures and fact sheets on various aspects of facial birth defects are available.

American Foundation of the Blind (AFB)
15 West 16th Street
New York, NY 10011
(212)620-2000

AFB was established to help persons who are visually impaired acquire improved rehabilitation services and educational and employment opportunities, and to aid those persons in daily living activities. Publications dealing with a variety of general interests and topics are available upon request.

American Society for Deaf Children (ASDC)
814 Thayer Avenue
Silver Spring, MD 20910
(301)585-5400
1-800-942-ASDC

ASDC acts as a clearinghouse for the exchange of information among family members of persons who are hearing impaired. ASDC provides general information about hearing impairments and raising children with hearing impairments, including deaf-blind children, to all inquirers.

American Speech-Language-Hearing Association (ASHA)
10801 Rockville Pike
Rockville, MD 20852
(301)897-5700
1-800-638-8255 (Voice/TDD)

ASHA is a membership organization of individuals with speech, hearing, and language disorders, their families, and interested professionals. ASHA is primarily concerned with public information activities and with advocating the rights of persons with communicative impairments.

Association of Birth Defect Children (ABDC)
Orlando Executive Park
5400 Diplomat Circle
Suite 270
Orlando, FL 32810
(407)629-1466

ABDC was established to provide information and support to families of children with birth defects of a nongenetic nature, caused by the mother's exposure to drugs, chemicals, radiation, or other environmental agents. The association also publishes a quarterly newsletter.

Association for the Care of Children's Health (ACCH)
7910 Woodmont Avenue
Suite 300
Bethesda, MD 20814
(301)654-6549

ACCH seeks to foster and promote the health and well-being of children and their families in health care settings. ACCH, as a resource for those interested in the care of chronically ill children and children with disabilities, offers a quarterly journal and a bimonthly newsletter, as well as bibliographies.

The Association for Persons with Severe Handicaps (TASH)
11201 Greenwood Avenue, North
Seattle, WA 98133
(206)361-8870

TASH was founded to advocate the need for quality education and services for persons with severe disabilities. Membership is open to families, educators, lawyers, medical personnel, therapists, psychologists, and social workers.

TASH has organized a parent-to-parent network of communication. By maintaining lists of parents with children with severe disabilities who are involved in local parent support and advocacy groups, TASH is able to put inquirers in touch with parents who have similar concerns. The association also maintains a register of professional contacts who are available for assistance with specific problems, such as education or training of personnel.

The Arc (formerly Association for Retarded Citizens of the United States [ARC])
500 East Border Street
Suite 300
Arlington, TX 76010
(817)261-6003

The goals of The Arc are to prevent mental retardation, find its cures, and assist people with mental disorders in their daily living. The Arc works on national, state, and local levels to communicate and interpret the needs of persons with mental disabilities to the public and to government agencies. The Arc answers lay and professional inquiries about persons who have mental retardation through publications or by letter.

Autism Society of America (ASA)
8601 George Avenue
Suite 503
Silver Spring, MD 20910
(301)565-0433

ASA is an organization of parents, siblings, professionals, and interested people who work for legislation, education, and research for the benefit of all children with severe communication and behavior disorders. Advocacy on the national, state, and local levels, particularly in the area of education, is a primary function of the organization. ASA publishes a bimonthly newsletter and an annual *Proceedings of Society National Conferences.*

Canavan Foundation, Inc.
320 Central Park West
Suite 190
New York, NY 10025
(212)877-3945

Canavan disease is an inherited childhood disease that is fatal. This degenerative disease is particularly frequent among Ashkenazi Jews whose families come from Poland, Russia, and Lithuania. The Foundation was established in 1992 to seek to eliminate Canavan disease through research and education.

The Candlelighters Foundation
1312 18th Street, N.W.
Suite 200
Washington, DC 20036
(202)659-5136
1-800-366-2223

The Candlelighters Foundation is an international organization of groups of parents who have or have had children with cancer. The foundation distributes bibliographies in the following areas: childhood cancer in general, materials for parents, and books covering cancer and dying for children at various age levels. Candlelighters also sponsors conferences for families, publishes a quarterly newsletter and a newsletter for teens, and serves as a clearinghouse on state and federal programs.

CH.A.D.D. National
499 N.W. 70th Avenue
Suite 308
Plantation, FL 33317
(305)587-3700

CH.A.D.D. is a nonprofit organization that provides information and support to parents who have children with attention deficit hyperactivity disorders. Through informative monthly meetings with guest speakers, newsletters, and the caring of other parents, CH.A.D.D. members form a close network to exchange helpful ideas about raising a child with an attention deficit hyperactivity disorder.

Clearinghouse on Disability Information
Office of Special Education and Rehabilitative Service
Switzer Building, Room 3132
Washington, DC 20202-2524
(202)732-1241

The Clearinghouse on the Handicapped, established by the Rehabilitation Act of 1973, is a resource information office designed to answer questions regarding legislation, publications, or programs affecting people with disabilities. Resource guides in such areas as recreation and leisure for individuals with disabilities, including descriptions of funding sources, have been completed. The clearinghouse also publishes a *Directory of National Information Sources on Handicapping Conditions and Related Services*.

The Council for Exceptional Children (CEC)
Information Services
1920 Association Drive
Reston, VA 22091-1589
(703)620-3660

CEC was organized to advance the education of exceptional children and youth, including those with disabilities and those who are gifted. CEC Information Services acts as an information broker for teachers, administrators, students, families, and others. CEC produces numerous publications on special education, awareness of individuals with disabilities, child abuse, recreation, parent–professional cooperation, career and vocational education, children with severe disabilities, and public policy. Bibliographies on topics of current interest and nonprint media are also available.

Cystic Fibrosis Foundation (CFF)
6931 Arlington Road
Bethesda, MD 20814
(301)951-4422
1-800-Fight CF

CFF was established to find the means for prevention, control, and effective treatment of this chronic degenerative disease, which involves the lungs, digestive organs, and other major organs of the body. CFF provides information on local group activities, as well as articles dealing with national programs, questions of higher education, marriage and family planning, and vocational training, which appear in its quarterly publication, *Commitment*.

Dysautonomia Foundation
20 East 46th Street
New York, NY 10017
(212)949-6644

Established by parents of children with dysautonomia, the foundation provides funds for research into dysautonomia and information on this genetic disorder to professionals and families.

Epilepsy Foundation of America (EFA)
4351 Garden City Drive
Suite 406
Landover, MD 20785
(301)459-3700
1-800-332-1000

EFA is involved in advocacy and a wide variety of services and programs for the person with epilepsy. EFA publishes pamphlets, reprints, books, cassettes, slides, films, a directory of clinics, and a monthly newsletter.

Exceptional Parent
1170 Commonwealth Avenue
Boston, MA 02134-9942
(617)730-5800

This magazine provides straightforward, practical information to siblings, parents, educators, and health care professionals involved with children and young adults who have disabilities.

International Rett Syndrome Association
8511 Rose Marie Drive
Ft. Washington, MD 20744
(301)248-7031

The association is an organization for parents, professionals, and other supporters interested in Rett Syndrome. The aims of the association are to provide direct support to parents and to find ways to encourage research, which may provide answers to questions about developmental difficulties.

Juvenile Diabetes Foundation International
432 Park Avenue South
New York, NY 10016-8013
(212)889-7575

This organization's primary objective is to support and fund research on the treatment and cure of diabetes, mainly juvenile diabetes (also called insulin-dependent diabetes), which has it usual onset from infancy to the late 30s. The organization publishes free pamphlets and fact sheets about diabetes and insulin for the layperson.

Kids on the Block
9385C Gerwig Lane
Columbia, MD 21046
1-800-368-KIDS

Kids on the Block provides a framework of educational puppet programs to teach about disabilities and differences. Several specially designed kits and programs, which aim to allay prejudices and fears about people with disabilities and to help children interact and work together, are offered.

Learning Disabilities Association of America (LDA)
4156 Library Road
Pittsburgh, PA 15234
(412)341-1515
(412)341-8077

LDA is an organization for professionals, adults with learning disabilities, and families of persons with learning disabilities. LDA provides general information about learning disabilities, as well as advocacy for educational and rehabilitative legislation affecting persons with learning disabilities.

Leukemia Society of America
733 Third Avenue
14th Floor
New York, NY 10017
(212)573-8484
1-800-955-4572

The Leukemia Society of America is concerned with finding cures for leukemia, the lymphomas, multiple myeloma, and Hodgkin's disease. Supplementary financial assistance is available to persons with these diseases, as well as funds for research investigating leukemia and related diseases. The society publishes pamphlets and provides audio-visual materials related to leukemia.

Little People of America (LPA)
P.O. Box 9897
Washington, DC 20016
(301)589-0730

LPA was established as a nationwide organization for people of small stature to provide fellowship and interchange of ideas, solutions to the problems unique to these individuals, and moral support. A special membership division provides opportunities for information exchange and group support to parents with children of small stature and their siblings. In addition to an organization newsletter, LPA distributes printed materials on equipment and aids, on social and vocational adjustment, and on clothing.

March of Dimes Birth Defects Foundation
1275 Mamaroneck Avenue
White Plains, NY 10605
(914)428-7100

The March of Dimes Birth Defects Foundation awards grants to institutions and organizations for the development of genetic services, perinatal care in high-risk pregnancies, prevention of premature deliveries, and parent support groups. It conducts the Campaign for Healthier Babies, through which information is distributed. Spanish-language materials are also available.

Mothers United for Moral Support (MUMS)
150 Custer Court
Green Bay, WI 54301
(414)336-5333

MUMS is a statewide, self-help group for parents, foster parents, grandparents, and professionals who work with children with any disabilities. MUMS provides information services and assistance in forming local support groups.

Muscular Dystrophy Association (MDA)
3561 East Sunrise Drive
Tucson, AZ 85718
(602)529-2000

MDA supports research into neuromuscular disorders. It also provides free medical care and other direct services to persons who have muscular dystrophy. Local chapters sponsor recreational activities (e.g., summer camps, picnics, outings) and organize self-help groups for persons with muscular dystrophy and their families.

National Association of the Deaf (NAD)
814 Thayer Avenue
Silver Spring, MD 20910-4500
(301)587-1788
(301)587-1789 (TDD)

NAD is the oldest and largest consumer organization of persons with disabilities in the United States. NAD advocates for people who are deaf or have hearing impairments, sponsors biannual national conventions, and operates a public information center.

National Association for Rare Disorders (NORD)
Post Office Box 8923
New Fairfield, CT 06812
(202)746-6518

NORD is a clearinghouse for information about rare disorders. NORD also promotes research, represents individuals with rare disorders, and educates the public and medical professionals about such disorders.

National Association for Sickle-Cell Disease (NASCD)
3345 Wilshire Boulevard
Suite 1106
Los Angeles, CA 90010
(213)736-5455
1-800-421-8453

NASCD provides an extensive public and professional education program about sickle-cell disease, its variants, and sickle-cell trait. A *Home Study Kit for Families* includes printed materials, cassettes, games, and other learning devices to help parents and other family members cope with related problems.

National Association for Visually Handicapped (NAVH)
22 West 21st Street
New York, NY 10010
(212)889-3141

NAVH provides information, referral, and direct services for persons with visual impairments and their families. The association acts as a clearinghouse of information for all services available to visually impaired persons, from both federal, state, and local government agencies and private sources. NAVH also publishes materials concerning problems encountered by visually impaired persons, as well as two newsletters, one for children and one for adults.

National Ataxia Foundation (NAF)
750 Twelve Oaks Center
15500 Wayzata Boulevard
Wayzata, MN 55391
(612)473-7666

NAF was established to serve persons with ataxia, identify persons at risk, educate the public and the medical community, and stimulate research. Free printed material and fact sheets are available.

National Center for Stuttering (NCS)
200 East 33rd Street
New York, NY 10016
1-800-221-2483

NCS provides information for parents of young children who are just beginning to show signs of stuttering. Information for treatment of older children and adults is also provided.

National Down Syndrome Congress (NDSC)
1800 Dempster Street
Park Ridge, IL 60068
1-800-232-6372

NDSC was formed by a group of parents and professionals interested in Down syndrome. NDSC members share their experiences with parents and professionals working for public awareness and civil rights of this population. An annual convention, a 10-issue newsletter (with a special sibling column) and a quarterly publication keep the membership informed about new medical, legislative, and educational developments.

National Down Syndrome Society (NDSS)
666 Broadway
New York, NY 10012-2317
(212)460-9330
1-800-221-4602

NDSS provides referrals to local programs and information on Down syndrome. Their major goals are to promote basic and applied research in fields related to Down syndrome and to provide information and services to families, professionals, and interested persons.

National Easter Seal Society
70 East Lake Street
Chicago, IL 60601
(312)726-6200

The society is the nation's largest and oldest voluntary health agency providing direct rehabilitation services to persons with disabilities. The National Easter Seal Society publishes a variety of books, pamphlets, and reprints for professionals, families, and persons with disabilities.

National Federation of the Blind (NFB)
1800 Johnson Street
Baltimore, MD 21230
(301)659-9314

NFB is a membership organization with 51 state chapters and 400 local chapters. NFB keeps up with federal and state legislation and state services affecting people with visual impairments. NFB conducts seminars on services available to people with visual impairments and what the law provides for in each state. Publications are available for concerned individuals, as well as a monthly magazine.

National Fragile X Foundation
1441 York Street
Suite 215
Denver, CO 80206
(303)333-6155
1-800-688-8765

The National Fragile X Foundation sponsors a biannual conference, promotes education concerning diagnosis, treatment, and research in fragile X syndrome, and provides referral to local resource centers.

National Head Injury Foundation (NIHF)
1140 Connecticut Avenue, N.W.
Suite 812
Washington, DC 20036
(202)294-6443
1-800-444-NHIF

(Note for second printing, January 1996: The National Head Injury Foundation has changed its name to the Brain Injury Association.)

Founded by families of people who have sustained brain damage and by professionals with an interest in the treatment of this condition, the National Head Injury Foundation assists persons with head injury and their families in seeking out needed resources and services. The foundation facilitates the formation of family emotional support groups, which exist in many locations throughout the country.

National Information Center for Children and Youth with Disabilities (NIC-HCY)
P.O. Box 1492
Washington, DC 20013
(703)893-6061
1-800-999-5599

Sponsored by the U.S. Department of Education, the National Information Center for Children and Youth with Disabilities collects and shares information and ideas that are helpful to children and youth with disabilities and the people who care for and about them. The center answers questions, links people with others who share common concerns, sponsors workshops, publishes newsletters, and generally helps the information flow between people who have it and people who need it.

National Mental Health Association (NMHA)
1021 Prince Street
Alexandria, VA 22314-2971
(703)684-7722

NMHA is primarily an advocacy and public education organization. NMHA and its 650 local chapters work for legislation affecting the rights and treatment of individuals with mental illness. NMHA offers a variety of publications, as well as a monthly newsletter, which informs members of news in the mental health field.

National Multiple Sclerosis Society
733 Third Avenue, 6th Floor
New York, NY 10017
(212)986-3240

The National Multiple Sclerosis Society provides funding for research, public and professional education, advocacy, and the design of rehabilitative and psychosocial programs. Direct services to individuals with multiple sclerosis are provided through 161 local chapters and branches.

National Neurofibromatosis Foundation (NNFF)
141 5th Avenue
Suite 7-S
New York, NY 10010-7105
(212)460-8980

The NNFF was established to provide information to individuals and their families, physicians, and other professionals, and to promote and support scientific research on the cause, prevention, and treatment of neurofibromatosis.

National Organization on Disability (NOD)
910 16th Street, N.W.
Suite 600
Washington, DC 20006
(202)293-5960
1-800-248-ABLE

NOD is a privately funded national organization on disability. Emphasis is placed on a partnership between individuals without disabilities and those with disabilities. A 30-page guide is offered, which discusses community goal-setting, dealing with the media, fund raising, working with elected officials, and more.

National Parent Network on Disabilities
1600 Prince Street
Suite 115
Alexandria, VA 22314
(703)684-NPND

Parent Network is a coalition of individuals and organizations dedicated to providing a linkage across the country to people serving other persons who have individual needs. Their first national conference included a session entitled "Siblings Speak Out." This network seeks to promote the interests of individuals with specific needs through the united action of parents and, to this end, hopes to establish a systematic information service for members.

National Rehabilitation Information Center (NARIC)
8455 Colesville Road
Suite 935
Silver Spring, MD 20910-3319
1-800-346-2742(Voice/TDD)

NARIC is a rehabilitation information center and research library. Information is provided on disability products, research, and resources. NARIC offers general brochures, publications, and flyers describing its services and materials.

National Reye's Syndrome Foundation (NRSF)
P.O. Box 829
Bryan, OH 43506
1-800-233-7393

NRSF was organized to promote awareness of Reye's syndrome. NRSF provides funds for basic research on the disease and support and guidance to families of children with Reye's syndrome. Brochures and newsletters are available from the Foundation, as well as an annual publication titled, *Journal of the National Reye's Syndrome Foundation.*

National Tay-Sachs and Allied Diseases Association (NTSAD)
2001 Beacon Street
Suite 304
Brookline, MA 02146
(617)277-4463

NTSAD is an organization that supports research, provides educational literature on Tay-Sachs and the allied disorders, and acts as a referral agency for families affected by Tay-Sachs.

National Tuberous Sclerosis Association (NTSA)
8000 Corporate Drive
Suite 120
Landover, MD 20785
(301)459-9888
1-800-225-NTSA

NTSA was founded by parents and concerned physicians of patients with this genetic disorder. Members of the association offer counseling, referral, and support services to other families of persons with tuberous sclerosis.

The Orton Dyslexia Society (ODS)
Chester Building
Suite 382
8600 LaSalle Road
Baltimore, MD 21204
(410)296-0232

ODS is an international membership organization for professionals and parents of children with dyslexia. Its purposes are to disseminate information related to dyslexia, and to refer persons with dyslexia and parents of children with dyslexia to available resources for diagnosis, remediation, and tutoring.

Osteogenesis Imperfecta Foundation
P.O. Box 24776
Tampa, FL 33623-4776
(813)282-1161

The foundation was organized by parents of children who have this genetic disorder. Information about medical facilities and service, care and management techniques, and equipment is available from the foundation.

Prader-Willi Syndrome Association
6490 Excelsior Boulevard
Suite 102
St. Louis Park, MN 55426
(612)926-1947
1-800-926-4797

The association was formed by parents and professionals who share knowledge and experience about the Prader-Willi syndrome and know how to manage it. The association's bimonthly newsletter contains tips from parents and professionals. *Prader-Willie Syndrome: A Handbook for Parents* contains information on behavior and learning capacity of the Prader-Willi child, as well as tips on management, diet, and exercise.

President's Committee on Employment of People with Disabilities
1331 F Street, N.W.
Washington, DC 20004-1107
(202)376-6200
(202)376-6205 (TDD)

The President's Committee on Employment of People with Disabilities serves an advocacy and public awareness role in fostering job opportunities for individuals with disabilities. Published pamphlets on architectural accessibility and education for youth with disabilities is provided along with information on employment. General information on the committee's activities and selected materials published by the committee are available upon request.

Sibling Information Network
The A.J. Pappanikou Center on
  Special Education and Rehabilitation
991 Main Street
East Hartford, CT 06108
(203)282-7050

The Sibling Information Network was formed to serve as a bridge for sharing ideas, programs, research, or needs regarding siblings and families of persons with disabilities. The network publishes a quarterly newsletter, *Sibling Information Network Newsletter.*

Siblings for Significant Change
105 East 22nd Street, 7th Floor
New York, NY 10010
(212)420-0430

Siblings for Significant Change is a division of Special Citizens Futures Unlimited, Inc. This organization is designed to unite siblings of individuals with disabilities for the purpose of advocacy, to disseminate information, to offer conferences and workshops for and about siblings and families of persons with disabilities, and to promote greater public awareness of the needs of these persons and their families.

SIBS
123 Golden Lane
London, EC1Y 0RT
England

SIBS is a support and information service for children, offered by the National Society for Mentally Handicapped Children and Adults (MENCAP). SIBS publishes a periodic newsletter for members.

Spina Bifida Association of America (SBAA)
1700 Rockville Pike
Suite 250
Rockville, MD 20852
1-800-621-3141

Organized as an outgrowth of the National Easter Seal Society, the SBAA places a primary emphasis on local support groups. Publications and public education materials are available through 100 local chapters in the United States and Canada.

Stuttering Foundation of America
P.O. Box 11749
Memphis, TN 38111-0749
(202)363-3199
1-800-992-9392

The Stuttering Foundation of America is a nonprofit organization that provides information to families, professionals, and individuals who are concerned with stuttering. Books, brochures, and pamphlets are just a few of the published materials provided by the foundation. Information packets can be obtained by contacting the foundation's toll-free hotline.

Tourette Syndrome Association (TSA)
42–40 Bell Boulevard
Bayside, NY 11361-2861
(718)224-2999
1-800-237-0717

TSA was established by patients and their families. The Association offers information and moral support to others affected by this condition through its more than 100 chapters in the United States, Canada, and Europe.

United Cerebral Palsy Associations (UCPA)
7 Penn Plaza
Suite 804
New York, NY 10001
(212)268-6655
1-800-USA-1UCP

UCPA programs and services are directed toward a twofold goal—prevention of cerebral palsy and meeting the needs of persons who are affected by cerebral palsy and their families. Publications are available upon request.

Williams Syndrome Association
P.O. Box 3297
Ballin, MO 63022
(314)227-4411

The association exists to offer support and assistance to families, to create a network and "family" for adults with Williams Syndrome, and to provide professionals with access to groups of Williams individuals for possible study.

Index